in a Headscarf

Muslim Woman Seeks the One

Shelina Zahra Janmohamed

Aurum
Press

First published in 2009 by Aurum Press Ltd
74-77 White Lion Street, London N1 9PF
www.aurumpress.co.uk

This paperback edition first published in 2014 by Aurum Press Ltd

Copyright © 2009 by Shelina Zahra Janmohamed

Shelina Janmohamed has asserted her moral right to be identified as the author
of this work in accordance with the Copyright, Designs and Patents Act, 1988.

All rights reserved. No part of this book may be reproduced or utilised in
any form or by any means, electronic or mechanical, including photocopying,
recording or by any information storage and retrieval system, without
permission in writing from Aurum Press Ltd.

A catalogue record for this book is available from the British Library.

ISBN 978 1 84513 549 2

10 9 8 7 6 5 4 3 2 1
2018 2017 2016 2015 2014

Typeset by SX Composing DTP, Rayleigh, Essex
Printed and bound in Great Britain by CPI Group (UK) Ltd, Croydon, CR0 4YY

To my mother and father
For everything

To Maryam and Aamina
Our future

To the One
You know why

'Love is the answer at least for most of the questions in my heart.
Like why are we here? And where do we go? And how come it's
so hard?'

Jack Johnson

'Love has nothing to do with
the five senses and the six directions:
its goal is only to experience
the attraction exerted by the Beloved.
Afterwards, perhaps, permission
will come from God:
the secrets that ought to be told will be told
with an eloquence nearer to the understanding
of these subtle confusing allusions.
The secret is partner with none
but the knower of the secret:
in the sceptic's ear
the secret is no secret at all.'

Rumi (*Mathnawi* VI:5–8)

'It is He who created you [men and women] from a single soul.'

Qur'an (6:98)

'And one of His signs is that He created pairs for you from
amongst yourselves, so that you find peace in each other, and He
puts love and mercy between you. In this are signs for those who
reflect.'

Qur'an (30:21)

Contents

Author's Introduction

Love. *Amour, ishq, hubb, amor, pyar.* All these are words in my lexicon to describe something delicious and mundane, irresistible and sublime. Love inspires great actions, absurd choices and inexplicable consequences. It directs lives and it makes or breaks hearts. It can arbitrate between life and death, and it can connect the body to the soul and join them with lightning. It is the essence of the human condition.

Civilisations do not clash over whether love exists or not. They may differ about what or who should be the object of love. They fight over the same lover. They disagree about how love should be conducted. But love, Love with a capital L, lies deep within every psyche and culture, and fills books with laments and odes in languages and paradigms from the beginning of time. In this modern day, when only what we see is allowed to have certainty, and when scientific data seems to hold the trump card for truth, when only what can be measured exists, love defies all of these strictures and dances joyfully before the eyes of human beings and teases them with the promise of the unknown.

Love has been lost to our generation, diluted to

ravishing and romance. We ask it to sustain us on a constant high and we feel betrayed and rejected when the adrenaline rush subsides into comfortable companionable love. We have shackled love by limiting its reign to the arena of candlelit meals and moonlit walks. When we talk of love in public, we have now diminished it. I wish for us to reclaim love for our society as a conscious and connected virtue of vast expanse and immense greatness. We each know inside us that love relates to friends, advisers, parents and those we live amongst. It takes patience, dedication and selflessness. Some, like me, may also feel that it connects them to the Divine, the Creator who has no shape, place or time, but who simply is.

The likelihood of a Muslim talking about Love in public is small. But like most societies and cultures, Muslims are obsessed with it. In fact, Muslim men and women spend a large proportion of their time wondering where on earth to find a partner. Finding that special someone is so critical to the fabric of Muslim existence, that almost everyone is involved – parents, siblings, aunts, uncles, Imams, even neighbours.

Beneath the translucent veils of Muslim women lie beating hearts, dreams of love, imaginations replete with fairy tales and princes, of happily ever after. Hidden behind the often misleading headlines of terror and destruction that are said to be in the name of Islam are Muslims: ordinary normal people who share that one thing that exalts human beings and connects the sublime within us to our mundane lives – that thing called Love.

Muslim women have many stories to tell. Some of these are horrific. The suffering, oppression and abuse that some women face in the name of religion, but which in reality is driven by culture and power, must never be forgotten and has to be stopped. I feel a double distress, sharing their pain as sisters in faith but also seeing the beauty of my religion misappropriated, misrepresented and abused to serve inhumane ends.

Stories like mine have remained unheard, as they do not fit neatly with prevailing stereotypes which tell tales of Islam's oppression or of those rejecting Islam. Nonetheless, such stories are just as crucial to our understanding of what it means to be a Muslim woman. Not every Muslim woman is subjected to a forced marriage, kidnapping or imprisonment. We are not one-dimensional creatures hidden behind black veils. Many Muslim women, like me, find Islam to be a positive, liberating and uplifting experience. We love our lives all the more for it. My account is dedicated to all Muslim women, so that humour, hope and humanity can once again become part of *our* story.

Muslim women come in many shapes, colours and flavours, and my story is simply the tale of one woman's experience. Hidden within my story are the human passions and hopes of many Muslims, both men and women, and of human beings of other faiths and no faith at all, all of whose own searches for love may have been as perilous, heartbreaking and entertaining as mine.

The search for love is a journey to find many different things. It is the search for a partner and companion, for the excitement of romance. It is also the search for a cherisher, for someone to nurture or someone to be nurtured by. It is a search for meaning, for the knowledge that you have achieved something, for a momentary acknowledgement or for immortality of your name. Love can be the name of the escape from the physical into the spiritual or from the mental into the carnal. The search for love is a resolute journey: to find out what it means to be human, and to share that humanity.

Love in a Headscarf

Prologue

I am keeping a very surprising story under my headscarf. I'd like to tell it to you, but you must promise not to keep my secret. If I'm bold enough to tell you my tale, will you be daring enough to be my friend?

My *hijab* is pink, the colour of an April sunset or a dusky summer rose. It is a long flowing piece of silk fading into a bold purple that reminds me of royal brocades and sacred discoveries. It is fragranced lightly with the scent of *bukhoor*, so that it surrounds me wherever I go, gentle but not overpowering.

It would be best for me to tell you this story over a cup of coffee – mine is a cappuccino, please, no sugar. We'll already be laughing far too much, and the sugar will only encourage us. When the tale becomes exciting we will need to clutch the cups in excitement or horror, our eyes popping at the incredulity of it all, like two teenagers at a pyjama party. When we reach the point of heartache, we can cast our eyes down into the dark liquid and sip in melancholy.

We should have cookies, too, white chocolate and hazelnut, in the shape of a heart. I will smile mischievously when you order them, but I won't tell you why, not yet anyway. You *must* have had a cookie moment too. We can compare notes. Remind me when we leave the café to take my sunglasses and their case with me.

Do you ever wonder what really goes on in the life of the Muslim women who you walk past in the street? I am quite different from the women you see in the newspapers or on television: I don't wear a black cloak or a veil. I don't live on a street with a mosque, but on a tree-lined road in suburbia. I'm not subdued or downtrodden. In fact, I think some people find me just a bit too cheeky and sometimes they can be a little intimidated. I think that's funny. Isn't that funny?

I want you to come into my world of being a British, Asian, Muslim woman. Sometimes it is quite complicated, negotiating your way round different cultures, histories and ideas. I'm not Asian as you might think Asians to be, I'm not Muslim as you might imagine Muslims to be. I don't fit into other people's boxes.

This story is about how I found myself, my faith and my love, but most of all how I learnt to be me.

ONE

The First Time

Good Headscarf Day   ☆

Samosas are frying in the kitchen, teetering between perfect bronze and cinder black. My mother is concentrating on the huge pan of bubbling oil, her hair wrapped up in an old towel, her mind focused on those who are about to arrive. They are important guests, perhaps the most important ones yet.

The doorbell rings. I am flicked upstairs with a tea-towel. There is panicked scuttling around the house. Cushions are plumped. Curtains are adjusted. The kitchen door slams shut and my father is assailed by a cacophony of shrieking voices: 'They're here! They're here! Open the door!' The house becomes acutely still. The lilies in the living room stand poised. My father, unflustered, strolls towards the front door and swings it open to face the man who might be his future son-in-law.

This is the first time that my family and I are to be formally *introduced* to a suitor. Choosing what to wear has been a struggle. I have to be attractive enough for the man in question, yet modest and demure enough for his family. The contents of my headscarf drawer are strewn colourfully across my bedroom floor in molehills of pink, purple, blue and green. Each scarf has been carefully draped and pinned in turn, and then analysed for aesthetics and impact. I choose one in dusky pink silk. The colour is soft and welcoming, feminine but not girly. I fold the square silk in half and place the triangle over my hair, pinning it invisibly under my chin and throwing the ends loosely in opposite directions. The fabric delicately swathes itself over my hair and shoulders. Fortunately, I am having a Good Headscarf Day.

My blouse, in the same shade of pink, long-sleeved with ruffles on the cuffs, contrasts with my sweeping cream skirt with frills that trails gently on the floor. The whole family is fussing about what to wear. The first meeting is a compulsory rite of passage. It might be my only meeting. I listen in vain for a deep booming voice to announce: 'Now

You Are a Woman.' Nobody says: 'Good Luck.' Nor does anyone glance proudly and parentally at me, recording my transition from child to adult. I am no different from thousands, millions of young women on the threshold of marriage around the world.

I stand in front of the mirror, staring nervously into my own eyes, trying hard to control my torrential pulse. I inhale then exhale. Breathe in, breathe out. What will he be like? What will I say to him?

I am nineteen and about to step into a world that I have been prepared for since I was a young girl. The weight of tradition, which has rested so pleasantly on my Asian Muslim shoulders since my birth, has been no less powerful than the innocent delicious wait for Love. Every voice inside my head is sure of Love. Hollywood rom-coms are certain of true glorious passionate love. Children's fairytales proclaim it. Islamic teachings promise each person a partner to complete them. Asian culture places marriage above all else. And love, sweet, spicy, all-encompassing love, blossoms at the heart of any concept of marriage.

The fact that I am meeting my suitor to see if we like each other is considered by some to be unspeakably modern. I always knew that I would meet my husband-to-be this way. Why, then, does my heart pound so violently? The man and his chaperones are coming to Check Me Out, and I, of course, am going to Check Him Out. The balance of Checking Out does nothing to ease my nerves. This is not just Blind Date, but Family Blind Date.

Cilla Black smirks back at me from my bedroom mirror. 'Will you go for Family Number One, the accountants from London? Or Family Number Two, the clan of doctors from Gloucester? Or will it be Family Number Three, the import-exporters from Birmingham?'

He might be the only Prince Charming I will ever meet, will ever need to meet. And what is wrong with that? I long for my own Prince and dream of being part of a loving, 'in love' couple. In reality I will most likely meet him through the formal introduction process.

On his visit to our home, he will be accompanied by at least one, if not more, 'grown-ups'. Getting to know his family and understanding his background is just as critical as assessing his ratings on the tall, dark and handsome scales. He and his family will be evaluating me in the same way: a communal date hinging on communal decision-making, and he and I will be the focus of attention.

I look at myself again in the mirror and practise my smile. Mona Lisa or Julia Roberts? I squirt myself with perfume and then collapse in a nervous puff on the floor. I recite some verses from the *Qur'an,* which will help to steel my nerves and restore me to normal working order. The rhythmic melody and the wisdom of the words make me feel calm. I put a few coins in a special charity box we keep at home, called *sadaqa,* and then straighten my clothes. Putting money towards those who need it is like chaos theory: a small flutter grows and magnifies until the positive energy comes back round to you. I need the good karma at this moment.

The front door opens; my breathing stops. Mr Right has arrived.

I scamper upstairs to watch the entourage from the window as they park their car. I kneel down so I can peer through the gap between the curtain and the windowsill. I note a greyish-brown Toyota. Or is it a Honda? Does the exact badge on a typical reliable Asian family car matter? My eyes scan to the couple clip-clopping up our path. The Boy, Ali, walks quietly behind them.

The guests trip merrily through our front door, pretending there is nothing unusual about their visit. Even in the introduction meeting itself, the purpose of the visit remains discreet and unspoken. The house tinkles with small talk. The guests look too innocent, too *nice* to be coming to turn my life upside down. Are they here to extract me from the bosom of my family? I like my family, I am happy here. Why do I have to leave? Their arrival has made me apprehensive. I flap my hands, panic-stricken, abandoned alone upstairs to pace soundlessly while I wait until the appropriate moment to descend into the lair. A girl on a date has to make an entrance. Everyone knows that.

I stop abruptly and berate myself. Don't I want to fall in love and live happily ever after? This man might be my Prince Charming. He might sweep me into a world of roses and Cinderella ball-dresses. Will I feel tingles and fall in love with him at first sight?

I know four facts, which I have categorised into 'important' and 'uninteresting'. That he is an accountant and 23 years old is important to know. That he is a 'nice' boy and from a 'good' family I find uninteresting. At nineteen these facts are irrelevant to my simple desire to fall in love.

I hear scuffling in the living room as everyone settles in. I creep quietly down the stairs and sit hidden so I can hear what is being said. They spend a few minutes discussing family ties and origins and assessing if we have any relatives in common. Asians talking about families is like English people talking about the weather: a safe preamble that can be pursued endlessly. Beneath the pleasantries it also provides critical clues about your conversation partner. What is their background, their history, their reputation?

The two parties converse until they find a mutual relative. Asian languages are well-suited for this purpose, having specific names for complex relations, making it quick to identify an obscure relative. I can identify my mother's sister's husband's sister in two moves rather than the four required in English, or my father's brother's wife's mother's sister's mother-in-law's sister's husband in three moves. Both sides are earnest in their desire to find a relative or friend that links them. A buzzer then sounds and a voice calls out 'Bingo! You have a match.'

After a few minutes, I instinctively know that it is time for me to make my entrance. I practise my smile again in the mirror: a small upward curl on the edge of my lips, or a big grin? Or should I bow my head almost imperceptibly as I enter the room? I tuck the rebellious wisps of hair back under my headscarf, straighten my skirt and stride towards the door. My heart thumps rat-tat-tat, my brow is moist, my cheeks volcanic. It is time to meet the man.

The door to the living room is ajar. I swing it open and walk into a room sizzling with conversation. I expect the room to fall silent and for all eyes to turn to me. Even though I stand there for several seconds, I am unnoticed. The good-natured small talk continues. Should I wave my hands? Should I speak?

My father suddenly sees me. 'O-ho!' he yelps, a distinct Asian word-sound. 'This is my daughter Shelina.' He looks in an explanatory way at the guests, as though my arrival may be a surprise to them.

Suddenly I am conscious of myself, standing alone in the middle of the room. Our lounge is a large square space painted in safe pale green with deep emerald velvet curtains. The patio doors overlook a picturesque garden lovingly tended by my parents. They adore the garden: the garden adores them back. The guests sit comfortably on soft leather sofas encircling the centre of the room – and whoever might be in it.

I smile quickly, nervously assessing my surroundings. As is the norm, the men and women adopt separate sides of the room. Where is the female guest? Courtesy demands that I move to greet her first. Where is Prince Charming? I must acknowledge him openly yet modestly. How have people arranged themselves and where is the space appropriate for me to occupy? Rapid and correct decisions are critical to making the right impression.

I move towards the female guest and say '*Salam alaikum*', the Islamic greeting meaning 'Peace to you'. She is Ali's aunt. I kiss her on the cheek and she kisses me back. The matchmaker's description of me must have been running through her head at this moment. What has she been told? Do I live up to expectations? The matchmaker is present even in her absence, holding great sway over my life and the lives of many single men and women.

I look around shyly, spot the Boy and nod courteously at him. I instinctively occupy an empty seat near the door. I sit neatly and clasp my hands daintily on my knees. I smile charmingly into the space in front of me. The conversation revives. I breathe once again and try to gather myself. I glance fleetingly at the suitor without looking at him. I am conscious of being assessed. He appears relaxed, leaning back into the sofa, chatting to my father. My father can talk to anyone, unperturbed by their rank, age or status. He is talkative on the outside, quiet and determined on the inside. He has a short white beard that befits his stature and dignity. He likes to tease me by rubbing it enthusiastically against my cheeks. His concession to the squeals he has evoked this way ever since I was a child is to shampoo and condition the hair to keep it soft, so he does not scratch my skin.

'Are you working or studying?' The room quietens. I stare blankly at the people around me. I am being addressed. I do not realise.

Eventually I squeak, 'You mean me?' I clear my throat to deflate the high-pitched cartoon voice. 'I'm studying.'

'Very good,' continues the older male guest, who is Ali's uncle. 'I hear you are studying Psychology and Philosophy?'

I nod mutely. My voice is upstairs in my bedroom in protest at this awkward social situation.

'Does that mean you can tell what I am thinking?' He chortles, and then laughs so heartily that he starts coughing.

'Shelina, *beti*, get him some water,' directs my father. *Beti* is an affectionate name for a daughter. It reveals his attachment to me.

I return with a glass of iced water and settle myself back into my seat. I sit quietly for a few minutes, until I receive an imperceptible nod from my mother. I exit silently, my feet padding on the soft carpet towards the kitchen. I fill up the kettle with water and switch it on, watching the red indicator burning brightly, waiting patiently for the water to boil. I stare vacantly and then return to the living room. I project my most sweet, most polite, future daughter-in-law voice and ask 'Would you like some tea or coffee?'

I suddenly feel more confident: I have a role to play. I smile in turn at each of the guests as I ask them what they would like to drink and how much sugar and milk they would like in their tea and coffee. I restrain my splutter when I am asked for four spoons of sugar and sweetened condensed milk, a staple of Asian tea drinking. This sugar-laden tea preference is not uncommon. I try not to look too much at the Boy whilst I take the orders. He looks as terrified as me.

I chant the drink requests mantra-like in my head. Cooking and hostessing skills are crucial in Asian culture as a sign of a 'real' woman, just as they used to be in Europe, too. *Every* woman must be a domestic goddess. It certainly would not be in my favour to make an error at this stage.

In the kitchen once again, I arrange the cups on the tray to match the seating plan in the living room. This will help me distribute each drink to the right person. I place teabags in cups, spoon in the coffee (it is instant, for convenience), distribute sugar, pour hot water, and mop up spillages. I straighten my clothes again and lift the tray. Trying not to trip on the hem of my skirt, I hobble towards the living room. I regret my choice of long flowing chiffon skirt as my feet step on the frills.

I put down the tray in the centre of the coffee table and place each cup carefully on a coaster next to the right person. I pick up the teacup for the Boy, and suddenly feel unsure of what to do with it. I approach his seat, just as I have with everyone else, and place the cup next to him. As I serve him, I lift my eyes briefly to look at his face. In my shyness I look away too quickly. Regretting my nerves, I raise my eyes again and find myself staring unexpectedly into his. Suddenly our shared gaze is over, and I step back into the normal space-time continuum. I flee to the kitchen, feeling flushed and haphazard.

Samosas

I pick up another tray that has already been prepared, of small plates and finger food. It includes my mother's perfectly browned samosas. 'Bringing in the tray of samosas' is a leftover *leitmotif* of what was once the meeting process: the only time that the girl came into the room where her future was being negotiated. It is now simply an ironic euphemism for the introduction of a girl to a boy.

This might be a girl's one chance to view the prospective bridegroom. The boy must also capitalise on this opportunity. This is not the moment to be out of the room using the facilities. Along with his whole family, he may have travelled many miles for this single brief moment, perhaps his only opportunity to see the woman with whom he will share the rest of his life.

Will his eyes sparkle when he sets his gaze upon her? Does he like the turn of her *dupatta*, the translucent shawl that Sub-continental women often wear on their heads in place of a headscarf? What if the fabric slips as she bends down to hand out the plates and he glimpses her long midnight black hair? The way she places the teacups on the table, or how she hands out the plates of *halwa* could change her fate.

'Bringing in the samosas' was originally designed for the groom-to-be and his entourage to cast their eyes over the potential wife. The girl was not wheeled out in order for her to have an opinion or play any part in the decision-making process. Her fate would be determined by the groom and his family. He was the hunter, she the hunted.

The boy would ask himself: was she attractive? The male elders would consider: was this a good match? The entire transaction would be sealed with a few glances of the groom at his bride-to-be. She might be so covered up that he could barely see her, or, as she served him his tea, she might have the audacity to raise her eyes to his and glance cheekily at him. It was the same moment, whether from a golden

Bollywood film or Jane Austen's *Pride and Prejudice*. The serving of the samosas was able to change futures, destinies and families.

The girl did not speak during this process. Her role was to be modest and demure. In very conventional circumstances she would not have entered the room beforehand, as I had done, nor – heaven have mercy – would she have spoken. The momentary connection that the crispy meat-filled pastries had created would determine the groom's decision. All the poor girl could do was to wait for the verdict. If the response was negative, and if she had already ticked the box of 'good' family, then what could she do but assume her looks had let her down?

The female relatives who have also come to visit will grill the poor young woman and deliver their verdict to the groom and the male decision-makers of the family. The boy will only know of the bride-to-be what the womenfolk have told him. The system does not allow for the fact that the boy may find a very different type of woman attractive than his female relatives might expect. He must accept that Mother Knows Best.

The importance of the female opinion is not to be underestimated. A marriage is not just between the bride and groom, but also between their families. Traditionally, a wife would most likely not have worked. She would spend more time with her mother-in-law and sisters-in-law than with her husband, as the extended family might live together. Even when the couple were to go out, she would socialise with the women while he relaxed with the men. Creating happiness in the extended family home was as much of a challenge for the new bride as creating sparks in the nuptial chamber.

I hand out the plates and snacks. This time when I come past Ali I shine a warm smile in his direction. Somewhere in that process I begin to find my confidence and personality, and it feels good. He smiles back nervously, but we have made a connection. 'Thank you,' he says – it is the first time he has spoken directly to me. I feel more focused as I return to the kitchen. I have walked into a room full of people who have come to visit just for me, I have smiled, I have spoken, and I have made radio contact with a boy who is not unattractive.

As I return to the kitchen, my mother follows me. She is small, with soft brown skin and a smile that can lift me out of even the darkest mood. I look at her lovingly, encouraging her to reveal her secret. She speaks to me in a silent whisper. My eyebrows rise in confusion to my hairline. She turns around and closes the kitchen door. 'You need to go into the other room and talk to him.'

The main act is about to begin: I am going to talk to a man about Getting Married.

I peer into the dining room to make sure everything is in order and then sit down. This is to be the arena for our negotiations. Like the living room, it is square, but this time decorated in shades of blue, with a large mahogany dining table at the centre. The chairs are dark brown with curving arms and cream damask cushions. In the middle of the table yellow daffodils burst out of a blue vase. I imagine where he might sit and wonder if the better profile of my face will be turned towards him. I turn my left profile in his imaginary direction, and then my right, and then sit and mimic speaking to him. I switch places to the chair I imagine he will sit in and pretend to be him responding to my statements: 'I think you are stunning and I have fallen in love with you,' he informs me solemnly.

I practise my smile again: a big smile, a cheeky one, a coquettish one, no smile at all.

It would not be appropriate to be too enthusiastic or jovial at this stage. I ought to temper my usual exuberance in case I scare him. I have been told repeatedly by the elders and Aunties that I am too confident and clever, and that boys don't like that. If I am serious about getting married, I will have to hide it. Showing a glimpse is fine, but it is crucial that the boys don't think I am *too* clever. The Aunties have even gone so far as to say that I must not study a Masters or – heaven forbid! – a PhD, because nobody will want to marry me. Then I will have only myself to blame. 'Nobody wants a girl who is too educated,' they advise me. 'Then you'll be old and left on the shelf. Better to get married first, sort out your husband, and then you can do as you please.'

The Aunties were always large and buxom, with strong accents that had a mesmerising yet grating lilt to them. Their voices echoed through my head like crazed Jiminy Crickets. They were loud and powerful and rang with the legacy of thousands of years of tradition and heritage. Who was I to disobey their laws?

'You know that girl Sonia,' one of them would begin. 'Such a nice girl, *so* pretty and *so* fair.'

'She got a proposal from a good family, and the boy was *very* handsome.'

'Good looking, heh.'

'Yes, *very* good looking.'

'She was only seventeen.'

'Yes, only seventeen, but very clever.'

'Yes, very clever.'

'And he had a good job.'

'Yes, a *very* good job in a big law firm. *Senior Partner*, you know.'

'So she married him. And now she has three kids. And by the time she is 45, she will have had her children. The children will also be married themselves and have gone to their own homes, and she'll be free. Then she can do whatever she wants. Study, work, travel.'

'She's already going to university to study. She has completed her degree and is doing a Masters.'

'What you need a Masters for to clean the kitchen I don't know!' guffawed the more buxom of the Buxom Aunties.

'Masters of making roti and biryani!' they both cackled with their gravel-laden, *paan*-tinted voices. Chewing *paan* leaves released stimulants into the blood, like nicotine, and left yellow stains on the teeth.

The Buxom Aunties raised the hairs on the back of my neck with their opinionated diktats. The unwavering confidence in their own view of the world threatened me at my point of greatest confusion: the intersection of being Muslim, Asian and British. I was not able to pull back the layers of culture that oozed from their Auntie-Jee pores to try to understand and assess the wholesome Asian wisdom that lay beneath. Even their title – 'Auntie' for respect and 'Jee' for further respect – reinforced their standing as bastions of heritage and tradition. I cast them as old-fashioned whilst I thought of myself as forward-thinking and modern. I felt youthful revulsion at the stuck-in-time stereotypes of women that they supported, and my teenage self rebelled against them and all that they represented of tradition. But I did not see any paradox in engaging with the traditional process of marriage, of which they were a pivotal part. If I wanted a husband, this was how things were done.

I hush their voices away as I sit waiting for this moment, this life-changing moment for which I have been primed. I tap my fingers on the table. Is someone whispering into his ear that he should move discreetly to the other room? Is he excited? Or embarrassed?

The door swings open gently and a little head pops around the side. 'Hello,' he squeaks nervously. He clears his throat. 'Should I come in?' He edges into the room, looking sheepish. We look awkwardly at each other. The pretence of normality is safer than admitting our apprehensions. Is it only those brought up on Hollywood romances that find these meetings contrived and embarrassing? Or do suitors the world over have to confront the fear of opening their hearts to a complete stranger in the hope of finding a life partner? I imagine a large poster on the wall: 'Marriage, yea or nay? Vote now!'

I wonder if I should stand up and help him with a chair, to fulfil my duties as hostess. Hospitality is a deeply entrenched and essential Islamic value. The British and Asian voices in my head insist I remain still: pulling out chairs is a man's duty in our culture, they say. The pursuit of marriage trumps hospitality, they advise.

Besides, my own voice echoes that it is a universal principle that a woman should leave a man to have pride in his own masculinity and to be sensitive to a woman's femininity. I empower the man be The Man.

We sit on the corner of the dining table, at ninety degrees to each other, close enough to speak but far from intimate. The door is wide open, allowing anyone to look in on us and hear what we are saying. The easy chatter from the living room wafts towards us, making our own silence even more voluminous.

I sigh, dropping my shoulders to relax. My mother appears with a tray carrying two cups of coffee, some biscuits and the unforgettable samosas. She smiles and speaks directly to Ali, 'You both forgot your drinks.' He blushes, I blush, and then she blushes and whisks herself out the door.

I might marry this man, I think. I imagine the dress I will wear at the wedding. He will carry me over the threshold. We would live in a lovely four-bedroom, two-bathroom house, and he will take me for a promenade in the evenings in our very own rose garden. Our first child's nursery will be painted lilac, with a crib handcrafted from natural oak.

The pause lengthens. He relaxes and at last seems pleased to be here. I wonder if he has brought an engagement ring with him in his pocket.

I look at him properly now. He has short, well-kept hair, a neatly clipped beard and small metal-rimmed glasses. He is wearing a blue shirt and casual cream chinos. His style is neither old-fashioned nor cutting edge.

He clears his throat: 'Your name is Shelina.'

'Yes.'

'This is your house?'

'Yes.'

'You're living with your parents?'

'Yes.'

'Were you born in the UK?' He lets his voice trail gently, tilting his head towards me encouragingly, cheerleading me to participate in the conversation.

I look at him desperately and wince: 'Ye-es.'

He persists: 'And you're studying at Oxford, is that right?'

'Uh-huh,' I agree. The Aunties tut-tut in my head at the poor impression I am already making. This couldn't have got off to a worse start.

'You must be, erm, very intelligent.' His face contorts. I think it is disgust rather than nerves. The Buxom Aunties are screaming, flesh wobbling. *See, we told you so. He is telling you already that this is a problem. But no, you didn't listen to us. You youngsters always think you know better.*

I gulp in despair and stare silently at my hands.

'What was that like?' He pursues the cul-de-sac desperately.

'Good. Hmm, yeah, good,' I stutter. I don't know how to break the deadlock between us, and his attempts are equally ineffective.

He waits for me to carry on.

'It was really, er, very good indeed,' I elaborate.

Our hands move to our cups to pick up the coffee. We lift them to our mouths and pause. As we are about to sip our gazes cross. We're frozen, eye to eye, lip to cup. I concede the face-off and tip the cup towards my mouth. The liquid is feverishly hot and explodes violently out from my lips in burning shock.

'Are you OK?' he asks, eyes huge, looking towards the living room. Will he be held responsible for my injury?

I smile by accident; and I step from opaque to translucent. I feel sheepish. He smiles too, concerned but laughing. I like the sudden vulnerability that I feel.

'What do you know about me?' he asks, his expression more relaxed and gentler now.

'Well, you are Ali. You are 23 years old. You are an accountant. How is that?'

'Most astute.' He raises his eyebrows as though he is both wise and impressed.

I match his floating eyebrow expression and raise the stakes: 'Is there more to know?'

'I was born in Nairobi and I came here in my teens, finished school, went to university and somehow ended up as an accountant.' He has an ironic twinkle in his eye now. He speaks softly and gently. The conversation is not eloquent, and barely trespasses on interesting, but it takes on its own life. We chat, sometimes smoothly, sometimes in stop-starts. It certainly isn't memorable.

It is a peculiar feeling to talk to a stranger in the knowledge that within a handful of conversations you may decide to marry this person. The veneer of pleasantries is geared to getting to know about what makes up this person, and asking questions that would be extraordinary in any other 'first conversation' context. The process is designed to allow the parties to ask fundamental questions about their life goals, their values and their hopes for the relationship.

'What kind of person are you looking for?' he asks me. 'Would you like children, and if so, how many?' I ask in return. We talk about our hobbies and interests and what we would like to do when we grow older. What kind of lives do we want to create? What jobs? Where does he want to live? What does his family do? What does he expect of his wife? Then the conversation veers back to the mundane. What is his favourite film? What kinds of food does he like to eat? And back again. He hopes I will continue my studies at university. I agree: that is a priority for me. He enquires: Am I ready to get married? I respond: Have you been thinking about getting married for a long time? And back and forth we continue.

Although the conversation may have started awkwardly, I don't find it unusual or strange that I might meet my future life partner this way.

Don't all relationships begin with a simple conversation to find out about each other, whatever the setting? Is this any different to chatting to someone in a bar, club or restaurant? At least I know for sure that he is interested in having a serious relationship and getting married, and I am not frittering away my time over someone with relationship-phobia. He is, at the very least, open to the idea of commitment. I already know instinctively the questions that cause people heartache at the beginning of relationships: 'Is he interested? Will he? Won't he?' The rollercoaster rides of films and romantic fiction only serve to underline the need for early answers to these questions. This type of introduction gives me those answers very quickly.

The process that I am engaged in is quite clear: both parties will have to make a statement about our intentions after the meeting, albeit through intermediaries. So it doesn't seem strange to ask huge, meaningful questions, interspersed with the basic facts of each other's lives and frivolities. These are the critical things that will determine if we can live a lifetime together, to share love, happiness and prosperity. I am, of course, trying to impress him. I don't want to be turned down. Who wants to be knocked back, especially the first time?

There is a tap at the door and a disembodied voice informs us: 'Ali, they are calling you, they want to leave.'

'Do you know what happens next?' I ask.

'I think you should talk to your family about our conversation and how you feel,' he responds gallantly.

I don't press him for advice. We are in the same position but not on the same side. We exchange closing pleasantries, and the awkwardness that we had managed to erase seeps back into the room.

As we re-enter the living room, I blush. They all know that we have been together, *talking*, in an open public space. I feel embarrassed, even though our conversation has been the key reason for the visit. I wonder with paranoia if they think we have been up to all sorts of *you know what*, but of course we haven't. And they know it. My embarrassment is a demon of my own making.

Unexpectedly, clothes rustle, pockets jangle and chairs and tables move. The guests stand up. Ali nods in my direction and I smile instinctively, then blush at being so forward. My mother, in tune, glances at both of us and smiles. We have to go, *faux*-apologise our guests. No, please, stay for another cup of tea, *faux*-responds my father, it's early yet. No, no, we have a very long way to get home, they counter-respond. Their answer reveals their participation in the etiquette of departure: they live only three miles away.

They shuffle towards the door, moving slowly enough to avoid appearing rude. Ali's aunt whispers into my mother's ear. The two women's words oil the marriage-making machine. They both agree that they will call the matchmaker who has set up the meeting in order to report back after the encounter. If the feedback to the matchmaker is positive from both sides, we will move to the next stage, which will involve meeting again and a more serious level of negotiation. Everyone else pretends to be oblivious to their conversation. Despite their whispers being inaudible, we all know why we are here and what they are saying. The rest of us pretend that this is nothing more than a Sunday afternoon social visit.

'Come again,' we chime. 'It is now your turn to visit us,' they chorus. 'We had a delightful afternoon.' 'Such a lovely house.' 'I'm sure we will see you at the mosque soon.' 'Please convey our *salams* to your family.' 'We should do this more often.'

Ali's aunt turns to look at me. She runs her eyes from my scarf down to my feet, and then pats my cheek. She turns to look at Ali maternally and then returns her gaze to face me. 'I heard a lot about you before we came,' she informs me knowingly. 'It was nice to meet you at last.'

'Thank you Auntie, it was really lovely to meet you as well. We enjoyed your visit.' I smile at her respectfully. She is my elder, and I offer her the courtesy that is her due.

The men look awkwardly around the hallway, wishing this would be over quickly. They do not enjoy the niceties of the process.

'This is in Allah's hands you know.' The woman turns pointedly towards my mother. Is she making a statement of her piety or is it a cover for an imminent rejection? 'It is a matter of destiny.'

They bid farewell and file out of the front door, trooping back to their respectable-but-anonymous car. My father stands at the door, one hand resting on the handle, the other held up, hinting at a sending-off gesture to our departing guests. He watches them climb into the car, close the doors and pull away. He waves vigorously for a moment, and then the car, and the Prince it contains, disappear into the suburban horizon.

We return to the living room and I flop into one of the armchairs.

'I'm so tired,' I wail. I unpin my headscarf and remove the hair-band that has been keeping my hair under control. I immediately feel more relaxed.

'Poor thing,' says my mum, patting me on the head.

I turn to my father who is sitting in his special chair, remote control poised to ignite the television and check the latest news. I interject between him and his news fix, 'What is your opinion, Dad? Did you like him?'

'He seems nice,' he confirms. 'It's up to you now. Whatever you think you want to do.'

I pout.

'We're your parents,' he continues. 'We can advise you but you are the one who has to live with him for the rest of your life.'

'What about everyone else?' I ask.

'I thought he seemed nice too,' says my sister-in-law, stretching her legs out onto the coffee table. 'I think he would make a good husband and you would be very happy. He's got a nice family, good job, he's religious, quite nice looking.' She pauses and then looks up at me mock-offended. 'What? What? I can't observe if a man is handsome?'

I turn to my mother for her opinion. 'You know many years ago a family would accept the first decent proposal that came along.' She pauses. 'He's a good choice. You shouldn't miss him.' Her hesitation belies her strong words. I can tell straight away that my feelings mirror hers but I value her advice. As a woman, a wife and a mother, she has already been through the journey that I am about to set sail on.

'He seems nice but that is what all of you keep saying: nice, nice, nice. How am I supposed to know? How do I know?' I look pleadingly at everyone.

Can you ever know? ask their eyes.

He was my first, a Prince amongst princes. Each one would offer me a very different life. How to choose?

Romance asked: *Does he make you tingle?*

The Buxom Aunties whispered: *Is he a good catch?*

Faith asked: *Is he a practising Muslim like you?*

I was bewildered by my own mistaken belief that there were contradictions in these different perspectives about love that came from faith or tradition, from popular or Asian culture.

It all came down to the same question: *Is he the one?*

Safura

The next morning the matchmaker called. She was a member of the Marriage Committee at the local mosque, a group of women whose *raison d'être* was to introduce families who wanted their sons and daughters to get married. When your child was ready to marry, you would approach the committee and inform them that you were looking for a partner for your child. The committee members would offer prospective suitors a wide network of contacts and an unconditional dedication of their time and energy towards meeting your needs. The community was always genuinely concerned that its younger members should be helped towards attaining fulfilled and happy lives. A well-matched and happy marriage was considered a critical component.

The very first time that the matchmaker had rung our home, she had offered a courteous preamble about the importance of getting young people married to suitable partners. It was up to the whole community to assist in the process, she had commented. The matchmaker's opening statement was both polite and heartfelt.

Marriage is a communal matter, and those who volunteer to be matchmakers play an essential part in protecting the existence of the family unit. In Islamic thinking, someone who brings two people together in marriage gains an immense spiritual reward for their good deed. The matchmaker pointed out to my mother that since I was now at university, it was a very suitable time to start on the search for a husband. It was accepted that a young woman would complete her education, if she chose to, before she got married.

'These things take time,' she had advised my mother learnedly. 'And if you find the right person, then Shelina can get married and continue studying, or they can get engaged and then marry after Shelina finishes her degree.'

Then she added ominously, 'The good boys get snapped up very quickly these days.' She paused and asked, 'Shall I start looking for someone for her?'

Both my mother and the matchmaker knew that the question was for decorum only. They were both searching already. Parental eyes are constantly scrutinising potential matches from childhood, making a point to come back to them when the possible suitors have grown up. It was important to think long term when finding a partner. Etiquette demanded a reply and my mother responded by thanking her for her concern, acknowledging the challenges that matchmakers face and re-iterating the reward they would gain for carrying out their Islamic duties with such diligence.

'I have someone to suggest,' cut in the matchmaker. 'A *very* nice boy.'

My mother responded with an encouraging sound and the matchmaker filled in the details. My mother listened carefully, making little scribbles on the notepad, nodding vigorously as the matchmaker listed the young man's virtues. She described his family and their connections until my mother knew exactly who they were. She elaborated on the details of the family's finances, qualities, reputations and education. She went on to make comments about the future mother-in-law and what she had specified as requirements for her son's bride. She closed her speech with a brief description of the boy himself.

'I will speak to Shelina and see what she thinks,' responded my mother. 'And then I will ring you back and let you know.' She paused. 'Thank you so much for thinking of Shelina, it is very much appreciated.'

My mother then relayed the details to me and the family. He was religious, educated, had a good job and was from a respected family. He was the right age and apparently quite handsome, too. 'He sounds promising,' I had commented. Everyone agreed, and my mother rang back to confirm our interest.

The next time the matchmaker rang was to confirm a date and time for the suitor to visit. 'They are very excited and looking forward to meeting Shelina,' she had added.

Now, post meeting, she was ringing again to gather our feedback. She would already have spoken to the boy's family – they were considered to be in the driving seat.

My mother switched the call to speakerphone so I could listen to their conversation. They chatted for a while, courteous small talk. Then, abruptly, she asked, 'What did Shelina think?' My mother jolted in shock, despite fully expecting the question. Her answer was, of course, the sole purpose of the conversation.

My mother manoeuvred deftly to avoid answering the question first. 'Why don't you tell me what Ali thought?' she asked in return. Offering an opinion was complicated. If we were the first to say that I liked him and they had said no, it would leave us vulnerable and embarrassed. If we said yes first and they said yes anyway, it would make us too forward. If we said no first and they had been planning to say yes, they would change their minds and say no to avoid being rejected, and so we would never know. But if they went first and said no, then if we said no, it would look like we had meant to say yes but were only saying no because they had done so. In addition to this, we were conscious that we would meet these individuals and their close relatives at the mosque and community events, and whilst the meeting would never be spoken of, everyone would be thinking about it. The denouement had to be handled diplomatically, to avoid anyone being insulted.

The matchmaker relented. 'He really liked her and wants to meet again if Shelina is interested.' It was quite common these days to have at least a second meeting, much in the style of the first, rather like second viewings to buy a house. In some quarters of the Asian and Muslim community the first meeting, which had once been risqué, was now standard. Now the boundaries of *cultural* acceptability were being pushed to a second meeting. Modernity was taking its toll.

It had once been quite common for the boy's family to make a proposal to the girl's family after one meeting. In fact, they may have sent the proposal even without a meeting: family references would have been sufficient. However, it was now more likely that there would be a second meeting, or perhaps even a third. By then you should know if he was the one or if she was your wife-to-be. And really, truly, having spent intensive sessions with them, and armed with details of their life, family, intentions, reputation and aspirations, why wouldn't you know?

You would have met in person to know if you liked each other's company. You would have a full reference history on their background, reputation, job (including salary), leisure activities, social participation, religious and mosque status and even their school grades and a CIA, FBI, KGB or NASA check if you wanted. Additionally, you would also know their family and their family history, including their track record as a unit of treating new spouses and their marriage and divorce rates. Your conversations would have been open and about the long term. You ought to know exactly what this person was about and where they were going. It was a robust and time-tested method that seemed to work. As the Aunties said, wasn't this the information you needed to choose the right person with whom to build a successful relationship?

Any risk that you might expect when marrying someone after such a short period was dealt with by community structures. Family would be on hand to support the new couple through their needs and worries, and parents and relatives would counsel the couple on any relationship-teething issues. And as one of the newly-weds you would be prepared for the relationship to take time to settle down before the Mills and Boon story kicked in.

The Aunties asked, what would make knowing someone for three years rather than three intense meetings a better match? It was hard to disagree with them on this point. They saw the world through a simple and practical choice between love – exciting, romantic, fireworks love – on the one hand, and a well-reasoned assessment of the practical sensibilities of life on the other. The first offered danger, exclusion, risk, a defying of convention. The latter had been proven out by history and offered respectability, a place in society and a recognition of status and worth.

It would take me many years to realise that I had been living their paradox of believing that this was an either/or choice but also longing and desiring to have both. I believed that I was special and could and *should* have both. It would take a search for my faith to reveal to me that my instinct was right – that love and practicality needed each other.

'Shelina . . .' began my mother

'Isn't he *such* a nice boy?' chipped in the matchmaker. '*Such* nice manners and *so* good looking. Ali said he thought Shelina was very nice and friendly.'

'Shelina . . .' my mother tried again, then stopped mid-sentence. 'Yes, he was very nice, and his family seemed nice too.' As my mother opened her mouth to say the next sentence, the course of my life was set.

'Shelina is not keen to go ahead with him.'

The matchmaker's eyebrows pinged to her hairline and her jaw clattered onto the floor. 'Oh,' she squawked, trying to hide her shock. 'Why not?'

'Well . . .' began my mother. What could she say that was both credible and conciliatory? Besides, she did not entirely agree with my decision. My family had encouraged me to meet with him a second time.

I was nineteen and he was the first man I had ever been introduced to, the first candidate I had considered spending the whole of my life with. It had been a constrained and artificial setting, and the signals, emotions and chemistry couldn't work their usual magic.

I was not aware that the artificiality of the meeting place had sucked away any instinctive attraction. In my ignorance of this fact, I did not understand that this was the reason why 'that feeling' was absent. I had set myself the wrong litmus test to find a partner. The ease with which

I rejected such a high-calibre suitor was naive. All that I had been looking for was 'that feeling'. At nineteen I had high hopes of Finding the One. I look back and think that Ali probably would have made quite a good husband. In fact, he did go on to marry, and his wife always looks happy and radiant. I sometimes wonder what would have happened if I had married him.

My family took their Islamic responsibilities very seriously. I had to agree to my future partner willingly and happily. What they were offering was an arranged marriage – something very different from a forced marriage.

As part of an arranged marriage, their job was to provide potential matches and offer advice, support and wisdom in choosing one. If I didn't like someone they presented to me, then so be it. My choice was the determining factor. In adhering to their faith as Muslims, it was quite clear to my parents that there was to be no coercion of any sort in my selection of a husband. Besides, they could never have forced me to do anything against my will: they were too respectful of me as a human being in my own right. On top of all this, if they had used force in sealing the marriage, then it would not be valid anyway. But there was nothing sinister in them helping to 'arrange' men to come my way. Who would object to help in finding the love of one's life? And they would also be on hand to help during the agreement process. Having someone to support the relationship as it became more serious was just as important as helping to find that special someone in the first place.

My parents were also learning through this experience. I was their first marriage experience with a daughter, and the rules seemed to be completely different for girls. Had they also known the complexity of the path that I was choosing to pursue, they might have encouraged me more vigorously to consider Ali, but I think they, too, believed that the perfect prince existed. How would they settle for anything less for their princess?

'Shelina should meet him again. It's always so hard to tell the first time, the poor little thing. He must have been nervous, she was nervous. They weren't really themselves,' twittered the matchmaker.

My mother wanted what mothers always want for their daughters: happiness and love. Whatever the positive experiences of their own lives, mothers want something even better for their daughters. So my mum fell back on a thoroughly modern phrase: 'She says that she just didn't feel the "click".'

I looked at my mum with adoring respect. She believed in the 'click'. This should have come as no surprise. One of her favourite stories from the *Qur'an* was that of Safura and Moses. Moses, a strong and handsome young man, has arrived in town and is watering his sheep at a well along with the local shepherds. Safura is waiting with her sister to water her flock but the other shepherds make it difficult for them because they are women. The chivalrous stranger intervenes and assists with their sheep. After Safura's encounter with Moses she returns home and recounts this incident of the strange man to her father. Her father has a business and she advises him that Moses would make an excellent employee because of his strength and good character. As a result of their conversation, her father dispatches her to invite him to dinner.

I often wonder if she tells her father of this Johnny-come-lately because she has taken a shine to him. It seems she was open with her family and that in such a setting there was no embarrassment in a daughter suggesting to a father that she has a special interest in a particular man. Perhaps Safura conveys her 'click' to her father. Moses is invited round to meet her family so he can be properly evaluated. Fast forward, and Safura and Moses are married.

My mother as well as my father had taken the analogy very much to heart. Despite the notion of 'click' being absent in cultural norms of marriage, they were open and conscious of exploring this concept as a result of what their faith described to them. They constantly wanted to learn from the stories of the *Qur'an* and the Prophets in Islamic history. Having the family involved was also no bad thing. It wasn't considered interfering: it was thought of as advice and support, and it was very welcome. Love and relationships were everyone's business because they affected everyone. Besides, parents had more experience and wisdom from life, which was helpful in making such huge choices.

In the process of making a decision to turn down one suitor, I had set in motion a greater journey: to look for the love of my life. The precedent was set: Finding the One was my mission, and in looking for love, I would find myself, my faith and Divine Love along the way.

I had declared the Search officially open.

TWO

Hyphenated

Innocence

At the age of thirteen I knew I was destined to marry John Travolta. One day he would arrive on my north London doorstep, fall madly in love with me and ask me to marry him. Then he would convert to Islam and become a devoted Muslim.

My school-friends had similar reveries, apart from the converting to Islam bit. I was a teenage girl with typical adolescent fantasies. Except for the matter of religion. Whoever was destined to be my Milk Tray man would certainly become a Muslim before any romance. This would lead directly to marriage, and it would be a short path between the two. There was to be no frolicking before the nuptials. Through my youthful eyes, I was sure that I was such an appealing prospect that conversion to Islam would be an obvious, uncomplicated and an easy choice for the lucky man.

I was told by the Buxom Aunties that I was an unattractive teenager, skinny, and with one curse considered by Asians to be worse than death: I was considered 'dark'. Asians are notoriously colour-conscious: to be fair is to be beautiful, to be dark is to be ugly. Being pale of skin is a sign of status and a hugely desirable quality in a future daughter-in-law.

It is most often the hero's mother that makes the selection as to who should be introduced to her son to consider for marriage. Mothers-in-law preferred to show off pale-skinned brides. I grew up believing I was unappealing and unattractive. When desperately searching for compliments, the Aunties would comment about 'how *charming* she is' or ask, 'Aren't her features *unusual?*' When faced with pale-skinned girls they would coo, 'My goodness, she's so fair and *beautiful!*'

As a child I had been both fair and adorable. I had thick glossy hair and rosy chubby cheeks. 'All the better to pinch you,' squealed the grown ups. I was extremely alert and very contented, happily playing for hours on my own.

My greatest distinction was being a diligent student, even from a young age. I loved going to school and doing my homework. Each evening I was questioned by my father as to whether I had completed my schoolwork, and often I would do more class exercises than necessary. In my childhood memories, my mother and father are both constantly present, spending as much time with me as they could. I basked in their love and grew up very much a golden child.

I was permitted to stay awake until eight in the evenings to watch television. It was only rarely that I saw those reflecting my skin colour and background on the small black window that stood in the corner of our living room. I was raised in the dark ages before the advent of the remote control. As the child in the family, it was I who was forced to jump between sofa and television to change channels at the whim of the adults. There were only four channels at the time, a very primitive situation. It was programmes like *Mind Your Language*, *In Sickness and In Health* and *It Ain't Half Hot Mum*, with their limited number of ethnic characters who had boot-polish painted faces and caricatured catchphrases that gave a window onto how Britain viewed the Asian and black immigrants they had once colonised and who were now slowly becoming part of British culture. We, too, were swept away by the rarity and simplicity of the portrayals, happy to see ourselves on television at all. At least the characters representing us in these comedies appeared human and humorous, not barbaric, oppressed or rebellious. 'You Pakistani *poppadom*!' we would chuckle to each other. 'You Indian *chappati*!' we chortled. 'A *thousand* apologies,' we waggled our heads without irony.

Even rarer were the occasional programmes about Muslims. After much turning of the pages of the newspaper TV listings, there would be a network of telephone calls to and from friends and relations to stay at home in the evening to watch a particular programme. This would be followed by a thorough post-programming analysis. We would gather in front of the screen and view each scene meticulously. Once we had a video recorder, each show would be captured for posterity. Mostly these programmes were inaccurate, plain and simply wrong about the tenets of Islam, showing shoddy research and a poor treatment of the subject matter. I remember vividly a series entitled *The Sword of Islam*, which depicted a besworded group of warriors thundering across Arabia and Asia, painted as all but a horde of vampires sucking blood from the necks of children. My parents were horrified that Islam was being portrayed in such an alien and stereotyped manner. We weren't converted by the sword, I reflected. Our family had been merchants who found Islam on their business travels. Even I knew that the sword story was a myth, and I was only a child. I concluded that the TV people really didn't know their stuff.

When I first started school, the question I found most difficult was: 'Where do you come from?' This was not a question to do with babies, whose origins were simple: they just appeared. They popped out of belly buttons and you knew their gender by looking at their faces. I was shocked at a conversation between my mother and her sister after her first baby had just been born. 'Why don't you have another child? You should try for a second,' said my mother to my aunt. I was puzzled. How could my aunt cause a child to happen? You couldn't just 'have' a baby. It was quite straightforward: children came only because God sent them, when God chose to send them.

It was my own origins that were much more complicated: a British East-African Asian Muslim girl in the bubbling ethnic mix of North London in the context of 1980s Anglo-Saxon monoculture made it hard for me to articulate succinctly my origins.

At the age of six, if you are asked, 'Where are you from?', the location of the house you live in is the obvious answer. It is the answer that anyone who does not look different would proffer. But you know they want more. They want to know why your skin isn't peaches and cream if you're from North London. They want to know why you wear those brightly coloured, strange-shaped clothes. Why your food smells strange and why you eat with your fingers rather than with cutlery like civilised people. Why, sometimes, you have strange brown tattoos on your hands. The questions were never verbalised directly at me in real life, as they were in the mouths of comic racist characters like Alf Garnett. But they sat accusingly, demeaningly, disparagingly, tucked between lips and teeth. It was always easier to hide, to deny, to keep things separate. As long as the worlds never overlapped, there was never any danger, but the fear of collision was constant.

I never revealed that we ate curry at home. I never prayed in front of my friends. I didn't tell them about going to the mosque. How to explain all this, when the students at my nice middle-class independent school all came from well-heeled, well-settled families with a professional father and a stay-at-home mother, the two of whom met at university, got married, bought houses in leafy Winchmore Hill, multiplied immediately and sent their children to relive their circle of life? Only later, as the world became smaller, as people's eyes widened at the complexities of global cultures, and as my confidence in my own faith and culture grew, were my answers delivered with edgy attitude about fusion style, tasty spicy cuisine and fashionable henna art; and about my faith and the belief that it had something strong to offer.

My great-grandparents had travelled from Gujarat in India to settle in East Africa in the late nineteenth century. They were part of a great wave of Indians moving from the British Empire's Sub-continental colony to its developing East African territories. The British encouraged many men to participate in the migration in order to provide labour to build the East African railways and start developing the region. Women undertook the migration soon after. Some went because famine was ravaging areas like the Gujarat and the Punjab. Others went to seek economic improvement. The Asian migrants spread to the tip of South Africa and as far west as the stylised 'Heart of Darkness' in the centre of the vast uncharted continent. That there were people already settled there who lived untouched lives with their own histories and customs was overlooked by the British. The Sub-continental Asians settled fast, turning areas like today's Nairobi, now capital of Kenya, from an undeveloped area, first into a vast tented metropolis, and then into a city, almost overnight.

The Asians joined a swirling mass of ethnicities. East Africa was occupied by both the British and the Germans. The French and Portuguese also held territories in the neighbouring Congo and Mozambique. The coastal areas had long been ruled by Oman, a great seafaring nation on the edge of the Arabian Peninsula that had grown rich through the frankincense it exported. Only on the south coast of Oman did these amazing trees grow with their dazzlingly hypnotic fragrant sap that was turned into perfume and sold at high prices around the world. They used their wealth and sea skills to expand their empire, stretching, in particular, southwards along the eastern seaboard of Africa. They named the now capital of Tanzania, where my parents spent the first years of their marriage, 'Dar-es-Salaam', the land of peace and safety, a name which persists today. The Omanis also called the coasts 'Sawaahil', according to the Arabic word, and the language that was created on fusing with the local dialects has come to be known as 'Swahili', the language of the coast. Today it is spoken as the official language in several countries, including Tanzania, the home of my parents and grandparents.

In the mid-1850s, before my great-grandparents had sailed from Gujarat to what was then Tanganyika, their small Hindu community had converted to Islam. Family histories point to people who embraced Islam with passion and simplicity, trying to create lives built around their new-found faith. The stories reveal a sense of innocent desire for spirituality and a bright-eyed recognition of truth. There was, of course, no internet, no high-speed delivery, no flying around the world to teach and learn. Instead such communities were sent teachers from the historic Muslim heartlands of the Middle East. The scholars who arrived from the traditional seminaries would then learn the local languages.

Books, including the *Qur'an* itself, were slowly translated from Arabic, Persian and even Urdu into Gujarati. The *Qur'an* lay at the very core of Islamic belief: 114 chapters which Muslims believe that the Prophet Muhammad received by divine revelation in small sections through the latter years of his life. It lays out the principal beliefs of Islam and guidance on how to be a good Muslim. It was preserved in writing soon after Muhammad died and the text has remained unchanged since then. Since the words are believed to be divine and each one carries a special meaning with multiple layers, the Arabic text is considered paramount. Translations in most languages have appeared, but these are only considered as helpful aides towards understanding the original text.

At that time individuals rarely learnt to read Arabic. My great-grandmother, even though she grew to a respectable old age, would rely on others, including her daughter, to read out loud any text in Arabic, never having learnt it herself. Slowly this changed, as reading in the original language became standard community practice, and many of the men learnt to speak both Arabic and Persian – the latter being the administrative language of India even into the twentieth century.

Within the context of a millennium and a half of Islamic history, my family and my community were relative newcomers to the faith. Even today, our youthful Islam is fresh and hungry. It stretches back for only a handful of generations and is seen through the eyes of India, Africa and now Britain.

My parents grew up in Tanzania, just as their parents had done. Their communities were mainly Indian, but from across the religious spectrum – Muslim, Christian, Hindu, Sikh. They lived happily as neighbours, sharing values and cultures, supporting each other in their religious practices. In my mother's family, educating the young women was important. In order to help my mother travel to school, her father purchased a bicycle for her, and she was the first woman in her town to ride to class. It was unheard of and deeply shocking. My grandfather insisted that it was important for her to attend school and that she should be safely transported there and back. Education was part of religion, and one of the great Islamic sayings from Muhammad was 'Educate yourself, even if you have to travel to China.' Back then, China was a distant and mysterious empire on the other side of the world. My grandfather's insistence that religion took priority over cultural expectations had a strong impact on my mother's faith, because setting faith over tradition still informed her approach to life.

Soon after my parents were married, Tanzania declared independence. My father's family had long been British Overseas Subjects. The new political situation forced him to choose between Tanzania and Britain. In the late 1960s, at a time of huge global and social change, he had to make a choice between the excitement of a newly independent state that he had grown up in and where his family lived, and a one-time-only offer to uproot himself with his young family and move to Britain, an unknown distant country, which held an unknowable future. Being a British subject, this country had been in his family's blood for many decades, and young, energetic and optimistic, he took the risk. They arrived on the shores of England with two suitcases and £75.

My parents recall it as a time of forgotten difficulties and magnified excitement. 'We overlooked the hardships,' they reminisce, 'because we were young and we wanted to experience the world.' They had exchanged living in a spacious modern flat in the centre of Dar-es-Salaam for a cold one-bedroom place in the suburbs of grey wintry London, with an outside toilet and a shared bathroom and kitchen. My father was refused jobs because he was of Asian origin. The bank manager insisted on a 50 per cent deposit when they bought their first house because he was Asian. The neighbours ran a campaign to prevent them from buying it. They withstood this discrimination and resolved to build a solid life for themselves. They had seen their own families living as minorities in East Africa, and the efforts they had gone through there to build up their wealth and status were still fresh and raw. Now that they found themselves in a similar minority situation in the UK, they got on with the job of doing the same in their new home.

The keys to success, in my father's eyes, were education and hard work. And by working hard he gave both his children a first-rate education. 'Give a man a fish,' he told us repeatedly, quoting from the well-worn proverb, 'and he'll eat for a day. Teach him to fish and he'll eat forever.' Success and material wealth were not to be relied on, he cautioned us. 'Did you see what happened to the Asians in Uganda?' he would ask rhetorically. 'They were good people living good comfortable lives, and then one day they had to leave everything behind and become homeless refugees. It shows you, wealth and prosperity can come easily and can disappear even in the blink of an eye.' The rise of bloodthirsty Idi Amin was a cautionary tale for migrant Asians who had been exiled with the threat of extermination from their homes in Uganda in the early 1970s.

Modernity has persuaded us that it is essential for us to fulfil certain needs: comfort, style, status, romance. But these are not the essentials. Instead, what the exiles had experienced first-hand was that life at its most threadbare is a desperate scramble for survival.

'How precarious is a person's position in any country?' My father would pause and remind us with cautionary love: 'The most important thing for you always, the thing that we teach you and urge you to always keep, the thing that will always keep you true to yourselves and to be good people in this world, is to ensure that you do not abandon your faith and to always remember God.'

My parents loved to travel. Perhaps it was something to do with the itch of the migrant in their blood. My school holidays were punctuated with trips abroad to interesting and exotic places, despite the fact that we were not wealthy. Every year we went away to see new places and explore their hidden treasures, and I gathered people, places and experiences in my memory. The visits embedded signposts in my wild, porous imagination and marked out the landscapes of a connected, multilateral reflection of a world that had yet to catch up with my longing optimism.

My first holiday memories are of a trip to Tanzania at the age of four to visit my extended family. We still have old projector film with movie clips from this trip. It's the kind of film you wind around a wheel and when it ends it makes a funny clicking sound and a white light is projected onto the screen. The scene that most surprised me years later was a vignette of me on the beautiful sandy beaches of Dar-es-Salaam. I am unaware of the camera's eye and unconcerned by social constraints. I am wearing my favourite red shorts and red *Jungle Book* T-shirt. It was only years later that I admitted that the T-shirt was too small for me to wear. I am busy with my bucket and spade, surrounded by a ring of young boys hanging on my every word and obeying my instructions, all of them trying to please me.

When I was three I began at nursery school. My parents had deliberately chosen to speak to me only in Kuchi, the dialect of Gujarati that we spoke, and so I didn't speak a word of English when I first started. Within weeks I was fluent. By the age of four I was reading children's English perfectly. At the same time my parents began teaching me to read Arabic script. They firmly believed that as a Muslim I should be able to read the *Qur'an* directly in its original language. Every evening I would sit playfully on my father's knee and practise reading a page of the children's manual to reading the *Qur'an*. I adored this intimacy with my father and I raced through the pages.

The Arabic script was a mystery that I took delicious pleasure in unravelling. It was not something alien in our home but part of who we were. It was like the fact that in my parents' bedroom the bed was pushed to one side so that there would be enough space for two prayer mats, one each for my mother and father. These were specific prayers that were done early in the morning, in the afternoon and in the evening. They combined special movements with words from the *Qur'an*, and all Muslims around the world prayed in exactly the same way, in the direction of Mecca. I would race to lay out the mats at prayer time and stand next to my mother who would gently direct me as to what to do. At the end of the prayers I would read out loud the most recent chapter from the *Qur'an* that I had learnt.

At the age of five I completed reading the children's manual and began the full Arabic text of the *Qur'an* itself. This I completed when I was six. I found it easy because the Arabic phrases had a simple melodious rhythm and the verses often rhymed, almost like poetry. At the age of six and a half I entered a competition at the mosque to give a talk about the Prophet Muhammad and what we could learn from his life. Diligently, and with the innocence and simplicity of a young child, I had prepared my own talk about the good behaviour and kindness of the Prophet. I admit to some plagiarism – I copied it almost entirely from a book about the Prophet, changing some long words I didn't understand and couldn't pronounce into six-year-old vocabulary.

At the end of the speech I added one of my favourite stories about the Prophet. Every day he was forced to walk along a particular street where an old woman would throw rubbish at him because she did not agree with the belief in one God that he was propagating. Each day he would come home covered in foul-smelling litter. One day he walked along the street but there was no rubbish. Instead of being happy at the absence of the woman as most of us would have been, he investigated why she was not carrying out her daily activity and discovered that she was unwell. He went to visit her to see if he could offer her any help. She was shocked that he would show such kindness after her long-standing harassment. Muhammad advised her that looking after even those who show you difficulties is what being a Muslim was all about. I was convinced that the inclusion of this story as the closing part of my speech would win me the prize.

The mosque was a small converted community centre. Some mosques were purpose-built, some were in small converted houses, others were old buildings of worship that had been closed down or in disrepair and then rescued and revived as a place of worship, but this time as a mosque. The floor was covered in large rugs, and as in all mosques, you had to remove your shoes in the cloakroom before you entered. The mosque was the centre of Islamic community life. Prayers were held there, along with *Qur'an* classes for children, lessons for adults, and other religious lectures and events. It was the hub of Muslim existence because it was a centre of learning and spirituality, but also a place to meet friends and family and fulfil your social needs.

When we arrived at the mosque, I would normally have joined my mother in the women's section, as women and men sat in separate parts of the mosque. Instead, in order to participate in the competition, I had to go into the men's side to give the talk. Since I was only six, this was OK. I felt slightly strange being the only girl in a roomful of men, all staring intently at me, waiting to see what a young child would say. The bright video lights were glaring and the cameras were rolling. I stood three foot tall and confident and reeled off my presentation, word perfect and carefully intoned, pausing at the right moments for effect. I spoke for five minutes and I performed the whole speech entirely by heart.

I was awarded only second place, runner-up to a ten-year-old boy, who was commended for his insight and deep analysis. I was disgruntled and reflected that of course his speech would be deeper and more insightful than mine: I was six and he was ten.

A few weeks later I was asked to prepare a short speech for a presentation day at the end of term at school, which would showcase the religions of all the students. Instead of the enthusiasm with which I had greeted the mosque competition, I was in fact deeply reluctant.

There was one other Muslim in my class, a girl whose parents were from Turkey. But it was I who was asked to speak about being a Muslim.

'Why can't *she* be the one to speak about Islam?' I whined uncharacteristically. I did not want to stand up in front of the whole school and talk about the details of Muslim life: that was reserved for my time away from school.

'Perhaps the teachers think that with your excellent speech skills you will do a good job of explaining what Islam is,' suggested my mother. I envied the confidence of her belief and the way it infused all parts of her life so naturally. Even to her friends who were not Muslim, she never preached, but her wisdom and advice, which were born of her faith, were naturally woven into her words and actions. She never elaborated about Islam but rather of living a good life. The separated worlds that I inhabited were a series of disjointed, uncomfortable hyphens. Her worlds were connected together with contented, respectful smiles.

I loved attending religious Sunday school. It was called *madrasah*, the Arabic word which simply means 'school'. The mosque was not large enough to provide suitable teaching facilities for the several hundred students who attended the classes once a week, so a local school was usually hired out for the morning. We were divided into groups by age and had four lessons, each taught by a different teacher, who was normally a parent who volunteered their time to prepare and deliver the class. Each week we were given homework and at the end of term we were given reports, followed by an end-of-term-celebration, just like at school.

As I was still in the primary classes, we spent our lessons learning the basics of religion. First was the declaration of faith as a Muslim, 'There is no god but One God, and Muhammad is the last messenger.' It was crucial to being Muslim to understand and really mean these two sentences. If someone wanted to become a Muslim, this is what they had to say. The first part meant taking all other gods out of your heart.

My teacher used to joke, 'Someone who says there is no god is already half way to being a Muslim!' One God meant that this Being had no place, no time and no physical shape. The belief that Muhammad was the last messenger was based in turn on believing that there were many prophets before him, like Moses, Abraham, Isaac, Ishmael, Noah, Joseph and so on. Prophet Muhammad came to give exactly the same message to human beings as all the other prophets: believe in God and be good human beings. I loved hearing the stories of all the prophets and all the different kinds of people that they lived amongst, and this was always my favourite part of *madrasah*.

We also learnt that Allah, which is the Arabic word for God, was kind, compassionate and loving. God had created the whole universe, and human beings were the best of all creation. It always appealed to me to be the best. I was, after all, the child of Asian parents: only the top grades in any situation were sufficient. Finally, we were taught that the world we lived in was not the End. There was something more to come, and it would be called *jannah*, 'paradise'. I imagined paradise would be like the inside of Willy Wonka's Chocolate Factory.

We were also taught about the actions we would have to carry out as Muslims. The first was *salat*, the prayer. I already knew the movements and words for the ritual prayers that were to be performed every day, because my parents had taught me. Next was fasting. Every year, for thirty days during the month of Ramadan, Muslims would refrain from eating and drinking from dawn until dusk, and spend their time focusing on their spiritual development. I didn't have to fast yet because I was too young. Then there was *hajj*, the famous, once-in-a-lifetime journey that all Muslims try to complete: to visit Mecca and the House of God, which is called the *Kaba*. Fasting, prayer and *hajj* were personal duties to connect you directly to God. There was also charity to give, and that had to come out of your time as well as your wealth.

I was the star pupil at the *madrasah*, so was selected to appear in a video for children about how to pray. My mother dressed me in my favourite green *shalwar kameez*, tied my hair into two thick plaits and pinned a white cotton scarf over my head. My father bundled me into the car and we set off to the other side of London to the house where the video was to be filmed. I was going to be the star of the film. Fame had called early.

My celebrity would spread far and wide, and marriage proposals would come flooding in. Not at the age of six. But it already laid the foundations of my public persona in the minds of our social circle and community. What my parents had implanted into my heart were the seeds of faith, love and community service.

In my own mind, my life would unfold according to the rules of a Disney cartoon. I knew that when I grew up, the mysteries of princes and marriage would be revealed to me. For now it was enough for me to read my favourite fairy tale: *Beauty and the Beast*. Butterflies fluttered in my tummy each time I read it. It was the perfect love story – full of eternal romantic truth. The hero of the story was undeniably handsome as the prince. As the beast he was dignified and patient. Whether monster or man, he was always true and dedicated in his love. The heroine was gracious, beautiful and saw the beast's inner beauty. The story hinged on a white rose bush. Each night the Beast would pluck one of the exquisite roses to present to Beauty as a token of his love, until she was won over by him. In our back garden at home we, too, had a magnificent white rose bush that burst forth with the same pure snowy petals as in the paintings in the fairy story. The roses fluttered, innocently fragrant, throughout the fairytale summers of my childhood.

Kulcha

It is a universally acknowledged truth that all Asian parents want their children to get married and settle down. It is the final and most important duty of the parent towards their child. It is also an Islamic responsibility to help your child find a suitable spouse. Only when the offspring are paired off can the mother and father sigh with relief. So momentous and significant is this obligation, and so huge is the impact of the choice of partner, that parents fret about finding that spouse from the moment the child is born. It is the job of parents, mothers-in-law and Aunties to network furiously and line up candidates. The girl and boy do not necessarily need to be involved. They can just turn up on the day, if they are required, in order to attend the communal meeting, as Ali and I had done.

Cultural norms dictate how the meeting of the two parties will play out. It may involve members of both parties being present, along with tea and civilities, and a subtle but rigorous scoping out of the other side. Or the boy and the girl might not even be there. The only certainty is that the meeting could change significantly the lives of the two people who are at the heart of the discussion.

The Buxom Aunties, those round matriarchal women in nylon *shalwar kameez* with their chiffon *dupattas* pulled deftly over their heads, therefore wield enormous power as matchmakers in the lives of young men and women and their parents who are searching for a partner for their child to build a life with. Behind closed doors, over cups of tea and crispy just-fried pakoras, the seasoned mothers-in-law, the nylon-clad *naanis* and the grandmothers, all of whom function as matchmakers alongside the Aunties, talk with the authority of wisdom and experience to those women who are wannabe mothers-in-law in search of a wife for their son.

Wannabe: I'm getting too old to look after Ahmed on my own.

Nylon Naani: It's time you got him a wife.

Wannabe: I know, but where do I find someone suitable? Someone who can cook, look after the house properly like we used to do and who will give me grandchildren and not go out and about abandoning her responsibilities. Girls these days are just all about themselves. They don't have the patience and tolerance that we had. You're a *naani* already, a grandmother, and you've sorted out your daughters-in-law so well. So hard with girls these days.

Nylon Naani: You're right, it's very tough. So many couples getting married and divorced willy-nilly. And your Ahmed is *such* a good boy. Have you talked to him about going back home and choosing a girl? They are the best you know, well-trained and obedient. They know how to look after a mother-in-law.

Wannabe: Talk to Ahmed about going back home to find a wife? Pfah! He doesn't want to even *talk* about getting married. He doesn't know I need someone to help around the house. Besides (and her voice softens here), he needs someone of his own and I'm getting old. Who will look after him when I'm gone?

Nylon Naani: That's your mistake. Boys are *never* ready, you have to just *surprise* them. Show them a few pretty girls and even the one who says *no, no, no*, he will fall for one of them. Boys can't resist a pretty girl. You might need to encourage and persuade him a little bit or perhaps even push him. But he'll thank you in the end.

Nylon Naani pauses, and then looks furtively in all directions, Godfather-style. Even with no-one in earshot, she leans in conspiratorially.

Nylon Naani: I'm going to tell you everything you need to know about finding a daughter-in-law. Only four things and you will be *laughing, laughing*, so happy. First, do not involve your son. He does not know what he wants and will only complicate matters. Next, avoid girls who are oh-so-independent. This is not a good quality for a daughter-in-law. They will not be committed.

Wannabe: Hmm, yes, hmm. So wise, *so* wise, yes, you are right. Such *wonderful* wisdom.

Nylon Naani: Three. Make sure she is pretty and she can cook. And the younger, the better. And last, look for a girl from the same culture, so that she can 'fit' with you.

When I am older, with many sons, fretting about finding them wives, I will write a sequel to my book. It will be called *Love in a Nylon Dupatta*.

THE BUXOM AUNTIES' RULES

The natural habitat of the Auntie is weddings, gatherings, dinners and other places where young unmarried women play together. They are normally distinguished by their fulsome breasts and round tummies, and often by their taste for chewing *paan*. They have either been married for more years than the Rolling Stones have been alive, and their multitudes of children are married and they have a small tribe of grandchildren, thus making them experts on marriage; or they are lonely spinsters, who now devote themselves to pairing off the younger generation.

As a young woman, I was deeply suspicious and cynical of the Aunties. They appeared to me like *jinnis* whose sole purpose was to make me feel small and useless. I was convinced that their entire reason for being was to make my life difficult and miserable by belittling my aspirations. In return I had to be polite and affable, as they might have access to my Prince Charming, my dream man, my life happiness. And, of course, I had to play by the conventions of the search that remained unspoken:

1. A third party, preferably someone considered as an 'elder' – the Aunties being the first choice – should be involved in mediating the search process. It is shameful social etiquette for one party to ring up the other and say, 'Hey, why don't our kids get it together?'

2. Both sides must make delicate enquiries amongst contacts to find out about the other side's family and the individual in question.

Only when sufficient information and recommendations are provided will the two parties move onto the next stage of arranging a meeting.

3. The first show of interest must be from the boy's party. The girl's party cannot make the first move, otherwise they will be considered 'desperate'. If the girl's party wishes to initiate a discussion with a potential match, they must do it through a third party who should make it look like it was the boy's party's idea.

4. The girl must be younger than the boy by at least one day. This is not so that he can avoid a wrinkly wife but so he can assert his authority. It is also in order that the girl will be 'mouldable', a word entirely peculiar to Asian matchmaking. 'Mouldable' means that she will 'adapt' to the boy's family's way of doing things. A younger woman will be less 'set in her ways'.

5. The girl should be shorter than the boy even while wearing heels. This is so the couple will be aesthetically pleasing when standing together. The boy can gel up his hair to gain extra height.

6. The girl should be less educated than the boy. The husband should be able to say in response to any question: 'It is because I am your husband and I am more educated than you, so I must be right. Do not question me!' in a surly yet dignified manner.

7. The boy's family should be wealthier so that he can look after the girl. The boy should have a 'good' secure job, ideally with a title such as Doctor, Dentist or Accountant.

8. The girl should be pale in colour.

9. It is important that she is 'homely and domesticated'. A domesticated girl is proficient in matters of cleaning, cooking, laundry and other kinds of housework. Being 'homely' describes a natural penchant for these activities.

10. 'Well-mannered, religious and from a good family, this is what you should look for,' I was told repeatedly. In Asian tradition, marriage is about becoming part of a new family, so choosing a 'good' family is a

critical factor. It includes people in the family having good reputations, which can be built on piety and religiousness, and acts of kindness and generosity, like dedicated community service and charity. Scandals could damage a family's reputation for years and they would directly affect the marriage prospects of the children. They were hushed away as quickly as possible. Also high on the criteria for 'good' family are: from the same country 'back home', from the same part of the same country, from the same town, from the same village. Most controversially in some communities, marriage proposals are only considered from individuals from the same caste, even though Islam, which is rooted in the principle that all human beings are of equal worth, is fundamentally opposed to the very idea of caste.

These unspoken rules of culture contradict the simple yet unheeded words of the Prophet Muhammad which sum up the criteria for a prospective partner with wisdom and simplicity: 'Do not look for wealth or beauty as these will last only a short time, and then you will be left with nothing. Look for piety and faith and you will get everything, including beauty and wealth with it.'

Despite all the unsaid cultural regulations, it is important for both parties not to appear too fastidious when it comes to selecting a spouse. Matchmakers lose interest in families who turn down prospective partners for nit-picking reasons. It is also important not to appear too eager. The stench of desperation is universally despised across cultures but the conditions are especially stringent in the Asian context. It is shameful for a girl herself to show any interest in getting married, no matter how much she may want to. This is because women are not supposed to be interested in worldly matters such as men. Perhaps in traditional societies where a woman used to have little choice in her partner, her interest would be futile. If asked by an Auntie or potential mother-in-law 'Are you interested in marriage?', the girl must blush shyly, look coyly to one side and whisper a platitude: 'Well, it's in Allah's hands. Of course all girls would like to get married.'

There was something in the very essence of this process that made young women squirm and even made young men run in fear. It was just so very embarrassing. We squealed at the agony of the ritual, both boys and girls. The parents, the mothers-in-law and the Aunties held it together. They were the cast and chorus, with cameos from the boy and girl. Things might not be perfect, they told us, but the Search According to Tradition had worked for generations. *Do you want to change the world, or simply find a wonderful partner and live happily ever after?* And who would dare to argue with that?

When I was a young girl, we had a family tradition of a Sunday afternoon drive. Part of this ritual was to listen to Sunrise Radio, the first big Asian radio station in London. The afternoon show was a phone-in for people searching for a marriage partner. It was aimed at the Sub-continental population, which included Muslims, Hindus, Sikhs and even Christians. Callers usually consisted of prospective mothers-in-law looking for wives for their sons, or of 'fresh-off-the-boat' Sub-continental men looking for wives, and the bonus of a British passport. Even as a child I found it extremely funny. I was blissfully oblivious to the impact that such attitudes would have on my life when I grew up. Perhaps that was why everyone else seemed to take it so seriously.

'I'm looking for a wife for my son,' the elderly lady would say in her thick accent interspersed with Urdu words.

'Tell me what kind of girl you are looking for,' the host would respond in her gentle but serious voice. I often wondered if she muted out her giggles. On air she always sounded deeply concerned and full of gravitas, an Asian Sue Lawley meets Claire Rayner.

'I'd like someone who is about eighteen, fair, homely and domesticated, and from a good family. She should be slim and white and have finished her schooling to A-level. Not tall, please. And fair, homely and domesticated.'

'OK,' continued Asian Sue Lawley, 'Tell me about your son.'

'He's 30, five foot three, well built, studying first degree in accounts.' I smirked. I waited for the velvet-tongued presenter to cut in and expose the contrast between what she was offering and what she wanted, but nobody seemed to notice the double standards apart from me.

'And what is his skin colour?'

'He is dark and he has put on a bit of weight but he is, after all, eating his mother's cooking,' she beamed radiantly through the air waves.

'And should the girl be working?'

'It's OK if she works until she gets married, we're very *modern*. Once my son has passed his accountancy exams, she can stay at home and look after both of us.'

With the mother-in-law's emphasis on modernity, I was sure they would have warped their beautiful names to something more 'English'.

'Thank you. That is Auntie Sugar from Hounslow looking for a wife for her son Harry who is 30, five foot three, dark and round, still studying and living with his mother, looking for a fair, homely and domesticated wife from a good family to stay at home and look after his mother. Number three-three-seven-eight for all you lovely ladies.'

It was an uneven playing field, but at least the rules were clear.

Intertangled

'Love comes *after* marriage' was the familiar refrain of the Imam of our local mosque. He was an indomitable figure in our community, much loved and respected. This was one of his favourite phrases about marriage. 'What is this "click" that people are looking for?' he would say. 'When you first meet, he does his hair all slicked back and puts on his best aftershave. And she puts on make up and smells oh-so-good. And you are both on your best behaviour, relaxed and showing only your good sides. And you both think "*Aaah*! I'm in love", "he is so wonderful", "she is the one". Only when you wake up in the morning and you smell his breath and you see her with her hair standing on end like a *jinn*, only then can you know what love is.'

This was certainly not the romance of *Beauty and the Beast* – or John Travolta. The Imam wasn't anti-romance, just anti-blind-romance. He challenged the prevailing narratives around me about Finding the One, Falling in Love, Getting Married, and Living Happily Ever After. He didn't spell it out, but he meant that films end abruptly when Sally and Harry get it together, when Seattle is no longer Sleepless, when boy gets girl. At the peak of precarious joy, the story ends. What was the reality of the After, when they said *Happily Ever After?* Was it endless summer breezes and dreamy flushed gazes? Or was it a negotiation around dirty dishes, unfinished DIY projects and unpaid bills?

Love was indeed a passionate human experience, of this the Imam was in no doubt. It could be transformative but it was a force to be tamed and channelled. Its rightful place was inside a marriage, where its transcendent virtues could shine without complications. Only within this structure of commitment, which gave formal security to both husband and wife, and only with the formal consent given by both the man and the woman to begin the relationship could love fully flourish. Marriage was an act of worship and love was the gift given in return.

The Imam was very clear about the importance of two things: agreement by both the individuals themselves and a formal written contract to underpin the relationship. In his words, marriage was the difference between a verbal agreement and a written contract. Whenever you dealt with matters of great importance, the law demanded a written contract in order to guarantee the rights of both parties and outline the nature of the relationship. When dealing with personal relationships, the same rules ought to apply, and so marriage would be a contract between two parties on the relationship they were agreeing to.

Talking about love, marriage and partnerships was a common and natural part of growing up for me. From a very young age, I was taught about Love. Not only about flowers and chocolates, but also about the hardships of love: its sacrifice, its divine meaning, and its joy and pleasure. The multiple and multiplying rewards of love had to be worked for, and that came with time and patience. Over and over again I heard this advice, this rhythmical lyrical preparation to love.

'Marriage and love are not grand abstract emotions that exist out-side of the realities of life,' the Imam explained. 'They come shackled to the drudgery of daily routine.' This was a fact most people, especially teenage romantics like me, preferred to ignore. 'And yet, everything you do as a Muslim,' the Imam elaborated, 'is an act of worship.'

'According to the Prophet Muhammad, being a human being is very simple, "Knowing God, and serving humanity." Even if you think they are dull and you don't like doing them, doing your bit in the world, even with things like laundry and mopping, can help you on the path towards enlightenment.'

The Imam's views were designed to be a walking, talking reality check about love. He encouraged people to be in love, but all the while remembering that it wouldn't be constant high romance. Housework and hoovering were just as worthy forms of devotion to God as prayer and meditation.

We attended many weddings, perhaps one every three or four weeks. They were always community events and everyone was invited, no matter how distantly related or how tenuously known. If they weren't invited, *it would look bad*. There would be hundreds and hundreds of people coming to celebrate the union of the bride and groom and the two families. Attending was seen as part of social obligation to the community, and any unjustified absences would be considered as snubs by the wedding parties and noted for the future.

Due to the sheer number of guests, weddings typically took place either in the mosque or in a large community hall. The weddings that I went to were usually segregated, with men gathering round the groom and his family on one side, and women unveiled in all their finery on the other. I loved the clothes that we wore. They were always in beautiful bright colours like crimson, pink, turquoise, emerald and purple, and embroidered with sparkling sequins, crystals and beads. They looked even more exquisite as they were made of luxurious feminine fabrics like silk, chiffon and georgette. I would wear a *shalwar kameez* or, when I was still a young girl, a small blouse with a skirt. The older girls and women would wear glamorous *lenghas*, which were heavily beaded silk bodices and long princess-like skirts. I wanted to wear these beautiful fairytale clothes too. I longed even more to wear a *sari*, which the women wore so elegantly and which flattered their curves, but young girls did not wear saris. I would have to wait till I was grown up.

The bride would enter the hall accompanied by her matron of honour, her veil hanging low over her face so she could barely be seen. Her hands and feet were exquisitely decorated with henna. Some brides wore red outfits; in our tradition we wore white. She might choose to wear a traditional sari, or if she was more 'modern' she would wear a *lengha*. When I was a child I would race to line the bride's path along with the other young girls so that I could look at her bridal outfit, and see how enchanting she looked. I would then race back to my mother's side and gasp, 'She's so beautiful! Can I have an outfit like that?' and my mother would respond, 'Yes, of course! Yours will be even more beautiful.'

The wedding ceremony began with a *khutba*, a short lecture given by the Imam or Shaikh, which was usually spent explaining the virtues of marriage. They reminded us that according to the Prophet, getting married meant you would 'complete half your faith', adding his words, 'Whoever rejects marriage is not from me.'

The marriage would then be conducted. Both the bride and groom would usually ask someone to represent them to participate in the *nikah*, the Islamic marriage ceremony. The bride's side took the first step in the ceremony by asking if the groom would accept her in marriage. This was to ensure that the bride was happy to get married. The groom's side would respond by accepting. The Arabic words were usually used for this exchange. The bride said '*Ankahtu*', I give myself, and the groom replied, '*Qabiltu*', I accept. As part of the marriage, the groom would give a gift to the bride, called the *mahr*. This was usually a small amount of money, as a token of the groom's affection, for when the two of them started their new life. The bride would tell the groom what she wanted the gift to be – and it could be anything, from teaching a skill, to a holiday, to a car, absolutely anything at all. Finally, the Imam would recite a prayer to bless the newly married couple. The whole marriage only took a few moments.

According to the *Qur'an*, God would put mercy and love between the couple. The *Qur'an* talks about this love with a special reverence, describing it with a sense of purity and spirituality that was dearer and sweeter than ordinary romantic love. This love, *muwaddah*, was reserved for those in a committed relationship and was a special gift for those who made that commitment. This is why I wanted to get married: in return for commitment, faith and dedication, there was a guarantee that love would definitely come after marriage, and that love would be sweet, kind and compassionate. Love and marriage were like, well, a horse and carriage. Or was that a carriage and a horse?

Before the wedding itself, there would be several celebrations held by the women of the two families. My recollections as a young girl are of sitting at such gatherings listening intently to conversations about how to make a marriage successful. The discussions about love and marriage involved the whole community, including youngsters like me. The desire to make marriage and family a success was drummed into us from an early age, and we were given the guidance and tools to do so. Even at *madrasah* we were taught how to select a future spouse. What kind of qualities should we look for? How should we nurture a loving relationship? How should we make it last long term? We might have been very young, but the lessons were designed to grow into our hearts and into the essence of our beings.

There was one thing that bothered me. All the advice and preparation seemed entirely aimed at the young women. It seemed unfair and unintelligent that the young men were not prepared in the same way. Didn't they also need to be ready for a relationship?

The *Qur'an* told me that men and women are a pair, designed to complete each other, equal and balanced. But the Aunties, who represented the conventions of culture, were quite clear in their views that the success of any marriage was in the hands of the woman. I was uneasy with this burden, as it clashed with my sense of fairness and my understanding of Islam.

On the other hand, my local Imam was constantly expressing his sadness and frustration at the over-inflated expectations of 'young people'. He thought people should learn to be more contented and understand the bigger picture, and that it wasn't possible to feel constantly in the throes of romantic passion. He felt that people gave up too easily. 'Couples on the verge of divorce come to me and they say "*Mulla*, I don't care for him anymore."' He would sigh the sigh of a man who has seen the world. 'You can't give up because you don't *care*. You are *married* to him. You don't come in and out of caring,' he would say. He was usually very laid back but you could see that this sort of youthful flippancy made him cross.

As a teenager I was given a book called *Marriage and Morals in Islam* to provide additional background reading as preparation for getting married. Producing printed material about marriage was an industry in itself, and like many other similar Islamic books, it covered the essentials of finding a partner, how to go about getting married, how to (cough, cough) have intimate relations and then how to be happily married. Its goal was to set young people's expectations of what having a relationship means and how to build a strong and lasting one. All of this was based on verses from the *Qur'an* and Islamic traditions. Whilst my friends read teen magazines about how to kiss wearing braces, I read about making sure I was dressed prettily and sprayed with perfume to spend time with my husband in the evenings, and how he should always be sure to compliment me on how beautiful and kind I was. We came to womanhood from different perspectives. They learnt how to say no if they didn't feel comfortable, I learnt how to be happy to say yes in the right circumstances.

I read and re-read several of these books, alongside the graphic tabloid teen magazines until the two merged into one.

'WHY MARRIAGE IS THE NEW BLACK'

Having a husband/wife* is a natural state of affairs. Human beings are not designed for loneliness or celibacy.

Marriage is a long-term commitment, and love and strength grows over time.

'Men and women are garments for each other,' says the *Qur'an*. Marriage is good for the goose *and* the gander.

S - E - X is a good thing, nothing to be shy or embarrassed about. It

*Delete as appropriate.

is a blessing and keeps a marriage strong. But it's got to be kept inside marriage.

And once the books had laid these foundations, they moved swiftly onto:

'HOW YOU KNOW HE'S THE ONE'

Personality, quality of character and faith in God are key. That way you know they will always treat you right.

The choice is yours. No-one can force you to marry anyone, and if there is no valid reason to refuse, then no-one can veto it either.

Wealth, race, caste, skin colour, family 'name' should not be part of the selection criteria, according to religion.

Looks are important, but should not be the decision-making criterion.

Look for a good parent to your future children.

The process of marriage threw up some baffling confusions about the complexities of faith and culture, which I was unable to decipher. The rules from culture and faith seemed to be at odds with each other, but separating them out was nigh on impossible. As I was growing up I didn't realise how different, even contradictory they were.

The Islamic guidelines created an aspiration for an achievable utopia for relationships. They seemed so simple and straightforward: find a good, decent man, get married and God will support you by injecting love and mercy into your relationship. The principles embodied the importance of respecting and loving people for who they were, not their superficialities. It was about faith, spirituality and being a good person. Race, wealth, culture and class were irrelevant. These rules allowed for Princess Jasmine, the daughter of the Sultan, to marry Aladdin, a penniless diamond in the rough.

Culture, which had a strong hand in dictating reality, appeared to be quite different from religion in the cut-throat world of bagging a partner. The process was oiled and managed by two crucial architects: the Aunties, of whom matchmakers were a sub-set, and Mothers-in-Law, which referred to the mothers of the grooms-to-be. The match-making process stretched back into the cloudy indefinable roots of cultural myth, which no one could untangle or clarify. The process was the way it was just because it was the way it was. You could not deny that it was down to earth: get the interested parties together, conduct an assessment, make a decision. Everyone concerned wanted a positive outcome: a good solid marital match, two happy families. And not to be entirely forgotten: a happily married couple.

The media culture around me had its own strong views about love and romance. I watched films like *Grease* and *Cinderella* over and over again, wide-eyed, yearning to find the man who would complete me. Which young woman would not be swept away by the romance of Sandy and Danny, of Cinderella and the Prince? I would be the Princess to John Travolta's Prince Charming. We would recognise each other and see true love shining in each other's eyes. Love would lead to marriage. And marriage would lead to us living happily ever after. This was the myth of romance at its most powerful. Films and magazines said it was true. But what 'love' meant was never clear, the stories always ended before explaining. Why was it important? What did it mean about how you lived your day-to-day life?

An opulent grand wedding was always the climax of a love story. This was how life was supposed to be for everyone, and if you didn't achieve it, you were a failure. Love was supposed to simply 'happen' if you waited long enough, *and* if you were beautiful enough.

Love for women was a helpless wait, like Sleeping Beauty's immobile slumber that stretches out passively till the saviour prince arrives. Finding Love was a paradoxical aspiration: it was mandatory but it could only be achieved passively.

The love story from within the parameters of Islam started at the opposite end. Two people got married. This would then complete their faith. They would be blessed with love, all the while remembering to work at creating a relationship of love themselves. And love would bring them happiness, romance, long-term contentment and a completion of the sense of self. Having a partner would help you to be a better human being, a better Muslim and to get closer to God.

Love was proactive. You, your family, the man in question, his family, in fact the whole community, would drive it forward. Finding the person was only the first step: it was how you addressed what happened after the wedding that was the key. The wedding was just the gateway, and all the magic happened when you put hard work into the marriage. But hard work is never as glamorous as romance.

The classes at Sunday school, the seminars at the mosque, the sermons at weddings, even advice from family members and mosque leaders all focused on what marriage was, why you should do it, and what would happen afterwards. There was just as much advice about how to find a partner as to how to keep them.

'Marriage is not a bed of roses,' the old uncles would waggle their fingers at us.

'It is going to be very hard for at least two years,' the Aunties would caution. 'Do whatever he asks you for during that time, and then he'll do whatever you want for the rest of your lives.' The whole approach was about staying the course in order to get the fruits of marriage. It was an investment plan for future comfort and happiness.

I wanted to find the One through the tried and tested traditional methods so that I could find romance, fall in love and complete my faith. And since the two of us would share the same faith, we would work towards finding the peace and contentment that as a married couple God had promised us. And then we would live happily ever after, amen.

I wanted a lot of things. I wanted Prince Charming, romantic love and to live happily ever after. I wanted to observe the cultural traditions of finding a husband. I wanted to follow the Islamic ideals of marriage. I also wanted to uncover spiritual love and harmony. I wanted to approach the Divine.

But what I really wanted was very simple: to make sense of the overwhelming contradictions and tangles facing me as a young Muslim woman.

THREE

Process Princess

Biodata

My first introduction meeting was followed by a steady stream of suitors. They swarmed in and then out through our front door, accompanied by parents, friends, Imams and distant relatives. Occasionally they came on their own, affecting bravado at being confident enough to face potential in-laws on their own. We were making samosas every weekend.

Despite the influx of potential husbands, it was important to be entirely focused on the task: finding someone compatible was paramount. There was simply no time to waste. My marriage, as with the marriage of any child in the family, was a collective endeavour, and I was the centre of attention. It was taken for granted that everyone would participate in the venture. My eventual husband would be selected from a pool of contacts collected by family, friends and matchmakers. The more people we all met, the wider our pool of prospects. Statistically, this would give me the greatest number of choices and the highest likelihood of Finding the One.

In order to enter the mating ritual, each candidate had to create a description of themselves, which would then be circulated amongst prospective families and matchmakers. This was usually done by word of mouth but was on occasion written as a document resembling a CV. It might even include a photograph of the individual. Once e-mail and internet had arrived, these were even sent electronically to speed up the introduction process, whizzing information about prospective partners around the globe, one love-hungry electron after another. These extremely personal details were then packaged with a description of the protagonist's character and the qualities and features they sought in a partner. The label for this package of information suggested an end-of-the-world-secret-services-hunting-down-dissidents film title: *Biodata*.

I was enthralled by the starkness of the word 'biodata'. But as a romantic seeker of love, it shot dread into my heart. This technical checklist drained emotion and humanity from the search. John Travolta would most certainly *not* have made the cut. I resisted putting together my own biodata as long as I could. I did not want to be dehumanised into a series of formulaic bullet points. However, without one, a prospective match could not be arranged, so I succumbed begrudgingly to the process.

It turned out to be an extremely useful document for those searching on my behalf. It helped them locate and identify suitable candidates in my absence, like head-hunters. I learnt that it was important that my criteria were clear, so that they were not presenting unsuitable options. However, it was also important that the criteria were not too specific as keeping an open mind about quirks and imperfections was critical. Also this would avoid the accusations of being too picky, too closed off to opportunities, too big-headed and stubborn.

I picked up a pen and a blank piece of paper, and started by creating a description of myself: a whole life, a whole person, an entire universe hidden in a soul: all of it reduced to a handful of words.

Early twenties, previously unmarried, university educated, 'religious', wears *hijab*. Five foot three, slim, nice family.

On the strength of these words, and the personal recommendation of the matchmaker or those searching on my behalf, as well as on my reputation and that of my family in the community, would my hopes of love and marriage rest. They were the foundations of who I was as a marriage prospect.

I now turned to finding the words to describe my perfect husband.

Good looking
Height 5'8" – 5'10"
Fantastic dress sense
The most handsome man in the world; it would simply not be possible for any other man to be better looking
Smells good
Handsome (Did I mention handsome?)

Was I thirteen? I looked at the list in horror. It had written itself, a collection of words that had travelled by osmosis via Mills and Boon, *Just Seventeen* magazine and Bridget Jones onto the page in front of me. It was the appendix to a trashy teenage conversation, an addendum to an adolescent dating encyclopaedia. All of this was a given – everyone assumes the need for looks and style, but they are less elusive than character. Hadn't faith and culture taught me to consider personality and character as paramount?

The self-description usually put forward by a suitor reveals nothing of their character, just as my words revealed nothing of mine. They would put on their finery, brush their hair and comb their beards for the process, which would bring them to you in this charming manner. In reality, the stress and constraints of the process reveal everything you need to know about their character. There are high stakes in play and even higher tensions. The suitor's true self comes out screaming their real character.

The goal of looking for love must never excuse the bad behaviour that some think it does. Rather, what you search for, the way you search and, most importantly, how you deal with the people your search takes you to showcases your own character. By outlining what I was searching for, it was time for me to reveal mine.

I wrote a proper description, sensibly categorising my requirements into must-haves and preferences.

ESSENTIAL

Male
Single
It was important to state the obvious.

Practising Muslim
This was crucial to me. I couldn't imagine marrying someone who wasn't a Muslim. I felt that this way I would be able to share my values and goals with my life partner. I didn't want someone who was identical to me but I did want someone who functioned along similar principles. Being a Muslim confirmed that scope and allowed this wish of mine to come true. I wanted him to be 'practising' so that he would want to understand religion and be inquisitive about it. It meant he would not blindly accept the tradition and cultures that pretended to be religion. I didn't want someone who just took everything around them at face value and repackaged this as faith.

In his twenties or very early thirties
I didn't mind if he was up to two or three years younger. I also thought that up to seven years older was fine. Matchmakers tended to draw the line at eight to ten years older as the maximum.

Involved in community activities
I wanted someone who would participate in the world around them and try to make it a better place. I had a strong sense of community and participated fully in community affairs. I wanted my partner to be the same. I did not want to be a football widow. I needed a man whom I could stand behind and be proud of our work together when we sat old and wrinkled in our comfy chairs in front of the fire, me knitting, him reading his newspaper.

Happy for me to wear *hijab*

I felt sad that I had to specify that a Muslim man should be happy for me to wear a headscarf and modest clothing, as this was my understanding of one of the requirements of Islam. It seemed that a lot of men were *not* happy for their wives to wear the *hijab*. He didn't need to advocate it but at least support my decision to wear it. I did not want to be shown off just for being pretty. I wanted him to be supportive of the choices that I wanted to make for my own life, rather than be conscious of how other people might react to his wife wearing the *hijab*. I wanted a man who wanted a wife he could be proud of and whom he respected. And to whom he would be irresistibly attracted in private.

Intelligent

I wanted someone sharp and quick-witted, who could challenge me, whose conversation would stimulate me. And surely an intelligent man would want an intelligent woman like me?

I carried on chewing the end of my pen, and then added '*someone I can talk to*'. The most important part of everything was a connection, a communication.

Muslim Man Travolta was beginning to take shape in my mind, and as he materialised I found I liked him even more than I had before. In the process of formulating my wish list for my perfect man, my father's most famous marriage phrase was coined. They were wise words, completely unheeded by the arrogance and optimism of my youth. 'If you have six things on your list that you are looking for, then if you get four, that is very good. You will never get everything.' But how to know which four would be enough? Why shouldn't I demand a full quotient of six? Why shouldn't everyone? 'Four out of six,' he repeated earnestly. His heartfelt and well-meaning advice was pitted against Mills and Boon, Hollywood, Bollywood and countless 'They Lived Happily Ever After' princess stories.

I focused myself on defining my list of six. I had included eight items on my list of essentials, but the first two didn't *really* count. I was left with the six must-haves that would guide me for the journey ahead: practising Muslim, within the right age bracket, involved in the community, happy for me to wear *hijab*, intelligent and someone I could talk to.

But I wanted more, craved more, desired more, needed more, deserved more. I should have it all! Yes! Yes!

From a practical point of view, I told myself that giving a more specific list would make Mr Right much more identifiable, more likely to exhibit the characteristics that were important to me. I rationalised the additions to my list by categorising them into a non-mandatory section.

DESIRABLE

Attractive
Oh yes, it crept back onto my list. Even Islamic guidelines said you should 'fancy' your spouse!

University educated
This would be a good indicator of shared experience, shared language, shared communication. It wasn't a must-have but I was convinced it would be a good foundation.

Born in or lived in the UK, Canada or USA since they were at least 18
I was presented with boys from all over the world, especially from 'back home', which for me was East Africa, but might also include India and Pakistan. I certainly would meet men from all over, but it occurred to me I was more likely to connect with someone with whom I shared some context. Having grown up in the UK, I felt I had a different

understanding and expectations of being married, of being a Muslim. I wanted someone who would be in harmony with that, not with whom I would spend the first years of my married life trying to adjust. It was worth noting that this criteria also meant that I would avoid those simply looking for a British passport. I wanted to be a wife, not a ticket to citizenship.

Has a social circle; does more than just work and play football
I came to be shocked at how many men this simple clause would exclude.

I was dreaming by now and let my imagination, my hopes and my heart run away.

Interested in reading, travelling, and generally a charming, interesting person. Wants to change the world and make it a better place. Vision and some sparkle. Cool and hip. Oh yeah, rock on!

I sighed. There he was, my perfect man. I wanted to just will him into existence. My heart told me that *of course* such a man was out there waiting to be found. My head wondered how he would be discovered. I held back on making my list longer. The voices of the Aunties in my head told me to rein in my desires. A girl should not be so demanding. How shameful!

I was fortunate. My family understood my description and were eager to cross-check their findings with me. It felt like we were a team working towards my happiness. I couldn't imagine looking for the most special person in my life without their support and encouragement, and they wanted to put all their resources into finding the person who would contribute to me living a happy and fulfilled life.

Their wisdom and experience forced them to temper my optimism with a dose of reality. They had read through my list and they had feigned seriousness about how they were to find this angelic hero.

'Are you expecting a man to fall from heaven into your lap?' my parents had asked. 'Perhaps you could find him for sale in Woolworths,' they teased me.

I pulled a mock face of horror. 'You couldn't think of somewhere more upmarket?' I gasped. 'What about made-to-measure from Harrods or Harvey Nichols?'

'We got *you* from Woolworths,' they reminded me, laughing affectionately. That was how they had explained where babies came from when I was a very young child, and the joke had stuck. 'Woolworths would be a good match.'

Partners do not come made-to-measure. My parents' description of Prince Charming being off-the-peg was much more accurate. There would always be something on the list that he would lack. But which qualities would I be willing to give up? When my father said 'pick four qualities', how would I know which two were dispensable? I refused to accept that I should downgrade my selection standards, so his wise and fatherly advice fell on deaf ears. Over time, his guidance was to settle for only three out of six. Finally his resolve weakened and as we entered the darkest hours he downgraded the requirement to only two out of six. 'You can't be too fussy,' he would tell me. Helpfully and realistically he would temper my expectations. 'Even two will be a blessing, *beti*,' he would counsel. 'We just want you to be happy.'

The search threw up the dentist from Birmingham, the doctor from South London, a lecturer from Bristol, various IT consultants, business-men, pharmacists and other unmemorable professionals. They were defined by the jobs they did. The higher up the professional rankings the matchmakers judged them to be – which didn't always reflect reality – the more they oohed and aahhed in honour of the prospective match.

The community liked pairing up well-labelled people. When certain engagements were announced it was like drawing numbers at bingo.

'Two doctors, how lovely, what a good match.' 'Two dentists, how nice, they will set up their own practice together.' 'They are both so fair and good looking, they will have such white and handsome children.'

On the whole, I would be the one to say no. The family generally presumed that the boy would take a shine to me. 'Who wouldn't?' asked my mum. 'You're beautiful, intelligent, nice, religious.' I would blush. 'You're my mum, of course you'll say that,' I would laugh at her. Every so often, it was I that would be turned down, and we would furrow our brows in surprise. *Why would anyone turn me down?* In this competitive world of finding a partner, modesty was a dispensable quality.

Funny Valentine   ☆

Faith and religious practice were an integral part of my life. I had been brought up as a Muslim from birth and nurtured within a Muslim household. I prayed. I fasted in the month of Ramadan. I gave money to charity. I read the *Qur'an*, the revealed scriptures of Islam. I wore the *hijab*. I tried to be good to my parents, contribute to my community and live a good life. I hoped one day to travel on the *hajj*, the once in a lifetime Islamic pilgrimage to Mecca. In short, you might describe me as a practising Muslim and one that was happy to be so. My life was centred around my beliefs and on the efforts to be a good human being as seen through Islam.

As a child, the choices that were made for me were based on an Islamic ethos as understood by my parents. Their Islamic principles guided them towards trying to live a good life and helping themselves, their children and their community to succeed in the here and now, materially as well as spiritually. Belief in a Creator, and a life after death, underpinned these ideas.

Even as a young child, I learnt to exercise choice based on these principles. Some were specific to being Muslim. Instinctively I knew I shouldn't eat pork or bacon, as this was forbidden by Islam, and I understood by the time I was four that I shouldn't eat sausages at school. They were made of pork. I also refused the shepherd's pie on the grounds the meat was not *halal*. The rice pudding I rejected on the grounds that it was disgusting.

Other principles were common between Islam and other codes of personal morality, such as caring about others, giving charity and respecting elders. The more I read, the more I listened and the more I learnt, the more Islam seemed to offer a holistic view of the world that made sense to me. It was concerned about my life and about showing me how to be happy. So despite the fact that I was born a Muslim, I made an active decision *to be a Muslim* because it made sense to me. It offered me peace and direction in a world that felt overwhelming and confused. It inspired me to excel, explore and discover. It pushed me to investigate myself and everything around me. It encouraged me towards success, which could be measured in affluence as well as contentment.

Islam had quite a few rules. Every human being has their own rules. Once they are part of your life, you don't notice them anymore. Outer rules always reflect inner meaning. I wondered if I had understood some rules properly, given I was fixed in time and place. Was it me, was it us, was it the here and now that was the problem in understanding? I thought about the intense conviction of Europe in the Middle Ages that the world was flat. Or how Einstein had created a new theory. Or how the notion that there is nothing left to discover never holds true: there are always new discoveries waiting to be made. I thought about how modern science had created a paradigm that had been unimaginable before. Wasn't that likely to happen again? And again?

I didn't start from the premise that the rules were archaic. The basic principles of being good, standing up for equality and justice and being kind and compassionate were sound. Instead I started to question which areas had become fuzzy with culture, power and mis-interpretation. Human beings like to twist things to meet their own selfish ends. They would mutate things for their own benefit and then claim this was The Truth. It was the challenge of the fresh eyes of each generation to re-examine and re-visit the truth of the principles that were accepted as universal.

I found it exhilarating that every part of my life was important and significant enough to warrant spiritual guidance. The delicacy and complexity of the layers of meaning and hidden depths hinted that a microcosm lay inside me, waiting to be discovered. I learnt about the map of my esoteric world through Islam. Through parables, sayings and teachings, the landscape of a human being and her soul was described.

I needed a partner to accompany me on this journey, and if I was to have a travelling companion, he would need to share the same map as me. How else could we journey on the same path?

My first Valentine's card was from a man who was not a Muslim.

I found it pinned to the door of my university dorm room early on the morning of Valentine's Day. I ripped open the envelope and devoured the contents. Inside was a handwritten poem, penned with traditional calligraphy. I read it slowly and then smiled. The poem had humour, rhythm and perfect rhyme.

Even though there was no name, I knew straight away who had sent it. I was very flattered. He was an intelligent, charming and generally well-liked young man. How delightful that someone could like me enough to send a Valentine's card with a poem he wrote himself!

Powerful emotions can be evoked with the turn of a phrase, an expressive manner, the run of elegant words that conjure up an image, or a feeling. Poetry was the ultimate path to seduction, and I was vulnerable to its magic spell like generations of women before me. I often thought that this was why the *Qur'an* was composed of poetry and poetic prose. Poetry is designed to inspire love, and Islam is about falling in love with the Creator of the Universe. The Arabic is simple and rhythmic and has layers of meaning that reveal themselves to you each time you return. The Arabs of the time were so taken aback by the elegance and mystery of the words, they called the Prophet Muhammad a magician. They recognised the power of ideas and eloquence to seduce the soul and create a revolution.

I saw the sender of my Valentine's Day card later that day. He was sitting with a large group of mutual aquaintances out in the garden, including my circle of close female friends. It was a beautiful early spring evening and the night sky was clear and full of twinkling stars. I walked along the gravel path, admiring the snowdrops and crocuses beginning to poke their heads bravely into the world. I had spent the afternoon smiling quietly to myself, wistfully imagining what might happen. The romantic teenager in me had sprung into life and asked the same questions I had asked at the age of thirteen about John Travolta. Was he interested? Would he become a Muslim? As always, the prerequisite was that he should be a Muslim. But the sender was nice, I thought, and I should explore these enormous questions of faith, belief and soul and see where we found ourselves. Even with the careful boundaries of modesty in place in our interactions, we could still talk. We could still see where life would take us.

I walked towards the group. I felt that courtesy demanded that I should acknowledge his actions. It must have taken much courage on his part to express his feelings. And of course the little voice of romantic destiny kept whispering, what if . . . what if . . . what if . . . he becomes Muslim?

'Hello,' I said to him.

'Hello,' he answered.

I smiled.

'Finished your essay?' he asked seriously.

'Thank you,' I answered incongruously.

'Thank you? For what?' His lips curled up cheekily at the edges.

'The card.'

He grinned. 'Will you have a cup of tea with me then?'

He knew I was different, and I think he liked that. He knew that I didn't drink alcohol, that he couldn't take me to the pub for a drink. He also respected my modesty and at the same time saw past my *hijab* to the person I was. Through later years I came across many Muslim men who were put off by the headscarf. It was something they just couldn't get past. They couldn't see *me* or want me for who I was. All they saw was a walking book of religious rulings, a miserable turgid caricature. But here was a young man, not Muslim, who was drawn to *me*. To *me*.

'I'm sitting out here right now, aren't I?'

We both smiled nervously, and silently enjoyed the night,

surrounded by our friends, as the chatterings immediately around us carried on.

I looked up at the sky, breathless from the sheer beauty of the stars. It was magnificent and indescribable. I wondered what lay beyond. But these were just physical things. What then was the Creator? Unimaginable, incomprehensible in majesty, the ultimate aesthete for creating these extraordinarily beautiful universes. I forgot that I was in company, and was lost.

Was it out in the sky that I should continue my search, where I would find the answers to who I was and what it all meant? Human beings for thousands of years had been mesmerised by the stars and heavenly bodies, even believing them to be gods. To me they were creations, beautiful breathtaking creations, which meant they had a Creator. That's how the Prophet Abraham talked to the stars. Were they gods, he had asked? As they faded away with the night, he knew that there was something greater. Was today's science like that? Did the twinkling light of scientific discovery hide from us the Creator behind it? Or did science actually reveal the wonders of God's creation and so reveal God Himself? That was to be my search, my journey – to know and love the Creator – and perhaps on the way I would get lost in the stars and their milky twilight.

'How did you know it was me?' he asked shyly.

'I just knew, maybe I have good intuition.'

'That's cool. You're cool.'

I blushed, and tried to change the subject. I wasn't very good at this.

'Aren't the stars beautiful?' I asked. 'Thousands of them, twinkling so far from us, yet so near. Who knows what it's like out in the universe where they are! What an incredible creation! I can't breathe when I look at them. I bet somewhere out there we could understand what life is really about and find a bit more meaning to bring into this world.'

I was lost in awe. There was a long silence and I forgot he was there. A few minutes later I spoke again. 'They make me feel like there is something bigger than me. I feel like they hold so many secrets, so much to be explored and found. I feel a sense of divine, whether that is with a small "d" or a capital "D".'

I looked at him, wondering if he understood what I was asking, what I was revealing about my quest for the sublime. Would he have provisions for the journey?

I was looking at him framed by the mystical crystal sky. The night was clear. The moon was bright. He paused and I smiled in anticipation. I waited for his charismatic description of the layers and veils of the universe and the unknowable yet tangible beauty of the stars and planets that shone mysteriously above us. I wanted to hear about his quest into his own soul, his fascination with the complexity, the enormity, the simplicity of it all. I wanted to know.

I asked finally, 'What do you think when you see the stars?'

He looked at the mysterious sky and said: 'I imagine joining the dots.'

Groundhog Day

Chez Shelina the ritual of the suitor's visit gradually reached a crescendo of perfection. Over weeks and months we worked our way slowly and methodically through a line of potential princes. I was able to be patient and give each man his due time and consideration. We had perfected the process: our family, his family, me and him; some tea, sweets and conversation. The morning-after call always came – from the matchmaker of course. Sometimes there would be a second meeting. More often than not it was a case of being philosophical and moving onto the next one. He must be out there. He must be. I told myself to make sure he was the right one. Finding the right man was important.

The suitor hot seat was filled week by week with an unexpected range of princely bottoms.

He was nicely built and good looking. The son of a friend of a friend, called Samir. I was immediately worried when I heard that he hadn't completed his university education, but I kept an open mind. Chemistry could sparkle in the most surprising places and between the most unlikely people. A variation in education was a minor point, perhaps even of no significance. Tick-box matchmaking on the basis of paper compatibility had its merits, and often worked, but it was the magic of the unexpected that produced the most interesting relationships in my view.

Samir had dropped out of school to set up his own business and was now an entrepreneurial meteor. He strode in and installed himself in my father's comfy chair. My father had given me his usual advice before Samir had arrived: if you are looking for a partner with six qualities and if you find four, that is the best you are likely to get.

Samir was full of confidence. He didn't bother to make conversation, responding curtly to questions posed directly towards him.

Otherwise he stared uninterestedly out of the window at my father's beautifully tended garden. My father exchanged pleasantries with Samir's uncle, spending a mandatory ten minutes establishing their family connections. Eventually they found a second cousin on one side married to a great aunt on the other.

Slightly nervous as always, I made my entrance, smiling and nodding my head and saying *salam* to everyone present. I sat in an empty armchair opposite the boy, my hands clasped, my breathing a little uneven. This time the vase was filled with scented crimson roses. He turned to stare disdainfully at me, and then turned back to stare disdainfully at the wall.

After a few minutes of polite conversation, I got up to make the tea. It was a welcome relief to have something to do. I returned with the correct distribution of teas and coffees, as well as the essential must-have home-made sweets. Again, I sat opposite the boy. My father and the chaperone flung open the patio doors and swept dramatically into the garden, leaving Samir and I sat abruptly facing the lawn, and awkwardly facing each other, like *budho budhi*, old man, old woman, staring at their garden in the autumn of their shared lives.

He looked indifferently at me and then at the ceiling-to-floor book-shelves that occupied the corner of the room. They were laden with books of all shapes and colours, so full that each shelf had books stacked up on top of each other and some were two rows deep. His eyes misted over at the overflowing reams of literature. He was mesmerised.

'Whose books are all of those?' he asked, in what I thought was wonderment and awe.

I smiled conceitedly. 'They are all mine,' I boasted.

He turned and looked at me witheringly and said, 'I hate books, I hate all books. I never ever read and I don't like people who like books.'

My friends Sara and Noreen were also looking for their own Mr Rights. They had grown up with me and were at the same stage of the marriage process. They too were university graduates, and were about to begin professional careers. Like me, they were involved in community affairs. They had similar stories to recount to mine. Sara, who wore *hijab* too, described the story of Fayyaz who came with the Imam who had recommended him. His biodata was promising: well-educated, religious, good family, wanting a woman who wore *hijab*, good job, liked to travel. He had his own flat already and so *he* was 'domesticated' and independent. His references were also impeccable.

She told us that the Imam – as is required of anyone in the pastoral professions – was chatty. We giggled at her description of the meeting: 'Fayyaz shifted his weight from buttock to buttock. At first he was patient, but then he kept throwing me desperate looks. Two hours later the forceful Imam turned to him and asked why he hadn't spoken to me yet.

'Fayyaz and I went into the other room. I understood immediately why the Imam talked so much.' She explained that Fayyaz was as quiet as his chaperone was talkative. 'Fifteen awful minutes of silence later we were summoned to return. Then the Imam chimes in: "You must have had a good chat" and gives me a wink. Then he says, "These meetings, ho-ho-ho! I had a friend who was an Imam too. He went on a visit on behalf of a friend of his to meet a girl. Liked her so much he married her himself! Ho-ho-ho!"' Sara, Noreen and I all squealed with horrified laughter.

Noreen had her own story to tell: 'Jameel was tall and good looking. He was a doctor and had been looking to marry for quite some time. He was intelligent and funny, and very charming. Everyone seemed to really like him in the family, including my Nana and my tiny little nephew. His stories were hilarious. And he said that he wanted a wife to embody both *deen*, spiritual life, and *dunya*, the world we live in. I thought he was perfect till his mum spoke to me.'

Noreen put on her lilting mother-in-law voice:

' "Such a nice boy, Always thinking of everyone else, especially his poor little old Mother." '

'I couldn't believe it when my own mum started gushing too: "He seems lovely, I'm surprised he's not been snapped up!" '

Noreen switched back into mother-in-law mode: ' "Well, he has liked a few girls, but you know, I never really liked any of them myself. He always says to me, 'Mummy, you know much better, you decide. I don't mind waiting for years until we find a girl you are happy with.' " '

Jameel remains unmarried.

Sometimes only the mother-in-law came to visit. I still served samosas and tea and tried to win their hearts. She might be visiting from abroad without her son, to set up a marriage tour. Once the prospective girls had been vetted and a critical mass had been established, the Prince would come to visit London and interview us one by one. His mother was the gatekeeper who had to be wooed. We had to pitch ourselves to get shortlisted to the next stage. I would make the snacks and cakes myself, and watch their eyes gleam with delight at the potential daughter-in-law who could cook heavenly strawberry gateau.

My greatest dread though was the mother-in-law meeting at the mosque. After the lecture or gathering was over, my mother and I would have to find the mother-in-law and stand with her in a quiet corner for my interview. Since there were only women in our section of the mosque, I did not wear my headscarf. My mother would ensure that my hair and lipstick were pristine, so I would look my prettiest. We were both apprehensive. Not only was the process itself difficult and unpleasant, but the environment was challenging too. In a few sentences I would have to win over the woman I would not be marrying.

Other women rushed behind us, stood in groups next to us, tittered in humorous gaggles close to us. We had to be discreet, otherwise gossip would start to fly the following morning about potential wedding matches before even a single glass of tea had been served to the boy's family. Questions would be asked: 'Who was that you were speaking to?' 'I hear she has three very good-looking sons. They were talking to the daughter of that woman over there before.' 'She's been looking for the oldest one for years. I'm sure they will settle for anyone who will have him soon.'

Habib cried when Sara spoke to him. Although his parents had divorced more than five years ago he was still very upset by it. He wanted to get married, but he would have a nervous breakdown if he had to go through a divorce. He was angry when she said this worried her as the basis of their first conversation. Sara described that he spat the words 'Reality, not romance! Reality!'

Then Noreen met Akil who said: 'I need to leave because I'm meeting my friends to watch the football.'

I was introduced to Bilal: 'My mum is getting old and she keeps telling me to get married. To be honest I think it's her that really wants the company. Personally I'm not so bothered.'

Sara got a visit from Javed: 'You're too clever. That's not for me.'

Mizan said to Noreen: 'I'm not really into this whole marriage thing but my parents don't get it. I wanna be single.'

And then Wadud confessed to me: 'I didn't really want to come, but it was this or get kicked out of home.'

Ahmed was not an attractive man. He was also not an intelligent man. I tried to ignore his looks and get to know him for who he was. When he came home to meet our family, he sat in the single armchair, surveying the room. He was aloof. His silence made me feel uncomfortable. On this occasion we hadn't been shunted off to the dining room. My parents had by now refined the art of moving seamlessly with the guests through the patio doors and into the garden, leaving us in situ, audible and visible from their new location outside.

Ahmed spoke little and responded less but when he did his tongue was very sharp. I tried all the techniques I had learnt to open up the conversation. His onion-seed eyes stared into me. I tried to break the frostiness with some humour as we talked about our friends working in the financial services sector. 'They are all accountants, overpaid ones,' I smirked in a slapstick over-the-top fashion to bring some humour to the conversation. I knew that I was making a simplistic and stereotypical statement, but in the Asian community being an accountant really can be a bit of a joke, so I played on it, trying to get both of us to bond over a shared caricature. He shot me a withering look and I felt my hair sizzle from end to root under my headscarf.

In a patronising voice he enlightened me: 'Accountants come in many different specialities and are quite different from other financial professions like bankers or actuaries, even though they are all considered financial services. It is a simple and obvious fact that even a mildly clever person would know.'

He thought I was thick, like a plate of gloopy blancmange. It was not something I'd experienced before. Other boys who had met me had said that I was too clever for them and so either they were not interested in me or were scared of me.

I did not care that Ahmed was the dullest and most difficult human being I had come across. I was more perturbed by the fact that he thought I was a bimbo.

A *bimbo*?

The matchmaker called the next day. 'What did Shelina think?' she asked my mother. I had briefed my mother on this boy's lack of social grace, his inability to have a conversation and the fact he was deeply unattractive, although to be fair, she had spotted this herself. She was aware that Ahmed had been extremely difficult and had shown no effort or interest in easing what is always an uncomfortable and difficult situation by engaging in conversation, no matter how meaningless. Even when two people know early on that the match is unlikely, both have a responsibility to make the situation as pleasant as possible and maintain a reasonable level of sociability and civility. Ahmed had missed this training session in his How to Find a Wife course.

My mother was brief and not complimentary. The matchmaker was surprised. I heard her popped 'Oh!' from the other side of the room whilst my mum was on the phone. 'But Ahmed really liked Shelina.'

This revelation elicited a corresponding 'Oh!' from my mother. I'd launched a tirade at her about Ahmed, so the fact he had enjoyed our meeting was unexpected.

'Erm,' began my mother. She gathered herself together and said, 'But Shelina said he did not speak, and that he looked very unhappy and she had to do all the talking.'

'Ahmed explained all this to me,' responded the matchmaker. 'He says it was a test.'

A test? Surely marriage and love were complicated enough. I didn't need a man who was rude or one who couldn't be straightforward and honest. I didn't have time to fritter away on a man who wanted to test me before he even knew me. And yet the matchmaker was still on the man's side.

'He said it was a test to see how the girl responds and Shelina did really well. He liked her.'

Huh?

'Does Shelina want to see him again?'

I began to despair. Where did these men come from? Was there something I needed to know about the male species?

They all seemed so normal but underneath they had these strange quirks. Sharing anecdotes with Sara and Noreen confirmed my suspicions.

'Have the men always been like this?' I asked my mum and her friends, to see if their experiences could shed any light on the matter.

'They are a strange bunch,' they confirmed. 'You have to be patient and let them do their thing. It's like having another child around.'

They weren't complaining about men or berating them. They smiled when they gave me this information. It was almost as though they wanted to add 'and that's why we love them'. Perhaps they grew up in more understanding times, when you just accepted men as they were. Maybe they understood that it was the quirks that made men perfect.

My generation was young and we knew it was just a matter of time and some effort before we encountered Prince Charming. We told ourselves that the strange men we had come across so far were one-off oddities.

We were optimistic. We had broken all the rules: we had been well educated, gone to good universities and had great jobs. We were attractive, interesting, well-spoken, religious and family oriented. Surely it was, to reiterate, just a question of time and effort.

I had learnt to be philosophical about these meetings. I had to be. It was important for my sanity to keep alive a small glimmer of hope that one of these Y-chromosome unmarried individuals might have something to tease me into marrying them. For weren't human beings full of surprises?

This continuing optimism, coupled with a good old-fashioned British stiff upper lip meant that I ploughed on with the search with stoic determination.

It was all a game of statistics. The big question was, which statistic: 'Finding the One' or 'Four out of Six'?

FOUR

Only Connect

Waiting

It was 4 a.m. Outside it was somewhere between the end of the darkness of the night and the pale grey light of dawn. My alarm was ringing wildly and my father's voice echoed through the hallway. '*Beti*, you have to get up.' It was time for the morning prayer.

How did he always sound so energetic and cheerful so early in the morning? My parents had already been awake for an hour, immersed in middle-of-the-night prayers.

'Allah loves this time of the morning the most, when His creatures give up their precious sleep to be close to Him,' they told me. Their eyes shone with excitement. There was something in the light from their faces – clear, contented – that resonated with their words.

'Whatever wishes you have, this is the time to ask.' It was so quiet, so uninterrupted, only your heart and the Divine. The answers become clear even before you ask the question.

I was not feeling so sublime that morning. 'Five more minutes,' I croaked. I hung my legs painfully over the edge of the bed, head between my knees, and then swung myself delicately out of bed, bleary-eyed, feeling slightly queasy at the few hours of sleep I had had so far. With the thought of having to get up again for work in less than three hours, I searched for a delicate balance between being awake enough to pray and not so awake that I couldn't sleep again. It took a force of will to stand up.

I could hear the soft patter of my parents moving about elsewhere in the quiet house as they prepared to pray. This was the magical period of *fajr*, a time when most people were sleeping. As the seasons changed, *fajr* would sometimes be earlier, as early as 2 a.m. in the summer and as late as 7 a.m. in the winter. It was the first of the five ritual prayers which punctuated the day and gave it rhythm. *Fajr*, to start the day right; *Dhuhr* and *Asr*, in the afternoon, to centre you during the busy work day, to remind you what the day was for and to pull you back from fatigue; *Maghrib* and *Isha* in the evening, for rest and peace, to give thanks for the day and to remember the Creator before sleeping.

To work out the beginning and end timings of each prayer, you could collect a printed timetable from the local mosque or access one on the internet. A simple matrix would help you calculate the timings: *Fajr*, starts 3.56 a.m., ends 5.53 a.m. You could pray your *salat* at any time in between, but it was always better to pray early. It showed you were keen, committed.

'If you had an appointment with a lover, your entire being would race through all the chores you had to do, and you would always do your best to be punctual,' used to say the Imam.

The principles to calculate prayer time are based on the movement of the sun, and so timings vary throughout the year as the length of day changes. *Dhuhr* was prayed when the sun was directly overhead, when shadows were at their shortest. *Maghrib* was prayed as dusk fell, on the cusp between day and night. In an urban lifestyle, the prayers created a much-needed sensitivity to nature's rhythms. 'The day was created for work,' says the *Qur'an*, 'and the night was created for rest.'

Before every ritual prayer it was a requirement to wash certain parts of your body, not only for physical cleanliness, but also for symbolic spiritual purification. Each step had a prayer that accompanied it. I washed my mouth: *please put sweet words onto my lips*. I washed my face: *let light shine from my face*. The words made me feel focused and uplifted. I washed my arms between elbow and fingertips: *let my hands do good, let them prevent bad deeds and injustice*. I ran my fingers gently across the top of my head: *when things get pressured, let me stay calm*. Finally, I wiped my feet, *let them walk me to places where I can do good*.

I returned to my room and unfolded my prayer mat. It was made of deep red velvet, about a metre in length and half a metre in width, with a small arch printed at the top, symbolically pointing in the direction of prayer. I laid the mat to face south-east, towards the *qiblah,* at the heart of which was the *Kaba* in Mecca. Hundreds of millions of other people, perhaps even a billion, around the world would face the same point throughout their day. I covered my hair with a long cloth, which swept over my shoulders and fell just past my waist. Beneath I was wearing my favourite blue satin pyjamas. I drew a deep breath and tried to focus.

First I stood upright, in *qiyam*, the standing position, and recited Arabic verses from the *Qur'an*.

Bismillah Ar-Rahman Ar-Raheem. In the Name of Allah, the Lovingly Compassionate, the Kind.

Alhamdu lillahi rabbil aalameen. All praise is due to the Sustainer of the Worlds.

I continued until the words were complete. Then I bowed down, my hands placed upon my knees, my back curved, my face looking downwards. I continued reciting:

Glory to Allah, glory to Allah, glory to Allah.

Finally, I bent down further and placed my forehead on the floor in *sajdah*, prostration, my hands on either side of my body, almost curled into a foetal position. Being in this humbled position, my forehead touching the ground, was the ultimate crushing of pride and showed that in front of no human being were you to fall so totally and humbly. Only the Creator was worthy of complete devotion.

I repeated these movements and completed the prayer. I sat on the prayer mat, at a loss. I reflected on my single status and the painful, heartbreaking process of looking for a partner, but never finding one. I felt so lonely. I didn't want to grow old alone.

I wondered whether it was my pride that had stopped me from accepting someone who didn't live up to the standards of my imaginary Perfect Prince. But I could not think of even one man I had turned down who could have made a suitable match. My head was tipped downwards, strands of my hair trailing over my eyes. I thought about how hard I had been trying.

'Wasn't effort to be rewarded?' I asked the Divine. 'You could magic up a perfect man in an instant if You wanted. You have power over all things. In the *Qur'an*, You tell us that You say "'Be' and It is",' I reminded Him petulantly. God clearly didn't need reminding of what He had said.

My eyes welled up, and tears started rolling slowly down my cheeks. I raised my hands, both of them open facing upwards. God wasn't upwards, wasn't in any physical place. But my hands moved instinctively, pleading. 'I really want to get married, have a husband, settle down. Haven't you told us that getting married means to complete half of our faith? I want to follow Your guidelines and I'm trying hard, so hard, to find someone. Why don't you send me someone?' I complained.

The tears came faster, unstoppable. I wept, blew my nose and cried some more. I was blessed in my life in so many ways: wonderful family, lovely house, good job, the opportunity to travel, close friends. This was the one thing I felt was missing. 'I'm only asking for something good, someone to be with and love, someone who will love me and bring me closer to You. It's awful having to go through this process week after week with all these strange people. I just want to get on with my life.'

'Am I not ready to be married yet? Are there more things I need to learn? Or is my Prince not ready for me yet? What are these things I need to know, to experience before I find the one who will complete my soul?'

I would have to be patient. The ability to wait, to hold yourself with dignity and thankfulness when you can't have what you want, or can't have it quite yet, is one of the hardest qualities to master. 'Allah is with the patient,' says the *Qur'an*. All good things come to those who wait, I reminded myself. I wondered how much longer I would need to be patient.

My life was on hold. School, tick. University, tick. Job, tick. Travelling, tick. Husband, big empty gaping hole. I was stuck, unable to move forward. But was it God who was teaching me to be patient enough to wait for what I needed, or was it only me who was holding myself back from living my life? If I was to embrace life, if I dedicated myself to growing inside my soul, experiencing new things and working for a better world, would my love arrive? What was the lesson to be learnt?

As time passes, the rules that govern our lives change. As I moved from early twenties to mid-twenties, I became less concerned with gossip. Gossip became less concerned with me. Where once I had only seen malice, I started to see genuine concern from Aunties and match-makers, albeit hidden under the same mannerisms as before. They were born of a different time and place. The function they performed would once have been utterly critical, upholding tradition and knitting together the fragile social fabric. They would have earned the right to be directive and they would have grasped the power they had. Marriage held the community together, and as its chief architects they would have been accorded deference and grace.

'We must get her married soon,' the Aunties would whisper, eye-brows furrowed with worry on my behalf. 'Soon all the good proposals will run out and then she will just have to pick anyone, anyone at all.' They meant to be supportive and encouraging but instead they invited the dark clouds of perpetual doom to hover over my doorstep. I refused to be cowed.

Young women were no longer beholden to marriage as the gateway to womanhood as once they might have been. Self-worth was no longer created through wifehood and children. The idea of marrying for the sake of social acceptability and status was slowly bleeding out of our system. This was sometimes misconstrued as rejecting marriage, rejecting culture, rejecting men. But this was far from the truth.

We were still besotted with getting married but not for the title or status; instead it was for companionship and love. No longer were we vulnerable to guilt or necessity as levers to push us towards marriage. It was not social pressure but rather that we recognised and accepted our needs as human beings: we wanted a partner and we wanted to be a partner. The change in mood that we heralded was seismic but the system had yet to catch up.

Being older had its benefits. The strictures of beady eyes and traditional processes started to become relaxed. Gossip focused on younger girls, and I was able to take advantage of newer, less formal ways of meeting suitors. There was a sense that a less structured setting might be more conducive to eliciting a proposal from the boy and an acceptance from the girl. And thus it was that I went on my first meeting outside my family home. Even though Sara and Noreen had been through the experience already, they teased me that I was going on a 'blind date'. 'All the meetings we have are blind dates,' I pointed out.

Syed lived in Leicester, about an hour-and-a-half's drive from central London, where we had agreed to meet. I wanted to be somewhere far from home and prying eyes. I had suggested a pretty little café in a popular part of town, with plenty of parking nearby, for a late afternoon coffee. Coffee was perfect: if things went well then we could have dinner. If they went badly, it could all be ended very quickly. We had agreed to meet at 5 p.m. He was an accountant, four years older than me, a graduate in science. We had spoken briefly on the phone to make arrangements to meet, keeping the conversation very logistical. His voice was light and breezy and I felt immediately at ease. He seemed good fun and very laid back.

I arrived five minutes late. I'd like to think I was fashionably, femininely late. I scanned the room. There was no sign of a man alone, wriggling uncomfortably or nervously. Each table was occupied with a couple gazing into each other's eyes. They held delicate china tea cups, and their pert cherry-lipped smiles created an angelic frieze. I wrinkled my nose optimistically: would their love perfume the air and infect us both?

I picked a table under a skylight to give us a bright setting. I sat facing the beautiful mural at the back of the café so that the sun shone onto my specially selected pale green headscarf. I was always advised to wear light colours. Apparently boys like pale colours. And apparently green is the colour of attraction. I took off my jacket and sat down, handbag on knees, rummaging around inside to find my mobile phone. I scooped it from the ocean-depths of my fathomless woman-bag and placed it expectantly on the table.

5.15 p.m.: In order to avoid causing injury and embarrassment by constantly turning to check the entrance, I swap chairs and face the door.

5.20 p.m.: I move my jacket from his seat to the back of mine.

5.30 p.m.: The waiter asks if I want to order a coffee. I shake my head, *I'm waiting.* He raises an eyebrow. Syed is 30 minutes late and he is coming from far away. I look at the phone: he hasn't rung to say he will be late.

5.35 p.m.: Should I ring him to find out where he is? I decide that would not be the right thing to do on a blind date.

5.40 p.m.: Is he alright? Maybe he's had an accident. Maybe he is lying in a pool of blood on the motorway. Maybe he is in an ambulance on the way to hospital. Never mind, I am the girl, I can't call him, and calling him won't help anyway.

5.45 p.m.: I order a cappuccino. Whether he comes or not, I still want the coffee.

6 p.m.: Does he have the right address? Has he forgotten to bring my phone number? It's been an hour. I decide to ring him. At least I will know. If he isn't coming then I can go home. Our meeting has other parties involved with their own vested interests in the outcome. I have to ensure that I have done my utmost to ensure the success of the date so I can step away blameless. It is important not to appear to give up.

I ring his number and wait. Eventually he picks up and I can hear the radio. He sounds relaxed. 'Oh yeah, I'm on my way, motorway you know, busy. Usual traffic. I'm nearby though, so don't worry, I'll be about half an hour.'

I sigh, half angry, half relieved. What is he thinking being an hour and a half late and not even bothering to ring? It says a lot about his manners. Do I want to spend the rest of my life with someone who runs this late and who is so thoughtless and inconsiderate as to not even let me know? He has revealed so much of his character before I've even met him.

On the other hand, it has been drummed into me that I should not jump to conclusions about people so quickly. Maybe there was a good reason? Maybe he couldn't ring while driving? Maybe the roads were treacherous and he had to concentrate? Maybe, maybe, maybe . . . There was no harm in having an open mind, was there?

Mainly I feel relief, and I try to make an effort to be excited again. I haven't been stood up. And I won't have to report back to the matchmaker with a failed meeting. I don't want her pity at being unable even to secure a man for a cup of coffee. Late or not, at least I am meeting a prospect. You never know, he might be the one.

6.30 p.m.: I am feeling hungry. I order cookies, white chocolate and hazelnut. I smile when they arrive, perhaps it is a sign: they are heart-shaped.

7 p.m.: I pick up the phone to ring him just as he arrives. Two hours late. He smiles broadly. He's five foot ten, slim, dressed in blue jeans and a crisp white shirt, short tidy dark brown hair. He smells fragranced, something soft and soulful.

He sits and stretches back in his chair. He turns to the waiter and orders a coffee. 'Long drive,' he explains. I nod supportively. He's no Indiana Jones, but he's pleasant to look at and he puts me at ease. Maybe the waiting was a lesson to be learnt.

'I need something sweet to help the coffee down,' he says by way of excuse. I point to the cookies but he wrinkles his nose.

'They do good cake here, too,' I smile conspiratorially at him.

His eyebrows shoot up. 'Reeeelly?' He looks thrilled. A dimple appears. My soft spot, *dimples*. The other is hazel eyes, but he doesn't have those.

He waggles his dimple enticingly at me. 'Chocolate?'

I nod again, encouragingly this time. I like chocolate too. He looks at me cheekily and then yells over to the waiter, 'Two slices of chocolate cake!' He turns back, grinning. I'm embarrassed at his yelling but impressed at the ease and charm with which he does it. The waiter seems happy to oblige. How does he pull it off, I wonder?

The cake arrives, dark, sticky, oozing. I eat mine in small tidy pieces, my fork weaving in between the layers of pure chocolate, whizzing into my lips, avoiding my lipstick. I am lingering over the sponge and rasp-berries nestling between the layers. I look up and his cake has vanished, his eyes are shining, his coffee cup in his hand. He is extremely likeable. But will he like me? I tell myself to try to be more fun.

We chat. He talks and I giggle. The two hours are long forgotten. We talk about travelling, we talk about the mosque. We talk about sports. He loves cricket. He really does love cricket.

'More than chocolate cake,' he smiles naughtily at me. I'm not a fan of cricket but I know there was a test match this afternoon.

'I'm sorry you missed it on my account,' I apologise in mock humility to him. I pause. 'Perhaps it was worth it?'

He smiles broadly. 'Maybe.'

I smile broadly back.

We chat some more. His work. My work. His family. My family. It's dinner time by now, and I'm getting hungry. I ask if he is too. He tells me he had a whole bag of crisps before he left home. 'Can't watch the end of a cricket match without wolfing down a big bag of cheese and onion crisps,' he advises. I don't like cheese and onion. They make me feel nauseous when I can't get the smell off my fingers afterwards.

He turns to hunt down a waiter. All the talking is making him thirsty. There is a big bubble expanding in my head, draining the oxygen, making me feel angry. I need to know exactly why he was late now. 'What time do you think the cricket match ended?' 'Oh, just after half past five,' he answers distractedly, still searching for the waiter. Puzzle pieces start to meld together.

'Did you watch the whole match at home?' I ask him, stunned. To control my trembling fingers I play with the cookies that remain untouched. He grins cheesily and then slurps down his iced mineral water. The cookie snaps suddenly, right down the centre. I offer him the ragged half. Whilst I was waiting in the café on my own for two hours, he was still at home, knowing with full audacity that he was going to be *two hours* late. I'm horrified. He is oblivious.

I stay as long as is polite to finish my coffee. I don't need to be as rude as he has been; I have my own character and reputation to protect. My instincts were right about him, and I should have trusted my intuition. The meeting has been revelatory. Without realising it, his actions have shown me a great deal of what lies beneath, enough to know that despite his charm and disposition, his character has the most fundamental flaw: disrespect and devaluing of another person. Cricket versus courtesy.

The advice from my parents and the Aunties about looking for someone who is well brought up with good manners rings in my ears. The religious advice to look for someone who will treat you well because he understands how to respect other human beings echoes.

I found this process amazing. It gave you access to the most instinctive behaviours of another person and then allowed you to see your own unmeditated response first-hand. The raw humanity of addressing the issues of spending life together made it the ultimate learning experience.

We were strangers but we had to talk deeply and intimately about our futures. Syed didn't need to explain to me in words how little he would really value his wife and how he would fail to respect others. I saw it in his actions. His words would only have told me what he wanted to believe about himself and what he *thought* he was like.

I began to ask myself the same difficult questions. Were my beliefs about myself at odds with my actual behaviour? Or had I managed to achieve integrity between my words and desires? After my experience with Syed it was very clear to me that just because you are meeting a potential life partner, it does not excuse a lapse in character.

My experience with Syed also reminded me to trust my intuition. After two hours of waiting, and without an apology for tardiness, I should have seen him for what he really was. But the rules of culture had told me to pursue marriage at all costs and to subsume my own mind and instincts to the process. Instead, I should have trusted my *fitrah*, the inner conscience that the Creator has put into each of us to recognise what is right, and to assert what is our due. *Fitrah* is an amazing part of a human being: the natural instinct that everyone has to know what is right, to want to do the right thing and to expect to be treated right.

My right was to be treated with courtesy. My culture had belittled the self-respect I should have had for myself. On the other hand I saw that my religion offered respect to me, telling me to trust that voice inside myself. I realised that my faith truly had something to offer me, and at that moment, I took it out of the books and applied it to my life: I was a human being and I deserved to be treated with respect.

Plus Ça Change

Good brains do not necessarily mean good character. Thus it was with Khalil. He was a well-qualified dentist. He had graduated first in his year and had gone on to set up a thriving practice. He was born and brought up in London, and my mother knew his mother, if only to say hello to. She told me that both his parents were very intelligent as well as attractive and religious too, and if he was indeed the son of his parents, he would be more than eligible. The matchmaker had rung my mother to find out if we were interested. He sounded like the most promising prospect we had had in a long time. We replied in the affirmative, and she asked if she could give Khalil my number to speak to me directly. 'They can have a chat and if they like each other then they can arrange to meet themselves,' she explained. This process made perfect sense and felt much more relaxed.

Khalil rang on Sunday evening, a beautiful golden summer's dusk. 'Hello,' he smiled down the phone. 'Hello,' I smiled back. We hit it off immediately, and chatted with both seriousness and levity. Fifteen minutes and two blinks of our eyes later, he told me he would ring again and I said I looked forward to it. He had described himself as five foot eight, slim and 'dashingly handsome of course'. I reciprocated with a sketch of my appearance. It made a phone conversation, however brief, much easier. His own mock arrogance about his looks made me laugh so much that I asked if he had any flaws. He put on a genteel accent and responded, 'My dear, a small case of sleep apnoea, but the ladies tell me that it is most charming.' I giggled, inexplicably allured by his confession of snoring.

He rang the next evening and we chatted again. He asked if I'd like to go to dinner on Friday, as we seemed to be getting on so well. I accepted. He had already ticked the critical box of 'someone I can talk to'. This was the box I found hardest to check. He rang spontaneously the following evening for another chat. I took this as a very positive sign. Two unprompted calls. I smiled. Our dinner was only three days away.

There was no call on Tuesday or Wednesday. He rang me on Thursday. His tone was quite different. 'There is something I need to tell you. I hope it won't change things, but it is important that I'm honest with you.' My heart raced. Oh no! What hidden secret did he have? Was he married? Did he have a fatal illness? Had he been in prison?

'I just wanted to let you know that I could never marry someone who is only five foot three,' he said in a very genuine tone. 'I know we get on so well. And I'm sure you are very attractive from what other people have told me. But you are just too short for me. So please don't get your hopes up when we meet tomorrow.'

There was a long pause. What to say now? He had upset the balance of power.

'But you're five foot eight, aren't you?' I furrowed my eyebrows at him over the phone. 'That's really not so tall compared to me. In fact some would say it's just perfect.' I wanted to salvage something of the situation, trying to persuade him not to destroy the hopes and burgeoning dreams for which I had been laying the foundations this week. It was so rare to find someone with whom I had such a natural spark.

'It's just the way I feel,' he said boyishly, trying to pass this off as one of his charming quirks. I recalled the issue of his snoring.

'Anyway,' he said brightly, 'Did you pick a restaurant yet?'

'I don't see the point of meeting,' I told him.

'You think I'm shallow, don't you?' he moped, conveying his disappointment in me. 'Well, if that's what you think, that's a real shame.' He paused deliberately to gather gravitas. 'Do you have a picture in your mind of the perfect other-half?'

'Yes,' I croaked, uncertain of his motives.

'I have a picture in my mind, too. She's taller than you.'

'Everyone has a picture,' I responded sharply. 'But I know that a real person may or may not be like that picture. I might find somebody completely unexpected, who doesn't match my imagination at all. They might be much better than I imagined. But how can you know if you have such fixed ideas? Would you give up the perfect person just because they were too short or too tall?'

'I would,' he said softly, unapologetically. 'But I'd still really like to meet you,' he cajoled. 'Please think about it.'

I recounted the sorry tale to my father, who was wiser and more perceptive. He made a simple statement: 'Tell him that women are not sold by the yard.'

Irrationally, I failed to decline his invitation and I did meet him for dinner. Curiosity? Attraction? Uncowed optimism? Attraction to doom? I should have noted that because he had already defined me as unsuitable, he had left himself with the option to carry on with the relationship but he had taken away any choice I might have had to reject him. He had kept all the power for himself and, weakly, I went along with it.

At dinner he insisted we 'go Dutch'. He reiterated that he had already made his intentions clear. We were simply friends. 'You are very pretty though. *Very* attractive,' he emphasised. 'But just way too short, it's a shame.' I wondered if he thought short people had no feelings.

I seethed inside at how ungallant he was. He failed to meet the universal standards of good manners that were present equally in British, Asian and Islamic etiquette. He was stingy. It would still be courteous of the man to pay, or at least to make a pretence of wanting to pay. I would have contributed anyway.

We left the restaurant. He insisted that he wanted to eat dessert. I was feeling bloated after our meal but I agreed to have some tea whilst he ate his pudding. I ordered tea, he ordered tea, dessert and after dinner chocolates. Neither of us had change to settle the bill, so we put in a ten-pound note each. The waiter returned the saucer with our receipt and the balance of the money. He took all the change and put his share as well as mine in his pocket without batting an eyelid.

I thought again about how the intensity of looking for love can reveal so much about a person. The feeling that Khalil had evoked inside me had made me forget how important character was. The words of the Prophet rang clearly in my head: 'Don't select a partner on the basis of looks or wealth, because those qualities will disappear.' Khalil had rejected me because he had a fixed idea of how I should look – and a completely irrational idea at that. It was not a companion that he wanted but a doll, a plaything built to his exact specification. And what should I make of the strange behaviour with the money? I wanted to share my life with someone who had generosity of spirit. That would be the kind of man who would take me closer to the Creator. I wanted to learn from my husband how to be a better person. I couldn't afford to marry a man who was miserly and didn't think anything of it.

Khalil's unrealistic and irrational expectations had denied him possibilities, including the possibility to be with someone who would make a good companion. And although he was polite and well-spoken, his actions showed how little respect he had for others. I couldn't spend a lifetime with someone who would control and manipulate, no matter how wonderful they seemed to be. In a few days of speaking on the phone, within a few hours of meeting, the starkness of the process had forced Khalil to show his hand. Had we been dating, he could have strung me along for months before revealing his preconceived ideas.

I confronted myself and challenged my own inner being to be honest: were my expectations just as rigid? Was I just as irrational and blind to any unrealistic demands of my own? The questions swam around and around in my mind, making me nauseous.

Soon after, I met Mobeen and tried to be more open-minded. Again we arranged to meet in central London away from the eyes of gossips. I was waiting for him outside the ice-cream shop we had chosen for our rendezvous when my phone rang.

'*Salam alaikum,*' said the voice.

I responded '*Alaikum salam.*'

'Er, hi, it's Mobeen.' He had a nice clear voice, smart and sophisticated.

'Hello, Mobeen,' I replied.

'Listen, I'm really sorry, but I'm running a bit late.'

Late. My life always seemed to run late.

'That's OK,' I answered. I wanted to be gracious, give him a chance, not pre-judge him, not find myself guilty as charged. Perhaps he had a genuine reason. At least he had called to let me know. But how was it that so many of the men were always late? I still cringed whenever cricket was on TV.

'How long do you think you'll be?' I asked him.

'About half an hour.'

'I'll see you then.' I closed my phone, tucked it into my handbag and walked towards the shops to browse. I would easily be back before he arrived and he could always ring me. No point standing forlornly in public. I became immersed in the window displays, making the best of the situation. I wouldn't let myself become distressed over a 30-minute delay. I resolved to make the most of the extra time.

A young Asian man approached me. 'Excuse me, I think I know you.'

My blind date is running late, and now I'm being chatted up by a complete stranger.

He looked at me with such assurance that I wondered if I just simply didn't recognise him. Maybe I did know him? If I told him bluntly that I didn't know him, and he turned out to be a family friend, then I would appear very rude. I was cautious in my response just in case I did know him.

'Where do you think we've met?'

He looked at me genuinely. 'At sixth form college.' He smiled, encouraging me to participate. I returned his gaze blankly. 'You know, in A level class together,' he added.

I'd caught him out. 'I went to a girls' only school, no boys in class,' I retorted, and turning heel I walked off. He ran after me.

Oh no, I thought, picking up speed, *I'm attracting strange men who stalk me in public*. I started walking more furiously.

'Shelina! Shelina!' he yelped. How did he know my name? I felt scared now.

'Shelina! Shelina! It's me, Mobeen!' I stopped and swivelled.

'Mobeen? But, but, you're running late!' I blurted out. Mobeen was 30 minutes away.

I turned to look at the spot where the stranger had just approached and propositioned me.

'But, you, but, just now, over there, but . . .' I looked at him in confusion and distress. He responded by grinning at me. He sat me down at a nearby café and ordered two coffees for us.

He smiled happily, like a little beam of sunlight, but I felt a dark menacing cloud inside me. I kept repeating my mantra not to pre-judge, not to be guilty of fixed expectations. Maybe he was a bit nervous, that was all?

'I wanted to see if you had a sense of humour,' he began, 'And so I thought I would play a little practical joke on you.' He smiled, happier still. 'You have a very good sense of humour, you took it very well!' He kept grinning. 'I really like that, most girls don't show such humour.'

I was pleased that I had passed the GSOH test. I was more pleased I had held on to my own respect and dignity. Sadly, Mobeen had not. In the race to think about what he wanted in a partner, he had forgotten that he was in the process of making an impression on me. And he had forgotten his actions would tell me more about his character than any number of words could have done.

*

My grandmother had recounted to me the process of selecting a suitor when she was young. If a boy presented himself to a family, and if they deemed that he was of good character and background, could earn a living and had no untoward characteristics, then the family had no choice but to accept his proposal. There was no exploration of 'compatibility' or 'attraction'. You couldn't be too picky. If a family kept a daughter in the house too long it was considered shameful. What reason could they give for refusing the first offer that came along? What if that was going to be the best or only offer that she got?

I asked my grandmother many questions about growing up as an Asian woman in the first half of the twentieth century in Tanzania. I don't believe that her experiences were necessarily unique to her being Muslim but reflected her time and provenance from the Asian community. I imagine her Hindu, Sikh and Christian Asian counterparts, who were quite numerous in the town where she grew up, would have experienced much the same as she did.

She told me that one day, when she was fifteen, her father – who by all accounts was a very kind, generous and compassionate man and also deeply pious – took her to the window of their house and pulled the curtains back slightly. He pointed at a small man walking away from the house and told her 'You are engaged to this man.' She was married soon after.

My grandmother recounted the story without surprise, as though this was an experience typical of her time. I believe this was the way things were done and that her father had nothing but love for her. My mother tells me that he was more loving to his daughters than his sons. When a son was born to his wife, he would give a monetary gift to the midwife and helpers. When a daughter was born, he would give them twice that. He had seven children in total. In a time when sons, as in many cultures even today, reigned supreme over daughters, this was an incredibly unusual, pioneering – and most of all Islamic – action. So I can only believe that the way he found partners for his daughters was with the same dignity, piety and love. How else was a young woman to be married and to have her own home?

My grandmother, like her peers, would most likely have had little knowledge of the men of the world, having been rarely exposed to them, and so she relied on her father's judgement and connections to find someone suitable. If she didn't marry at around fifteen, what else was she to do? A young woman would be quite mature by this age and considered to be an adult. Even today, girls of this age are physically and mentally adult, and even have children of their own.

If the young woman didn't marry, she would be 'holding up the queue' for any younger siblings. A younger sister could not marry until the older one had, otherwise the elder sister's chances would be blown forever. Every choice a young woman made, or every action she undertook, was a communal affair – driven by, but also impacting those around her. Just like all human beings, the young woman did not – and still doesn't – live in a vacuum. The destiny of those around her is intertwined with her own.

A young woman had to get married: for her to remain at home with her parents until she grew old would not allow her to fully flourish in the society of that era. It was also clearly impractical. Women were not able at that time to be entirely financially and socially independent – as was the case in Western societies, too – and society was family based. Once her parents died, who would look after her? What autonomy would she have? From a social and cultural perspective, marriage was a way for a woman to get status and some control over her destiny. It was believed that she could flower into womanhood in her own home, where she would be running her own show and experience a new level of happiness. From an Islamic perspective, both men and women were thought to be at their most complete when they were married. Besides, rightly or wrongly, it was believed that what women wanted most was to have their own home under their own control and then to have children.

The marriages of that time reflected the socially accepted split of responsibilities between the husband and the wife. The husband would bring in the wages: the wife would look after the home and the children. The Islamic marriage contract that bound them together does not enforce these duties on a wife. The husband certainly is responsible for providing maintenance and shelter for his wife and family. She can participate in meeting their financial needs if she wants to, or if she needs to, but she doesn't have to. Her official obligations as a wife do not include cleaning, cooking or even looking after the children. Her responsibility is to be a good companion to her husband. But in all aspects of Islamic law, *shari'ah,* a person's obligations are set at the very minimum limit. If you fulfil those obligations then you have followed the letter of the law but not its spirit. As a Muslim, you are encouraged to be compassionate and kind and go beyond the rules and give more than you expect to receive in return. In marriage, certainly in my grandmother's time, that meant men should support their wives in the home and women should look after the husband and family in return. The rules do not make you do any of these things: it is your love for each other that inspires you.

My grandmother had ten children. I remember her as constantly smiling, her *Qur'an* in one hand, her rosary in another. She had woken up every night for more than 50 years to pray her middle-of-the-night prayers, and she stayed awake until the morning, reciting verses from the *Qur'an.* On the occasions she stayed, when I came down for breakfast in the morning she was already wide awake, making tea, smiling, always smiling.

She had the most radiant energy of anyone I remember, and this has left a lasting impact on me. No matter what troubles she faced, she was always contented. My mother said that she was like that ever since she could recall. I could only attribute it to two things: her calm demeanour and her constant consciousness of God. She was always with her Creator, always thinking of her Sustainer, always connected. Her love for husband, children and community was intertwined effortlessly with her Love for the Divine. I found her very comforting and soothing. I wanted to know her secret. But she didn't appear to have any mysterious methods. She was simply dedicated to the Creator, and made sure to treat everyone with kindness. She was the embodiment of 'Islam'. She was an ordinary unsung person, who hadn't changed the big world out there. But she had completely changed the world inside herself, she had won over all the people around her, and all of that made her a hero in her own life.

She told me her stories of being a married woman and prayed that I would find a good husband. 'Be kind to them and they will be kind to you,' she advised. 'Look after your community. Work hard. There will be ups and downs in marriage. The way that the relationship within a marriage will work when you are married, will be the same today as it was when I got married.

'You must look after your husband. I know people have different ideas today, but if you look after him, then he will look after you, remember that, even when it feels hard, even when you don't get what you want. Once you get married, then comes the difficult part. Remember to say sorry, even if it is not your fault. Men are different from women. When we are upset we hold it inside, men get it out of their system and then forget. In fifty years' time, who will remember if it was your mistake or his? You're on the same side, so does it matter if you apologise and he made the mistake? What he will remember is that he had a wife who loved him, and who he still cares about after so many years.'

Then she would smile and laugh loudly. 'Look at me, an old woman giving you advice.'

'*Naanima*,' I would answer, my heart bursting with love for this radiant light that was part of my life, 'will you pray for me to get a good husband?' She put her hand on my head and said with the voice of a mother and the light of another world, 'I pray for all my children to be happy. God will guide you and bless you. It is in His hands, just pray to Him.'

Her love would then melt into her huge smile, and I knew she was about to tease me about getting married.

'You're a bit skinny,' she would laugh. 'Is that what the men like these days?'

Lightning

I longed for 'that feeling' I believed would come from romantic sunset walks or watching the moon rise. But I also knew that this wasn't the reality of life. Even the most handsome poetic romantic princes would struggle under the harsh fluorescent light of the kitchen when you both examined the mouldy contents of the fridge. Which man or woman could be perfect for more than one snapshot in time? Every human being is perpetually evolving, and so while they may be a romantic hero today, tomorrow there may be a discovery that reveals something new about them.

My dreaminess was not an affliction unique to Muslim women: it was shared by many other women and men. I reflected that if we were just to get on with it all and get married, so much of the energy, focus and heartache we expended on looking for love would be freed up for other activities. I wondered how much time, effort and money were spent across the country in pursuit of love, lust and relationships. I wondered if the government had statistics on the potential for wealth, volunteerism and happiness that had been lost in the all-out pursuit of love.

One Thursday we got a call about Karim. He was not from an East African background but rather of Indian origin. My mum was asked whether this was an issue? She responded, 'Of course not, as long as he's a good Muslim.' He sounded promising. He worked as a newspaper photographer. He was *not* an accountant. He had studied Fine Art at a prestigious university, was a year older than me, born and brought up in the UK.

My mother spoke to his mother to arrange a time for the meeting, and reported that she had sounded friendly and personable. They agreed to come over on Saturday at 3 p.m. There was no need to delay. If this one didn't work out, we would have to move onto the next, and so there was no point postponing an introduction. *Time is of the essence*, I kept being warned. We had told Karim's mother that we had to leave at 6 p.m. to attend a family wedding. We calculated that three hours was sufficient to drink some tea and have a preliminary meeting. They lived close by, so if things went well, we could always meet again; if they didn't, at least we had a credible exit strategy in place.

By 4 p.m. they hadn't arrived. They hadn't called to say they were late either. We didn't need to rush quite yet, but with only two hours to go, the proceedings would be constricted. Introductions require a certain amount of protocol and therefore can only be compressed so much. It would be rude of us to accelerate the meeting. My mum tried to call them to see what had happened. No answer. We assumed they had left already. We didn't have a mobile number to ring them en route. She kept trying and at 4.30 p.m. she eventually got through.

'We're waiting for my husband,' explained Karim's mother. 'I'm sure he'll be home very soon and then we'll leave. Don't worry,' she said.

We didn't worry, we fumed, smoke-from-ears fuming. They hadn't even bothered to tell us they were going to be late. Eventually they arrived at 6 p.m. In order to make it to the wedding on time, I had changed out of my elegant, subtle skirt and shirt, and into a bright turquoise silk *shalwar kameez* with rich embroidery. It was perfect for a wedding but quite out of place for an introduction. I was also going through an experimental phase at the time, and to relieve the boredom whilst waiting for Karim, I painted my nails turquoise blue to match with my outfit. If he was cool then he would think it was just a bit of fun.

When they arrived I was dumbfounded. He was gorgeous. He had a beautiful face and amazing hazel eyes. He was courteous and charming, and had a gentle, warm presence that eased all the tension from the room. Although I was cross that they were so preposterously late, I was deeply excited. This was the first time in all the introductions made that I'd had this reaction to someone. I felt a poetic connection.

We chatted for a short time, delaying our journey to the wedding, prioritising this meeting and feeling that even though it was they who had turned up three hours late, we had a duty to be polite and host them. Karim was intelligent and charming. He was also deeply connected to his faith as a Muslim, and that appealed to my spirit. My heart raced as I spoke to him. His smile sent shivers through me.

For once I felt tongue-tied, but he had enough skill and grace to carry the conversation. Although we only talked briefly, I felt that there was magic. At 7 p.m. we all exited our house. They returned to their home and we went to our wedding.

I was still annoyed at them for being so late and for the lack of courtesy, but I was smitten. He scored six out of six on the Shelina-Suitor-Scale of *Essentials*. The qualities I found so hard to locate elsewhere were abundantly present in him: he was a practising Muslim who was deeply involved in running youth activities at his local mosque, he was looking for a wife who wore *hijab*, he was the right age and a smart human being who was easy to talk to. And looking into his beautiful eyes, he met a few of my other *Desirable* qualities too.

Finally I had found someone who shared my vision of faith and who I felt compatible with. I kept thinking about him, hoping that he had felt 'that feeling', too. I was sure that he had. All the signs were there. He had looked right in my eyes as we spoke and his smile had a certain warmth. Most importantly of all, he had told me how nice I was, and how refreshing it was to meet someone like me. I was sure that we would meet again.

Several days later we had still heard nothing. It wasn't proper for my mother to call them. The girl's family could not be so forward: the next move had to come from the boy's side. We all grumbled about how we were at the mercy of the boy's side and how humiliating it was that they controlled the whole situation. We pointed out to each other how

Khadijah, the Prophet Muhammad's first wife, who was herself a successful business woman, had taken the initiative in sending a marriage proposal to Muhammad. And yet despite this, we felt through the force of cultural standards that it would be too shameful to call them.

As the days went by, I lost hope and licked my wounds. I mourned that when I had finally found someone who was suitable and who I liked, he didn't like me. Maybe it was the blue nail polish.

Three weeks later, on a Friday afternoon, we got a call. It was Karim's mother. 'We'd like to visit you tomorrow, Saturday at 2 p.m., so Karim and Shelina can meet again.' We were all shocked. We hadn't heard a squeak for three weeks and now they wanted to come over tomorrow. Stunned by this revelation, my mum forgot to remain cool and agreed to her request, despite the fact we already had guests arranged. She rushed to reschedule. Suitors always took precedence: you never knew when you'd get the chance again.

At 10 a.m. we cleaned the house. At midday we made samosas and sweets. At 1 p.m. I started to get dressed to make sure I achieved a look that was both cute and modest. At 2 p.m. we waited. At 2.30 p.m. we continued to wait. At 3 p.m. we waited further, getting agitated. At 3.30 p.m. we grew furious. At 4 p.m. they arrived. I saw him and I melted. We talked and talked. He smiled at me and his beautiful hazel eyes lit up. I sank into them. What more could I ask for? I could feel the sparks flying. We exchanged mobile phone numbers and e-mail addresses at the end of the meeting. As they left, his mother gave me an enormous squishy hug. She looked straight into my eyes and in an adoring manner told me, 'You are a very lovely girl, Shelina, I like you very much.' I smiled with affection. I was in with the mother!

Since Karim and I had exchanged contact details, my parents assumed the official liaison between them and his parents was over and left it to the two of us to negotiate further developments. They would, of course, be keeping a wise and guiding eye on the proceedings. I hadn't done this before. The rules of meetings were changing, morphing. With new technologies and changing attitudes, mobile phone calls and e-mails were now possible. By Tuesday, I had heard nothing from him. I decided that as a modern woman I too could grasp the reins of my future and get in touch with Karim. I sent him a brief e-mail.

Salam alaikum, Karim
It was nice to see you again on Saturday. I hope your weekend went well. It's always tough to go back to work on a Monday. I'm a bit bored right now so I thought I'd drop you an e-mail to let you know that I'm off on holiday next Monday to Canada to visit my grandmother who is living there. Can't wait. I've been to Toronto several times before, but this time we're going to drive to Montreal as well and spend a couple of days there. Really looking forward to it.
What's new with you?
Shelina

I felt this struck the right balance between nonchalant and leaving the door open for him to respond without feeling pressured. I had deliberately closed with a neutral question so he had to respond but did not feel that it held weighty meaning. The note also created a time line for him to get in touch as I was going away.

I got no response.

The following Monday, I sat on a plane ready to take off for Canada. I succumbed and wrote a short text message to him. 'Off to Canada today. Hope all is well with you. Catch up with you after my return at the weekend. Shelina.'

It took me half an hour to frame this message in order to achieve a tone midway between interest and detachment. I felt like a teenager. I was excited, breathless, truly believing that he was the One. In

Montreal I bought him a T-shirt as a souvenir. I'd never done that before. I wasn't sure how or when I would give it to him, but I already felt a connection. I knew that somehow he was going to be special in my life.

A week after my return I'd still heard nothing back. I tried one more e-mail but got no response. Karim's mother called my mum the following weekend. She was distressed.

'I like Shelina so much,' she told my mother, 'She is so nice, so religious, wears *hijab*, pretty. But my son, I don't know what to do with him. Whenever I ask him, he says "yes, she's nice" but then doesn't *do* anything. I want to see him get married, and he needs an educated, religious wife, and I show him Shelina and he is ignoring me. He says he is busy trying to set up a new business with his friend and he's going to give up his good job. What should I do?'

My mother was trapped between counselling this poor woman and trying to secure her son for me. But she was also annoyed at this dilly-dallying. We'd been through too much of this before and firmly believed that clarity and honesty was the best way forward. She also knew from hard experience that when someone like Karim came along, turning our noses up in a snotty huff would do us no favours either.

My mum told her about the e-mails and text messages, and then gently consoled her and told her to be patient.

A few days later, I got a reply to my email.

Dear Shelina, *salam alaikum*
Thanks for your messages. I saw your first e-mail and just before
I was going to respond our house was struck by lightning!
    There was a power surge to my computer, which I had to fix.
I think the hard drive was corrupted, and I lost your e-mail and
your e-mail address. I will give you a ring later in the week.
    Take care
    Karim

I never heard from him again.

I can't do this anymore. I can't I can't. How can they all be so awful, and the one I like doesn't even give me a second thought? Maybe my father was right – maybe there isn't any such thing as the perfect man. Should I stop looking for Prince Charming? Will that crackling chemistry never materialise? Perhaps my ideal of Prince Charming was just that – an ideal, a dream, something that could never be real.

Or perhaps the problem was with me. Did I expect too much? Surely I couldn't really imagine that falling in love would mean living happily ever after? Despite pretending that I was immersed in the depths of my faith, and saw marriage as part of completing that faith, I had to admit to myself that it was Prince Charming from the fairytales that I was looking for. I demanded such a person from the Creator. I failed to reciprocate with the right attitude. If I saw my partner through the right eyes as a companion in life and faith, then he would be perfect indeed.

Perhaps I should have learnt from Karim that there would not be a perfect man. He had shown that despite meeting all my criteria on paper, and apart from the huge fact that he had evoked 'that feeling', he lacked both the character to treat me well and the desire to be with me.

My rejection should have pushed me to assess honestly what I wanted in a partner and what the reality of choosing my companion should be. I should make a choice based on who would treat me well, and then trust in God to put the mercy, compassion and love between us, as promised. My experience in meeting Karim should have reinforced how important integrity and manners were – more important than that elusive spark.

Instead, I still prioritised 'that feeling' above all else. I was still waiting for my romantic dreams to be fulfilled and believing that they would bring me a sense of completion and happiness. But that love, the love that we describe through 'that feeling', is not an understanding of the eternal and universal truth of Love. That superficial feeling of attraction is about as far from the Divine Love as it could be. Despite knowing the words to explain that, and regurgitating what I had learnt as a Muslim about my faith and the extraordinary universality of love and its connection to the Divine, I didn't really *know* it. It is easy to *say* you know something, but a completely different matter to *live* it with your being. I would have to fall harder still before I would be able to pick myself up and look directly into the face of love.

FIVE

None of the Above

Six Stages of Self-pity

As time passed, the quality of the men being presented by the Aunties began to decline even faster. My parents exchanged worried glances as the introductions were made and yet another suitor was rejected. They were concerned that I would never find anyone to be my exact match and that I should think carefully if any of the men that we had met so far could be a strong contender. 'Three out of six,' said my dad, referring to the diminishing number of my requirements that I should look to find in a man. I asked them, if we could go back in time and have our pick of the boys we had met, which of them would they like me to reconsider. With great sadness, they agreed that none of them had been a suitable match. We were sitting in front of a blank drawing board.

Life was on hold until I got married, and it was the same for my friends. Girls were offered two life settings: before marriage and after marriage. So until I found a husband, everything else had to wait. Soon I would realise that this was a false dichotomy, and that actually I could quite happily get on with my life and search for a partner at the same time.

I would get together regularly with my friends Sara and Noreen to compare notes on our search. We looked forward to sharing these intimate thoughts and the emotional stresses we were facing in order to gain inspiration from each other, as well as consolation.

Each time we met, our conversations followed a similar format: the Six Stages of Self-Pity.

1. (MUSLIM) WOMEN ARE AMAZING

'I don't understand,' I would begin, initiating the well-worn format of our conversations. 'You're both so beautiful, so smart, so funny. I just don't understand why men aren't falling over themselves to marry you.'

Noreen started giggling. 'We could ask you the same thing . . . You could have married Syed and his cricket addiction. Or you could have grown three inches and said "yes" to Khalil, the dentist who wanted an exact-height wife.'

'Don't laugh!' I chided. 'The state of men like that isn't funny.'

'It's not, it really isn't,' she confirmed, sobering up her expression.

'I don't get it either,' said Sara, ignoring Noreen's premature dive into hysteria. Commentary about all the awful men we had met did not usually take place until Stage Three of the conversation. Sara carefully returned us to this first stage of our discussion: to eulogise about how talented Muslim women were and how they were excelling in their education, careers, communities and spirituality. 'We've worked so hard to become the women we are today, it hasn't been easy at all.'

Noreen and I both nodded in agreement. Our parents had arrived as part of the immigrant waves of the 1960s, 70s and 80s. During this period, Britain had been changing socially and culturally, while at the same time the world was becoming more connected and we all started living in a 'global village'. We were all the first generation of our families and communities to be born and brought up in Britain. That meant we had to navigate our way through the challenges that faced all Asians and all Muslims. Many of those challenges were the same that any second-generation child of immigrants might experience in creating a solid sense of identity that combined both their parents' culture and the culture that they found themselves growing up in.

Muslim women had risen to the challenge and were using all the opportunities presented to them. They were outstripping Muslim men at school, university and in some cases their careers too. They also seemed to be more confident in their identity and in finding a way to integrate together their faith and their Asian and British cultures; and they were more open about these different elements that made up their lives. In our circle of friends, all the Muslim women we knew were university-educated and professionals of their trade.

There was one area that was particularly clear though – the Muslim women we knew were still very much connected to their community, their mosques and their faith. In all these areas they were much more visible than men, and worked hard to keep them together. In our experience, Muslim men only seemed to return to these spaces after they were married. Muslim women were pushing forward the debate about our community's understanding of Islam. We were questioning 'how things were' in the way that our faith was practised. Our spirituality and faith were important to us, and we wanted to have our voices heard and our questions explored. We were confident that we would be the ones who could create real and positive change in the Muslim community and in extricating the faith of Islam from the cultures that had taken root in its practice.

In that far, far away alternative universe, where hard work, effort and creating positive change was directly rewarded, and where it was known that we deserved wonderful men in our lives, we would not need to hold regular heartbreak sessions with our girlfriends about not being able to find a husband. Real life should have been like that, but it wasn't.

'If it makes you feel better, it's not just Muslim women like us who are amazing and having difficulty in finding amazing men,' I consoled the girls.

'You're right, I have so many incredible friends who are female and they are all finding it hard to find the right man,' agreed Noreen.

'Nope,' said Sara shaking her head emphatically, 'that does not make me feel one bit better at all.'

2. WHERE ARE ALL THE DECENT MEN?

'They must be out there,' said Noreen, 'somewhere.'

'But where?' chimed in Sara. 'I've looked everywhere. Are they invisible?'

We had been searching for so many years and yet we hadn't found any decent specimens. Where were they hiding?

'The good ones are all married,' sighed Noreen.

'But maybe they only got "good" once they'd been whipped into shape by their wives?' I was thinking out loud to the girls. 'Maybe living with a woman is what turned them into "decent men"?'

'So maybe what we need to do is spot the potential in a man, marry him and then magically, just by living with us, he'll turn into the perfect Prince Charming!' Noreen threw her hands into the air in excitement.

'Or maybe,' said Sara breathlessly, 'they are all hiding from us, frightened that we'll pounce on them. They might be hidden in some kind of underground bunker or on a desert island, and if we can just find them then we'll have our choice of men galore!'

I placed my hand on Sara's forehead. I wondered if the intensity and stress of the search had made her delirious.

It wasn't just us as single women that despaired about the absence of eligible men. Mosques and community leaders did not know where to find them either.

'I met a couple of nice boys at a wedding last month,' Noreen told us. Weddings were always a good place to meet previously unknowns. They were rarely present for more mundane social activities but were required by family intervention to attend such significant events. 'Both of them seemed like good possibilities. One was setting up his own business, the other was an architect. Both of them very nice, intelligent and charming.'

'Very smart,' said Sara, intrigued. 'So, what happened?'

'We exchanged details but I never heard anything back from them.'

'Did you contact them?' I asked, and then added cheesily, 'There's no point being backwards in coming forwards.'

'Yes, I did,' declared Noreen, 'but I've heard nothing. I don't mind making contact, but I'm not going to be desperate.'

'I think these men are not looking for women through the traditional routes of family and friends, maybe they think it's just too "old-fashioned",' commented Sara. 'And because they meet us in these environments, they think we're too "traditional" and can't see us for everything we are, even though we need someone like them who is out in the world.'

'Where are all these men hiding?' I asked again.

Sara responded: 'More importantly, who are they marrying?'

3. MAYBE THERE ARE NO DECENT MEN LEFT

'If nobody can find them, maybe they don't exist,' wailed Noreen. 'Everyone knows everyone else or knows someone who does, so by now between us we ought to have met any half-decent single, breathing man.'

'You're right,' agreed Sara, 'there aren't any. We're going to have to live out our lives as lonely spinster Aunties in our nylon *shalwar kameez*, fixing up matrimonial matches between the new batch of girls and boys.'

'I'll tell them to take the first one they get,' said Noreen seriously. 'I wish I had done that, at least I wouldn't be in this hapless, manless situation.'

'Maybe these men have let their mothers search for their wives, and because we don't fall into the mould of "good traditional wife", we've been excluded!' Sara was cross: she was starting to think mean thoughts about these men and their spines. I could tell it was going to get very ugly very quickly.

'We've had to work so hard to find a partner, and these men just waltz in and take who they want and expect us to fall in line. That's not being a decent man! Even though I love cooking and looking after the house and I want to have lots of children, that doesn't mean I want someone who just expects me to stay at home all day in traditional servitude!' Sara's cheeks were burning neon red.

Noreen put her arm around Sara's shoulders to comfort her and calm her down, but Sara had another furious complaint. 'Why are all these men going "back home" to marry? We want to marry men who have had a similar upbringing to us and share the new identity and perspectives that we've had to create to find our place. I can't marry someone from "back home" because I can't talk to them and they just don't understand the new environment that we're in. The men don't seem to care, they just want to find a traditional wife and have an easy life. No wonder there are no decent men – they are all marrying "back home" and we are all left with nothing.'

'I know, I know,' soothed Noreen, but there were tears in her eyes too. 'The boys are encouraged by community and family to marry "back home" without worrying what is going to happen to the single women who are here.' She cleared her throat and tried to lighten the mood. 'I have a cracking story to add to our list of terrible introductions.'

Sara and I inhaled in mock horror: 'Another one! Who would believe it!'

Noreen continued, 'I met a potential match for a coffee last week. Thirty-five years old, VP of a multinational corporation. He brought his mother along as a chaperone.'

'No!' gasped Sara and I in unison.

'And she told me that next time we met I should bring my passport so she could check I was really a British subject . . .'

'No!' we repeated in a higher pitch.

'. . . and that I wasn't out to marry her son for his citizenship or his money.'

With the inclusion of the latest story to add to our anthology of awful experiences, Stage Three was complete. Now it was time in the conversation to turn up the expression of our pain to 'full'.

4. MAYBE WE ARE THE WRONG KIND OF WOMEN

'I was cornered by some Aunties at the wedding,' Noreen divulged. She rolled her eyes in horror. 'They were in fine form, raising their eyebrows and waggling their fingers energetically at me.'

'Oh, yes, and what was their wonderful advice to you on this occasion?' asked Sara with irritation, still emotional from her outburst.

Noreen tried to imitate the rhythm and accent of the Aunties' voices. '"We know that things are *changing*. We *know*, my dear, we're not *so old-fashioned* like you think. We *know* that it is good for you young girls to work, but we *told* you, we *told* you so many times, to find yourself a man and get married first, then you can do *whatever* you want. Just start by looking *after* him and *then* worry about this independent modern nonsense later. Men like to have independent women as *friends*, but when it comes to *marrying* and having a wife, they all want the same thing – a *nice* traditional woman who will look after them. Men are *men*, you can't change that."'

We all growled, but were we upset because they were wrong or because they were right?

We were following the 'traditional' process because we felt it fitted well with our faith as Muslims. But we had rejected the definition of a 'traditional' wife when 'traditional' was restricted to mean 'wife-is-second-to-husband'. We wanted to pursue our understanding of a more *Islamic* marriage relationship, where the minimum obligations were defined, and where love and companionship were the fundamental pillars. Maybe that's why the process wasn't working for us, because even though we were playing by the rules, we were not abiding by them in spirit?

The crux of the matter was this: whatever we thought of being a traditional wife, or of falling into the traditional process and being the kind of wives we thought boys and their mothers wanted us to be, we seemed to be the only ones that were suffering. The boys were still getting married. We girls were left single and unloved, wailing to our friends and families.

We thought we had created a strong equilibrium in forging a path through the complications of culture and faith, and through it all we had maintained our relationships with our faith, family and community. By pioneering this balance, were we paying the price for not being traditional enough for 'traditional' men (and their mothers) and being too 'boring and religious' for 'modern' men?

'The Aunties tell us we're not traditional enough . . .' said Noreen.

'. . . and the men who have the qualities we are looking for tell us that we are too traditional,' added Sara.

Were we (a) wrong about our ideas, or (b) the wrong kind of women?

5. OH MY GOD, WE ARE NEVER GOING TO GET MARRIED

'There are no decent men out there,' wept Sara again.

'And we're the wrong kind of women,' I howled once more.

There was only one conclusion, and Noreen was poised to make it: 'We're never going to get married.'

Were we – single, educated, twenty-first century (Muslim) women – a time-bomb waiting to explode in the society we lived in? If a whole generation wasn't married because there were no suitable partners, what would the repercussions be, not just for us, but for our communities?

'We're going to die, old, wrinkled and single, cats running round our house,' added Sara with theatrical drama. 'We're never going to find someone and we'll never, ever get married.'

6. THE PERFECT MAN IS OUT THERE JUST WAITING FOR US

We had indulged in mutual misery, and reached the depths of despair. It felt good to share our pain, but we knew for sure in our hearts that there was someone out there waiting for us. Perhaps he wasn't ready for us yet and still needed life to polish him up. Or maybe it was us that life needed to polish before we were ready for the One.

It was heartening to know that we were not alone in this situation. A good conversation with friends had turned sadness into solace, and returned us back to hope.

You, not Me

Since that very first prize-winning speech as a child, I had regularly given short lectures about Islam at the mosque, as well as at other social and community events. At the wedding of a close friend I was asked to say a few words during the henna party, which was held a few days before the marriage itself.

The henna party is a women-only event, like an old-fashioned hen night. The bride holds a celebration with her female friends and relatives to prepare her for her married life to come. It is an event where women celebrate their femininity, share the wisdom of their relationships, and when mothers, daughters and aunts bond over the happiness, tears and struggles they all face together as women. Those who are married recall their own weddings and pass on their experiences, those who are not married have blessings and prayers showered on them by everyone else that one day they might be the woman at the centre of attention. It is a gloriously female festival. At the end of the party an artist paints henna onto the hands and feet of the bride to make her look beautiful for her wedding day and new husband.

As this was a women-only event, I picked my most sparkly outfit, had my hair specially done for the occasion and put on a full face of make-up. There was not a sign of headscarf, veil or long cloak. I chose a beautiful crimson skirt that flowed with grace and elegance, which was embroidered all over with little twinkling crystals. It was matched with a small bodice with the same crystal embroidery and a silk shawl that draped glamorously over my arms. I had chosen long jewel-like earrings and a delicate necklace to finish off the look. I felt like a princess. I loved to dress up like this and the beauty was for me and those close to me. I loved looking beautiful: all women do, it is part of being a woman. But in public I wore the headscarf and more modest clothing because I did not want my looks to be what defined me.

In deciding what I would speak about at the party, there was only one subject that seemed appropriate: the Love and Compassion of the Divine. The topic was perfect for a wedding: having a partner was all about love and compassion.

'Allah always begins any chapter of the *Qur'an* with the words "In the Name of Allah, the Lovingly Compassionate, the Kind",' I began.

'When you first meet someone that you are attracted to . . .' I paused and smiled conspiratorially at the bride. She giggled. '. . . Or when you are making an introduction and hoping that a marriage will come from it . . .' I now turned to face the mothers, Aunties and matchmakers who raised their eyebrows. I could see them all wondering if I was about to compliment them or present them with a platitude or say something shocking, '. . . you always begin your introduction with something beautiful. You choose the quality that you think is the best thing about that person and you begin the introduction with that.'

I smiled with joy: 'The thing that Allah, the Creator and Cherisher, wants us to know most about Him is that He is *Rahman,* full of Loving Compassion, and *Raheem,* full of kindness and mercy. These are two of His names that we are most familiar with and which He repeats about himself most often.'

God had many names by which to know Him, and the most common of these were the famous 'Ninety-Nine Names'. These were 99 ways in which God described His nature so that we could find a connection to the Sublime. There were names like Power, Majesty and Strength, but also names like Gentle, Loving and Generous. Reflecting on the names and their qualities would help to gain an understanding of God. Human beings were made up of all the same qualities, we just needed to uncover them and develop them in ourselves in order to become better individuals and get closer to the Divine.

It was time to come back from the sphere of the sublime and think about the wonderful romantic wedding in front of us. 'Getting married is the perfect time to learn about kindness and compassion. These qualities are the groundwork for the relationship and reflect the love between husband and wife.'

During the rest of the party, one of the wedding guests approached me. 'You stood up and you looked so pretty and so fashionable that we thought, "What is this modern girl all dressed up, no headscarf, all trendy, going to be able to tell us about religion?"'

I bit my tongue at the implicit idea that fashion and faith were mutually exclusive. She was not the only one who made that assumption. Those who were not familiar with Muslims and Islamic teachings often thought the same as her but in reverse: that wearing a headscarf meant a high quotient of zealousness and an inability to be fashionable.

I let her continue. 'But not only did you look beautiful, you also spoke beautifully. You touched our hearts and we were very, very moved.'

I had overturned a mistaken assumption.

Shelina, One. Stereotypes, Nil.

The Prophet Muhammad was born in 570 AD in the city of Mecca, which lay at the heart of the Arabian Peninsula. The Arabs were a tribal people who took great pride in their ethnicity and looked down on those of non-Arab origin. Muhammad was born into one of the leading tribes called the *Quraysh*. It seems that he did not share the sense of self-superiority of his fellow Arabs, but encouraged the tribes to be united. His family had for generations looked after *Kaba*, which had been built by the Prophet Abraham in Mecca as a house dedicated to the One God but which now contained hundreds of idols worshipped by the pagan Arabs. They thought themselves to be highly knowledge-able and advanced for their time, and were particularly proud of the beauty and eloquence of their poetry, some of which still survives today. Alongside the polytheistic Arabs lived tribes of Jews and Christians.

Some of them believed that their scriptures indicated that a prophet would come soon.

Muhammad's father died before he was born and his mother died when he was only six years old. He went to live with his grandfather, who was considered one of the statesmen of the tribe, but he passed away very soon. He then went to live with his uncle, where he grew into a man who was noted for being of exceptional manners and excellent character.

Mecca was at the crossroads of several trade routes, so, like many people who lived in that region, Muhammad became a merchant, travelling to buy and sell goods. Since he had an excellent reputation as a hard and honest worker, he was employed by a wealthy business woman named Khadijah, who was known as the Queen of the Arabs because of her business empire and possibly because of her beauty, too. She was a smart, sophisticated woman who knew what she wanted and how to get it. When I read stories about her, I admire not only her dignity and grace, but also her determination and self-confidence.

She was impressed by Muhammad's commercial acumen, and the profits he brought back to her business after leading trade caravans to other cities on her behalf. She was more impressed with the honesty and dignity with which he carried out his affairs. She knew that Muhammad had a reputation as *sadiq*, truthful, and *ameen*, trustworthy. She saw in him a worthy companion and partner, and made enquiries about him with regards to the possibility of marriage. She asked a relative if he would take her idea of marriage to Muhammad to see what he thought of it. Muhammad was delighted and accepted, also seeing in her a worthy companion and partner for himself. The marriage, by all accounts, was extremely strong and intimate, and even years after her death, Muhammad said that she was always the one for him and he would never forget her. No-one could ever take her place.

The story of Khadijah's proposal and subsequent marriage to Muhammad was often recounted as part of the discussion that Muslims had about the rights of women in Islam. The subject of women, their status and their treatment was always a hot topic. It was often raised by the media and society around us, as well as by Muslim women themselves. How could we see the physical abuse, suffering and torture of Muslim women around the world and not ask why this was happening? We didn't believe it to be part of our faith, but how should we stop it? The news would present images of women in black cloaks and veils and ask, 'Are these women oppressed?' To understand our heritage and the principles which underpinned our story as people of faith, we looked back at the individuals like Muhammad and Khadijah who had laid the foundations of Islam. *You have to know where you've come from to know where you are going.*

Khadijah was a woman who found a man she believed would make her ideal partner. It seemed that a similar process of arranging a marriage existed then as it did now – it had stood the test of time. But instead of waiting for the man to propose, Khadijah took the first step to approach this potential husband and sent a proposal to him herself through an envoy. This is hailed as very liberated and empowered by many Muslim men and women. I agreed with them, but I found myself asking, if this is such a wonderful thing for a Muslim woman to do, why is it considered so shameful for the girl's family to approach the boy's family to talk about marriage?

There was a twist to this story: Khadijah was much older than Muhammad, perhaps up to fifteen years his senior. Again, this was held up in discussions about Muslim women to show that marriage was about finding the right qualities in a person rather than securing a good match on paper. I found myself wondering why, if the relationship at the very heart of the birth of Islam had a woman who was older than Muhammad, was there an unspoken yet rigid rule that the girl should be younger than the boy?

It was enough to get me thinking about the discrepancies between what people *say* is Islam and what Islam *actually* is.

Muslims like to dwell on how Islam gave rights to women long before similar rights were granted in other parts of the world, including Europe. Muhammad explained that women were equal in value to men, and that the best of men and women were those who worked hard to be good human beings. In this, he said clearly, men and women were no different. He laid out laws which gave rights to women to own their own property and not be forced to hand it over to their husbands. Women were not items of property that belonged to men, nor did their own property belong to men. European laws only accorded women this status hundreds, in some cases a thousand, years later.

Even though Islam had been pioneering in its time, *radical*, you could say, it had buried that vision under layers and layers of dense culture over time.

Muslims should just be honest with themselves, I reflected.

It would be simpler to admit that the fundamental idea of equality had got blurred and to reignite it than to defend as Islamic those ideas that had crept in from culture over time. I found it worse still that some Muslims tried to stop Muslim women from raising these questions by calling them sell-outs, and westernised feminists, as though these were dirty words.

But if we can see discrepancies, then it is our duty as thinking human beings to challenge them, I thought.

The intimate bond between Khadijah and Muhammad lay at the heart of the new Muslim community, which slowly attracted people to the new ideas that Muhammad brought. Alongside his key message that there was no god but God, one unified single Divine being, he said something that was so simple that it was profoundly shattering: all human beings, regardless of age, gender, creed, race or colour, are totally equal. It was a remarkable statement for a society which was hierarchical and racist, and oppressed women. One of Muhammad's closest friends was Bilal, a black African slave who was tortured for his beliefs as a Muslim. Another was Salman, who was originally from

Persia. Both were taunted for their non-Arab origins, and looked down upon. Muhammad did not accept this racism and appointed Bilal to a position of status as the *muezzin*, the one who announces the call to prayer. He also gave Salman the title 'the pure one' because he was so spiritual.

I thought Muslims found it easy to look back on this stand against racism and claim credit for the equality that lies at the core of Islam. But my experience through the marriage process was forcing me to ask difficult questions about whether the 'rules' that we were socially obliged to follow really did adhere to the fundamentals of our faith. If they did, why was it considered almost unheard of to marry someone from a different ethnic group? If you were from the Asian community, marrying a Salman would be frowned upon, despite his excellent character. Worse still – and it would be impossible even to suggest such an idea without creating a tsunami of horror – would be the idea of marrying a Bilal.

Such contradictions finally forced me to understand that faith and culture were completely separate, and I would have to learn to deal with them as separate things. Culture was a wonderful, beautiful, textured human experience to be upheld and treasured. I wanted to hold onto all the culture that was part of me. I loved cultural traditions, processes and quirks. I found beauty and history in them, as well as simplicity and elegance. So often they found a simple solution to a complex question. Sometimes, though, culture had got it wrong. There was no shame in admitting it; culture needs adjusting from time to time, and that is why so many prophets were sent to people – to ensure that the errors of culture were corrected.

My faith as a Muslim is what created my vision as a human being. Where the two came into contact, and where there were contradictions, faith had to take priority. I could no longer ignore the discrepancies that kept coming up. The delicious irony was that the marriage process was one of the most traditional components of Asian culture, and it was the very act of going through this marriage process that had unmasked the double standards between what was said about Islam and what was actually done about it. Once I had realised this, I had to take my own steps to free myself from the ties of culture that constrained me from living my life, and from questioning, exploring and practising my faith to the full.

This decision had real consequences: I would have to brave the instruments of social compliance that culture employed to keep individuals – particularly women – in line: reputation, gossip, social inclusion and of course, access to marriage.

It is easy to damage someone socially. It is possible to use all four of these tools very quickly and in a matter of words to destroy someone, particularly a young woman. Picture this seemingly harmless vignette: two Aunties chewing *paan* and discussing the latest news. 'Do you know what that girl got up to? [Insert spiced up anecdote here.] No shame, absolutely no respect for our culture. Tell your daughters not to spend time with her anymore, otherwise they'll be tainted and their reputations destroyed. I had such a nice boy in mind for her, but how could I suggest a girl like her to his mother. No, no, she's off my list.'

It was time for things to change. It was okay if the change was slow. But, as Gandhi had said, I had to *be* the change that I wanted to create. I smiled at how far I had come, and how once I would have seen my decision as courageous. Now it felt straightforward and sensible because I had embraced my faith as the most important part of me. And in using the vision of Islam to make my life and the lives of those around me better, I made a decision: in order *to be the change*, intelligence and humour would be my weapons of choice.

The first thing I decided to do was something that nice girls didn't do. I decided to climb a mountain, a very big mountain. Kilimanjaro to be exact, the highest point in Africa, sitting just inside the border of

Tanzania. It was a special thrill to embark on such an adventure in a country that had a close family connection to me.

'Nice girls don't climb mountains,' an Auntie told me.

'Why not?' I asked

'Because it's not the kind of thing a girl should do.'

'Why not?'

'Because it's not nice. And people will talk.' The argument then changed tack. 'What need have you got to climb a mountain?'

'No need, I just think it will be exciting, and a challenge.' I let the argument circle around the edges of culture and personal development.

'There are other exciting things you can do.'

'But God says that we should travel in the world and see His creations. In fact, He says several times in the *Qur'an* that we should travel His earth which He has created for us.' Exposing the discrepancy between 'how things had always been done' and Islamic teachings meant that there was no argument to be made in response.

'Don't think you are a boy, that you can do whatever you like. You're a girl and you have to know your place.'

I was not surprised by this turn in the discussion: it simply evoked a long-standing incredulity about what is and isn't right for girls and boys to do.

'Are you sure that it's OK for boys to climb mountains but that girls should not climb mountains?'

I raised my eyebrows and smiled cheekily. I was sure that I was very irritating at this moment.

In my head I wanted to ask her: 'You don't want to phone a friend or ask the audience? Is it your final answer?' Instead, I paused and slowed down my pace, adopting a more serious tone.

'I love the stories of the Prophet, and I particularly like the story of his wife Khadijah. Don't you? It must have been very moving for her to be married to a man of such spirituality. She was very dedicated to looking after him. Often he would go to a special place to "get away from it all" and to meditate. This place, called the Cave of Hira, is where he received the first verse of the *Qur'an* and where the Angel Gabriel told him that he should announce to the world that there was only One God, and that he, Muhammad, should spread this message.'

This was a moving story about the very first days of the Muslim community, and every Muslim knew the details of these moments.

'The first person he shared this news with was Khadijah, his wife, and she accepted his message. She was one of the solid foundations at the birth of Islam.'

There was irritated coughing. 'This is, of course, a lovely story, but this doesn't change the fact that nice girls don't climb mountains. You have to take care of your reputation otherwise no-one will marry you.'

'Oh, but this does change everything, Auntie. This story changes absolutely everything if we take it to heart. This Cave of Hira is at the top of a very steep mountain which it is no easy task to climb. Khadijah would climb this mountain every day to visit the Prophet as he sat and meditated. The wife of the Prophet climbed a mountain. And I'm going to do the same.'

There was only one path I could choose that would let me look back on myself and have no regrets, and that was to choose the rules that I believed were the truth and to live by them. I had made my choice: it was Islam. And then, no matter what people said, there was only one overarching principle: *To thine own self be true.*

I stood at the highest point of Kilimanjaro at midday one October morning. The first three days of the journey had been a gradual climb, first through tropical forest, then into watery clouds and then a rest day to acclimatise to the altitude. The fourth and penultimate day was a long unending trek across an almost lunar landscape to the base of the crater. We camped at the foot of the great peak, agitated by the lack of oxygen at this height, hungry, but not wanting to eat in case we were sick.

At midnight we began the final ascent up the steep crater wall to reach the rim of the volcano. It was dark and our feet stumbled on the rocks wedged invisibly into the almost sheer mountain face. As dawn was breaking, we arrived exhausted at the rim. There, at the top, I met two English men with a thermos flask. 'Tea?' they asked.

After climbing through the night, and now at 19,000 feet, every step was an unimaginable effort. First my legs refused to participate and I had to focus all my determination on placing one foot in front of the other, one by one. I took off my gloves so that I could pull out a bar of chocolate from my rucksack and found that the temperature at minus 25 degrees had turned my hand deep blue. The cold and fatigue were affecting my resolve to reach the peak. I had made it to the rim; would it make any difference if I got to the highest point or not?

I will never know where the inner determination came from, but inch by inch I dragged my legs, my body and the entirety of my being to Uhuru Peak. I made it to the top of Africa. I was padded out like a teddy bear with six layers of thermal clothing, two hoods and a baseball cap over my headscarf, my hands Prussian blue in the cold as I handed over my camera for a photo to be taken of me standing exhausted, elated and proud at 19,314 feet. I had made it to the very highest point. It was a glorious and unforgettable moment. *I did it.*

We prayed at the top of the mountain through sheer joy and thanks for arriving safely at this most amazing place and for being blessed enough to experience something that so few people could enjoy. We looked out over peaceful snow caps and majestic glaciers that shone with an other-worldly aura underneath the immanent sun.

It was no easy task to have achieved this and I felt proud of myself. It was an exercise of both mind and body. I had climbed uphill physically and metaphorically to a goal which 'people' believed I should not set myself. During the four days of gruelling climb I had been in awe of the creation of the Divine and learnt that I could achieve things beyond what even I myself believed I was capable of. I could push my body harder than I ever had. I could push my inner being further and with more focus than I could have ever imagined.

Through the encouragement of my faith I had seen the beauty of creation, something I would never have done otherwise. The experience had revealed the obvious: *nice* girls can achieve whatever they want.

After climbing the mountain, I decided to buy a convertible racing car, a glamorous James Bond-style model with *va-va-voom*. Boys were allowed to buy exciting cars, in fact they were *supposed* to buy an out-of-the-ordinary car. Nice girls were *not* supposed to. People might get confused and think it was the *girl* that was racy, not the car.

I was advised *not* to take the car to the mosque because people might get the wrong impression of me. They had known me my whole life, but the small matter of owning such a car would completely wipe out my previous *nice reputation*.

Girls who wore headscarves ought particularly to avoid such cars. It was not seen as befitting their piety, nor suiting the reputation of sobriety that they were forced to maintain. I should be aware that *people would talk*.

'Let them,' I shrugged. 'If the most interesting thing that these people have to talk about is my car, then I feel sorry for them. If it helps to spice up their gossip and make their lives more enjoyable, then consider my new car to be an act of public service.'

I pulled my sunglasses out of the glove compartment, put the roof down and *va-va-voomed* into the sunset.

Hijab Marks the Spot

It was an average Tuesday at work. In the office our row of desks looked out of the full-height glass windows of the fifth floor. We were perched above the Thames and could see the Houses of Parliament at one end, and past several bridges and into the blurry, crowded money-scape of the City at the other. Behind us was a busy London street.

The weather was averagely autumnal; dry, crisp leaves colourfully littering the streets; collars now upturned on the city types who click-clacked their smart city shoes on the gritty pavements as they rushed home on the ever-so-slightly-closing-in September evenings; thicker and longer than average coats on the slick all-in-black media women.

I sat next to Emma, an unpredictable Anglo-German woman of highly strung intensity and brow-furrowing naivety. Behind me were Elaine and Nicola, two women, about my age, who were excited about moving to London after graduating from university. Opposite me was handsome, well-travelled, courteous Jack. He was a tall, affable all-American college boy who charmed effortlessly and unknowingly, pulling wonky faces at managerial nonsense and participating in peer-to-peer banter with good will and kind heart. Jack was optimistically American and realistically New York savvy. His humorous self-deprecating cynicism meant he had blended in nicely in London.

We sat punching away at our keyboards, post-lunch, pre-home time. E-mails flew backwards and forwards, the internet was surfed and digital decisions were made. On the other side of the room there was a whisper.

Heads lifted across from me and I heard a voice shout, 'A plane has crashed into the World Trade Center.'

I looked up. The room was full of agitated rustling, eyes squinting, eyebrows rising. Everyone was restless but there was as yet no sense of shock or fear.

I heard the words again: *a plane has crashed*. I imagined it to be a small glider and wondered how it could have entered a well-monitored area like Manhattan and then lost control. I didn't imagine it to be anything other than a horrible accident.

I carried on typing. Suddenly, there was a loud, frantic shout: 'Oh, my God, I think we should watch this on the large screen in the canteen.'

Chairs scraped, shoes clattered and bodies moved hurriedly. We raced to the open space where we sat and ate our lunch every day. As we ran, our eyes remained glued to the large television screen above us that was playing a live news feed. The camera was static on the stark image of two of the world's most famous buildings standing tall against the autumn blue sky. We were stunned: the World Trade Center had swathes of menacing black smoke billowing out of it.

We remained frozen with horror. It was completely unbelievable; we couldn't understand exactly what was happening. Then, before our eyes, a second plane came into view and crashed into the second tower.

I was in shock as they kept replaying the second crash. This can't be true, I thought, this is just a sick Armageddon Hollywood blockbuster.

No-one knew what to say. The events were inexplicable. Nothing like this had ever happened before. This was the first attack of its kind on America that we could remember during our lifetimes. After we could no longer bear to see the same crash scenes anymore, we returned to our desks. We couldn't make sense of what had happened.

Jack and I searched the internet in a frenzy to find out more, something, anything. The BBC website was down, CNN was down, CBS was down, Fox News was down. They had all been broadcasting from the Twin Towers, and those that hadn't were just unable to cope with the number of visits to their websites and their servers froze up. We were among millions of people looking for information, and right now we didn't have access to any at all. Jack had friends who worked in the building. My friend's fiancé worked there, too. There was panic on our floor as everyone recalled a friend or colleague who worked at the Twin Towers.

Who could have done this? A Palestinian group claimed responsibility, seeing an opportunity for raising awareness of their organisation. Then they withdrew, realising that the pretence was more than they could handle.

I returned home, and stayed glued to the television screen, like all of my friends and colleagues. London fell into a stillness that none of us were used to. The minutes ticked by and still we had no news, nothing was clearer. We sank into a chasm of fear and distrust. Which city would be next? There was so little information about who had carried out this attack or what their motivations were that we assumed London would soon be a target.

George W. Bush announced the culprit was Al-Qaeda. Al-Who? I had never heard of them. The world's most wanted man was suddenly Osama Bin Laden. I'd never heard of him either. We were told that Bin Laden and his associates had carried out the attacks. They were Muslims and had declared *jihad* on the West. Nine days later George W. Bush announced his own war in response, the 'War on Terror'. It felt like it was declared on me, on us as Muslims. I felt stigmatised and cornered. It was not the autumnal air that gave me chills.

Just like the rest of the public I felt angry and frightened. It was easy for people to lash out in fear, and ordinary Muslims like me, despite sharing the same panic and dread as everyone else, became cast as murderous, hateful, barbaric villains. *Double whammy*, I thought to myself. We now faced fear on two sides.

My headscarf was suddenly a neon flashing light as I walked along the wide-eyed fearful streets. The horrific tragedy in New York and the thousands of innocent deaths were, it seemed, my fault.

Every channel was full of discussion, debate and analysis. Jack returned from a short visit he had made to New York to ensure his friends and family were OK after the attacks. He described how groupthink patriotism had spread itself over the tragic remains of Ground Zero. 'Why do people hate us?' was the question Americans were asking, he told us. He also said that to do what he was doing now – questioning, analysing, wondering what could have led to this awful situation – was socially forbidden. People first needed to grieve.

We were told that the perpetrators had been inspired to carry out their hideous actions 'as *jihad*', based on the belief that they would become martyrs for their faith and then reach paradise. I was horrified. As a result of this, the whole world seemed to think Muslims believed their religion encouraged killing innocent people. This was incomprehensible to me and to most other Muslims, whose fundamental belief is to ensure peace and harmony in the world around us. Even the very name 'Islam' means peace. It was hard for us to come to terms with the question: how could people who called themselves Muslims do something like this?

Jihad had been terribly mistranslated by Western commentators as 'holy war'. It had been terribly twisted by the criminals who claimed that they were Muslims and that their violent acts were *jihad* against their 'enemies'. *Jihad* actually meant 'spiritual struggle'. It meant doing your best to live the highest moral and ethical life. It had its own place in religious terminology because it was an activity in its own right, and a tough one at that. It was a fight to stop the dark side of your conscience from behaving in a way that prevents you from being fully human. The only time *jihad* was allowed to become a physical struggle was if you were required to defend yourself from attack. *Jihad* did not permit the killing of innocent civilians.

As the hours and days progressed, the investigations into what had happened continued. We learnt that there were nineteen men involved. We also found out that in the last hours before embarking on their plans, these men were busy getting drunk and having intimate relationships with unknown women. It didn't make sense. If they were the dedicated puritans that the media described, they would not have engaged in these activities which were outside the bounds of Islamic behaviour. And if their acts were not motivated by religion, why would they blow themselves up along with thousands of other people?

The shock that America experienced brought the world to an emotional standstill. On their home soil this huge and powerful nation had been attacked, and its citizens had never experienced such a thing before. They were in deep turmoil and anguish, and the world was with them. All other countries put their own devastation and pain into second place to share America's moment of bereavement. Innocent people had been killed and this was intolerable. Islamic – human – etiquette demands that even a single innocent death must be mourned, irrespective of who that person is. The value of a lost person is not dependent on what else is happening in the world. One human life lost, wherever or whoever, is the loss of the whole of humanity.

Muslims from around the world sent heartfelt messages of condolence and denunciation, but it was never enough. No matter how much we condemned the atrocious acts, we were informed that we were actually supporting them. We were told that we ought to condemn them more fervently and more passionately. So we condemned them some more, and then we were told we were insincere. When we tried to explain the peaceful humanitarian principles of Islam, we were told that we were being false – otherwise how could these men have carried out their atrocious activities saying that they were 'Islamic'? We also explained that their interpretation of the teachings of Islam was erroneous and they were criminals trying to justify their disgusting actions any way they could. Speaking out just attracted more attention, more vitriol, more hatred. But keeping quiet was not an option. Keeping quiet would allow others to suffer and the War on Terror to spiral out of control. I felt frightened – as though I had been identified and badged as 'evil' and a 'terrorist'. I was fearful of what lay ahead for me as a Muslim.

This was the first time that I was encouraged to say 'not in my name'. It was demanded of me as a Muslim to denounce what had happened, distancing myself from something that was not my responsibility. I wholeheartedly rejected the outrageous attacks, and it came from my very soul to state my horror at the deaths. I denounced the actions as a human being, as a citizen of the world who abhorred violence and the killing of innocent people, and the wilful destruction of people, property and symbols.

'Not in my name' as a human being was a universal statement. But I felt angry that it was expected of me to say 'not in my name' as a Muslim. Even though I was a Muslim, I had no connections to the evil men who had done this, so why should I have to say 'not in my Muslim name'? Why should I create a link that didn't exist? I was as little involved as anyone else. I had been taught only peace and harmony. That was the very fundamental basis of faith – to be at peace with the Creator, at peace with one's self and at peace with others.

'Not in my name' still echoes, after 7 July in London, and is still demanded whenever a Muslim is linked to violence. I am asked to become an apologist for the actions of others, connected to me only as much as anyone else in the six degrees of separation. But I should only be held responsible for my own actions: that is a human principle, an Islamic principle.

After 11 September 2001, and again after the events of July 2005 in London, my colour, my name and my headscarf marked me out and tagged me with the label 'terrorist'. It was 11 September that marked the date of the very first time that I felt subhuman in Britain, and the first day that I felt scared to live in my own country.

Many days before the awful events in New York, I had arranged to meet with a group of Muslim women to build a Muslim women's social network. This was to have been our first meeting. Our purpose was to drink tea, eat muffins and make new friends. It was 12 September and the girls felt nervous.

'Not sure we should be out,' said Sara.

'I'm feeling scared,' said Noreen. 'We'll be exposed and in danger. People will be watching us, wondering what a group of Muslim women is talking about.'

I was worried too: we could be targets. Would we be attacked verbally or even physically? My uncle had two fingers aggressively thrown up at him; my father had been jostled by two men in the supermarket that morning.

Everyone was frightened to be out in public – what if London was next? The streets stank of fear, people were eyed suspiciously and footsteps rattled swiftly across pavements to take their owners quickly home to safety and the never-ending stream of news analysis on which we were now all fixated.

We were the same as everyone, just as worried, just as fearful. But we carried a double burden: targets for the terrorists and targets for those who were now boiling with anger and fear because of the attacks on the Twin Towers.

We took a decision to meet anyway, in a small coffee shop. There were five of us who refused to be cowed by the fear that the terrorists had invoked in all those around us, five of us who refused to be targeted by those who stereotyped us as terrorists, too. Five of us who needed a strong cappuccino and some marshmallows. We were just as shocked as the rest of London, just as horrified and just as opposed to the violence. But we had to get on with life.

My faith had been quiet and broadly unknown, but suddenly Islam was discussed constantly. Some commentators reiterated our vehement arguments about Islam's opposition to violence and the killing of innocent civilians. Politicians outlined new policies under the mantle of the War on Terror. Afghanistan was the first casualty, and would be bombed to evict Bin Laden. We despaired for the innocent civilians who would be killed there as collateral damage to find him. Their deaths would not bring back the innocent Americans who had died. It was awful to contemplate that one attack on the US meant thousands and thousands of innocent civilians being killed in Afghanistan. Soon Iraq was to follow.

It became difficult to engage in ordinary activities if you were a Muslim. If you were boarding an aeroplane, you would be subjected to extraordinary and unwarranted checks if you had a Muslim name, even if you didn't fit the simplistic descriptions of what a Muslim was supposed to look like. My friend Shahnaz was stopped ten times in one multi-destination trip 'for no reason'. She was told it was 'just routine'. Another friend was detained on his way to an interview 'for no reason'. He told them his interview time, and was then held back and released deliberately a few minutes after his appointment. My friends who worked in banks were told to freeze accounts of people with 'Muslim-sounding names'. As I disembarked from a flight returning to London after a work trip, a woman from immigration was waiting with intent at the exit of the plane. She barked at me to step aside, uninterested in any of the other passengers. She insisted on looking at my passport, and I asked why I was the only one being checked, as hundreds of others walked past me. She repeated her demand. I asked her again why she wanted to see my *British* passport but she ignored me. 'If you don't show me, we'll have to take you for questioning. Who knows how long that might take,' she whispered ominously.

One morning later that winter, Emma pulled me to one side as I arrived in the office. I was wearing a black headscarf to co-ordinate with a smart black suit that I had just bought. Since it was an icy November morning, I had pulled on my long black winter coat to keep out the cold, as most of the other men and women in the city had also done. I hadn't thought twice about the combination of black headscarf and black coat. It was cold midwinter and black was the order of the day.

'I really don't think you should dress all in black,' Emma whispered.

I was baffled. Was wearing black now a fashion *faux-pas*?

Her eyes crinkled with concern. 'People might get the wrong impression, you know, with all the stuff going on in the news. You might get hurt.'

Emma meant well, of this I was certain. She was someone who cared about the fact that I was a Muslim. She cared about whether I got hurt. She saw what other people perhaps didn't see: I was a person like everyone else underneath. I loved her for this.

'Thank you, Emma, I really appreciate your concern.' I smiled warmly at her and gave her a gentle hug. 'Consider the all-black French spy look gone and forgotten.'

'You don't mind me saying anything?'

'Of course not. I like it that you are concerned for me.'

Emma's comments reassured me that things could get better, that we could aspire to a society where we treated individuals on their own merits and cared for their well-being. I was hopeful that there were other good-hearted Emmas out there. The world needed more people who looked out for each other.

Her comments made me worry, too: would it be enough to avoid wearing black? Those who ignorantly held me responsible would seek out vengeance, whether their target was marked clearly and stereo-typically in black or not. If I removed my headscarf, that would make me less noticeable. There was discussion about whether women who wore the headscarf would be advised to remove it for their own safety. I was adamant that this was not something I would consider. I was firm in my belief and I would stand up for it. I refused to change the way I practised my faith or to let fear stop me from carrying out what I believed in. If I did that, I would have failed in my duty as a citizen.

I worried about the stereotypes of Muslims that were being perpetuated. Emma's idea that those who wore black coats and black headscarves would be seen as terrorists was one of those stereotypes. I was deeply touched that she was worried on behalf of my safety. And I understood her dilemma about whether to convey the stereotypes that other people might have of me. But by conveying those stereotypes, she was in small part accepting them and even reinforcing them. How was I to change the world if even the good people who were concerned about me couldn't help me reject the prejudice that was out there? Accepting the inherent prejudices that people had would make me live my life in fear, constantly worried about how people were seeing me. I needed to be brave and shatter those ideas.

It wasn't easy. Fear and violence were affecting all of us. One of my headscarf-wearing friends was punched and her nose broken as she sat quietly on the train home. Her aggressor muttered profanities about her faith and her 'terrorist activities' as he went on to terrorise her himself. He inflicted shattering pain on her face and then walked off at the next station. Even when he was gone, the other passengers left her to bleed.

As a Muslim who believed in peace and dialogue, I had to face fear and aggression from several quarters. Those who had conducted the attacks on the Twin Towers had attacked the very core of Islamic belief that we should be working towards peace. They claimed aggressively that people like me were weak 'moderate' Muslims. Paradoxically, as had been my experience over the previous weeks and months, I was associated with those who had perpetrated the acts, and labels like 'violent' and 'extremist' were applied.

In amongst all of these stark opinions were the ongoing discussions about the position and treatment of Muslim women. The views that I had seen on television as a young child, painting Muslim women as oppressed and abused, had changed very little in the intervening years. Islam was held almost entirely responsible for all the violence conducted in non-Western countries against Muslim women, even though such horrible acts were usually driven by culture, the cycle of under-development and a lack of education. The suffering that women in these areas had endured was compounded by wars that left them in poverty, barely able to survive. As for me, even though I had chosen to wear the headscarf, the public discussions about Muslim women – which rarely included the voices of Muslim women themselves – identified me as too repressed to know my own mind; so repressed, in fact, that I wasn't allowed to speak for myself in these debates. By wearing the headscarf, I was said to be participating in my own oppression.

So many labels were stuck onto me without me having a voice:

Oppressed, repressed, subjugated, backwards, ignorant
Violent, extremist, hateful, terrorist, jihadist, evil, radical
Weakling, moderate, sell-out, self-hating, apologist

Labels and boxes, I hated all of them. I was none of the above.

My search for love offered me no escape from the boxes either.

Nice Asian girl
Overly pious, sour-faced Muslim *hijabi*
Smarty-pants bossy-boots
Boring, always praying, stay-at-home dullard
Non-traditional, modern rule-breaker, independent, unsuitable, unmouldable

I was weighed down by expectations and labels from so many cultures and narratives, each trying to tell me what I should or should not be, each pretending to speak on my behalf. As just one person, how many stereotypes could I shatter?

I resolved to create a voice – my own voice – that would stop people speaking on my behalf, and that would be dedicated to answering the questions: Where does the truth lie? What is the right thing to do?

I broke all the boxes that people wanted to put me into with one simple statement:

I am me.

The different cultures, histories, religions and heritages of being a British Asian Muslim woman had made me who I was. Those different strands were not burdens, but instead gave me a unique perspective so that I could see things from many different angles. I could bring together my cultures, my faith and the clear vision that Islam offered to start building a more hopeful future.

I felt abandoned trying to deal with these huge questions on my own. My heart was disintegrating in the solitude, in my increasingly lonely, empty inner world. Would I be able to find a man to share these questions with? Where was the one who could empathise with me on this journey, who was also determined to throw over the stereotypes and live his own path?

I am me, I reflected again, *but who is he?*

☆ ☆ ☆

SIX

Semiotic Headscarf

What Is It Like Under There?

The events of 11 September 2001 put Muslims under a global spotlight. The *Qur'an* shot to the top of the bestseller list for books, with more people reading it than ever before. *To find out who Muslims were*, they said. I could sense that people at work wanted to know what I thought, and whether what they heard about Islam was true or not, but they seemed afraid to ask. I heard their whispers, trying to unravel the different ideas that were portrayed about Muslims on television and then trying to reconcile them with their experiences of me, the resident office Muslim.

As the days passed I was surprised that they did not approach me with their questions. I wondered if it was fear of breaking the jovial façade we had created between us. Did they feel that they would be invading my privacy? I *wanted* to talk to them, I *wanted* to explain the context of what was happening in the news and share information I thought would be useful to know about Islam and Muslims, but I didn't know how to do it without appearing to preach. What should have been an easy conversation discussing the news coverage and what it was like to be a Muslim turned into a wariness on my colleagues' part of bringing the personal into the workplace, and a disappointment on my part that no-one seemed to want to discuss the huge world issues that affected all of us – but very visibly affected me. The violent acts of 11 September, then 7 July 2005 and other attacks, injected fear into the most critical of activities: we were frightened to talk to each other.

Despite the fact that all the terrorist acts were carried out by men, it was the Muslim woman's headscarf that turned into one of the targets for attack, both verbal and physical. Suddenly, this scrap of material on our heads was the focus of attention. Many Muslim women wore the headscarf like me and went about their daily lives quietly and peacefully. We considered it a matter of faith and personal choice to dress this way. For me, wearing a headscarf was not a political decision, nor a form of public statement, it was just one part of my everyday clothing. 'It's just a little piece of cloth,' I mused. 'It's not the end of civilisation as we know it.' I underestimated how upsetting my headscarf could be.

'WHAT IS YOUR HAIR LIKE?'

All eyes were on my hair. 'It's my hair,' I thought. 'I can do what I like with it. It's not any of your business to look at my hair if I don't want you to.' Again, it seemed I was wrong. The public demanded the right to see my hair. My lovely hair, that was part of me, that was part of my physical being as a woman, was now public property. Whatever happened to a woman's right to control her own body?

It was the men who were curious about my hair; the women never asked. I wondered if this was because the men found it hard to comprehend my femininity without my hair. I had withdrawn one of the visual cues by which they could define and categorise me. I didn't find their questioning offensive, in fact I found their curiosity both innocent and amusing. I could tease them and they would never really be able to define me on their terms. They would have to accept what I wanted to tell them about me. I could tell by the feigned reluctance to ask the question that they had probably been thinking about it for quite some time.

'It's a blonde Mohican,' I told them, straight-faced. They nodded, acceptingly.

'Doesn't it get squashed?' they asked innocently, avoiding looking at the top of my head. Then they realised that I was Asian with brown skin and dark brown eyebrows and eyelashes.

A grin spread across my lips, but I kept looking them straight in the eye with seriousness. 'I actually don't have any hair.'

Now they were sceptical. They realised that I was deliberately confusing them.

'So what is your hair really like?' they asked again.

This time I was more serious. I felt very protective. I didn't want to be imagined. 'I feel it's my private space. I've covered my hair, because I don't want you to see it. What would be the point of telling you what it looks like?'

What they didn't realise was that Muslim women were as pre-occupied with their hair as everyone else. We kept it styled, trimmed and coloured, just like women who didn't cover their hair. It might be covered up out in public, but it was just as much an object of feminine attention in private. It was part of feeling womanly. Wearing a headscarf didn't mean denying your physical femininity, it just meant celebrating it in the private sphere.

'Wearing a headscarf' wasn't just about hair either, despite the emphasis on the 'headscarf' part of the dress code. It was about a whole way of dressing based on being 'modest'. Many Muslim women did not wear a headscarf but still observed modesty in their dress and behaviour, and that was the most important part. With all the focus on hair and the head, the philosophy of modesty that lay behind the headscarf was overlooked.

'DOES YOUR HUSBAND MAKE YOU WEAR A HEADSCARF?'

I sighed wistfully, 'If only I had a husband.' It seemed the greatest irony that as a Muslim woman it was assumed I was under the thumb of my husband, and yet here I was, unable to find my Mr Right.

Before anyone else pursued this line of questioning I would add, 'My father hasn't forced me to wear the headscarf either.'

For Muslim women, wearing the headscarf landed us right in the middle of a double whammy. It polarised feelings with passion and intensity. Traditional Muslim men insisted that Muslim women *should* wear it in order to defend Islam. The voices in the media that hinted that Muslims were to be feared as stuck-in-the-dark-ages-violent-terrorists insisted that Muslim women *should not* wear the headscarf.

'Could I say something, please?' I thought.

I opened my mouth to speak but a Muslim man stepped in to defend me: 'Islam has given you Muslim women the headscarf as your right, can't people see that? Of course you are proud that you are liberated.' I agreed with his statement but felt annoyed that my right as a Muslim woman to defend *myself* had been taken away from me.

'I'd really like to say something for myself,' I thought again.

Once more, before I could speak, I was pre-empted. 'Muslim women have been brainwashed. You think you want to wear it because your religious leaders tell you that that is what a good Muslim woman should do, so you're complicit in your own subjugation.'

'Complicit in my own subjugation?' I reflected. That sounded complicated and slightly kinky.

I was cross. How dare other people speak on my behalf? If I have been liberated by Islam to be fully human, with full rights, then I am liberated enough to speak for myself. If you think I am oppressed then stop oppressing me further by telling me what to say and think.

I had spent a lot of time considering how I wanted to dress and what impact I wanted to make on the world around me. Wearing a headscarf was not an easy thing to do, as I looked immediately different from everyone around me. With the tense political and social climate, it also made me more vulnerable, more stigmatised. In choosing to wear the headscarf it meant being willing to address these difficulties and these tensions because they were worth bearing, in order to practise my faith and try to make the world a better place by challenging stereotypes of women, Muslim women in particular. As a woman, I had a choice about what to wear, and I fully exercised that choice. It was my decision.

I was hopeful that asserting my own decision would add my small voice to the calls to change the lives of women who were oppressed in the name of any religion. I had made my own choices, but there were Muslim women who were forced to dress and act in a certain way, and that was wrong. Some were forced into marriages, and that was wrong, too. Others were denied education, healthcare or the right to work, or had violent cultural customs forced upon them. It was the same words that had to be said again: wrong, wrong, wrong. Any kind of coercion was absolutely forbidden and utterly opposed to the spirit of Islam. Those who perpetrated such horrible acts of violence and oppression ought to be exposed for what they were really after: power and control. They should not hide behind their false claims that it was in the interests of women, Islam or humanity. The actions of a Muslim always had to be taken with free will, otherwise there was no point. The *Qur'an* was very clear, 'There is no compulsion in religion.' You can't and you *must not* force anyone to do anything they do not want to do.

'IS IT HOT?'

The prevailing imagery of Muslim women showed us covered from head to feet in black. The headscarves were long, black, flowing pieces of fabric, draping over a long black cloak, and sometimes with a *niqab*, a veil, over the faces too, also usually in black. The photographs were taken to make the women look eerie and inhuman, alien to Western eyes. But underneath each one was a life, a story, a heart, which was denied by those who saw them just as a ghost covered in black cloth. Those who saw them as anonymous creatures were complicit with those who tried to make them anonymous by imposing this uniform style of dress. It made me feel uncomfortable to see women – Muslim or otherwise – dressed in identikit clothing, whether that was the 'little black dress' or the black outfits of the media *luvvies* or the black cloaks of Muslim women. It was strange that the colour black was the recurring theme.

This style of long, shapeless black clothing was deliberately adopted by many Muslim women as a way of controlling for themselves the external projection of their persona. They were fed up with the imagery surrounding us of female perfection and nothing less: thin, tall, blonde, glamorous, perfect hair, perfect skin, perfect make-up. That was still women being told how they should dress and what they should look like. For them, the long black clothes were a way of reclaiming control over their image.

Not all women chose to dress like that. For me, personality and aesthetics were important. 'God is Beauty, and God loves beauty,' is a famous Islamic saying, and I believed that meant incorporating beauty into your clothing to complement its modesty. After all, it was modesty that was the Islamic value at the heart of the discussion; the headscarf was only one component of that.

The *Qur'an* advises the 'believing men and the believing women' that the first step towards modesty is to 'cast down their gaze' when looking at someone of the opposite gender. The words suggest this either literally, or perhaps metaphorically, as a form of respect to another person not to see them for their sexuality. Take that out of the equation, and social relations become less tense and less fraught with the complications of sexual tension. People want to be judged for who they are, not what they look like, and sadly, it seems to be women who suffer most by being judged on their looks and sexuality.

Modest behaviour is accompanied by modest clothing. For women, that meant clothes that were loose and covered up to the wrist and down to the ankle. Most Muslims, but not all, believed that it meant covering the hair as well, and a very tiny number believed that it meant covering the face, too.

By introducing modest behaviour and clothing into the public space, the aim was to make life easier, less tense and less judgemental for everyone. If I wanted to make society a happier place to live, I was willing to spend a little more time and care on choosing my clothes and wearing a headscarf. For me, it was a matter of faith and a contribution to making the community we live in better. The ever-visible headscarf was therefore only one element of the dress choice. Sometimes it was a bit hot, but it was worth it.

'WHY DON'T MEN HAVE TO WEAR A HEADSCARF?'

As the *Qur'an* had described, men were just as obliged to behave and dress with modesty. Often men thought they could get away without it, sometimes going as far as wearing tight jeans and skinny-fit T-shirts. If they were abiding by their Islamic values, then they ought to dress respectfully too. According to most Muslims, men were required to dress modestly but weren't required to cover their hair as part of their modest dress in the way women were. The curiosity that I'd found men had about my hair, where women had not had the same curiosity, and the way they used hair to complete their visual imagery of me, made me consider the possibility that hair was an essential part of a woman's beauty and mystique in a way that it simply wasn't for men.

Irrespective of whether it was an obligation for men to cover their hair, in many Muslim countries it was in fact common for men to do so. In Oman they wore a turban-like head covering called the *mussar*. In Saudia Arabia they wore a white cloth called a *ghutra*, held in place by a black coil. In the Gulf as well as the Levant the men wore a *keffiyah*, a checked cloth held in place in the same way. In the Subcontinent it was a small hat, often white, called *topi*, and in Malaysia the men donned a cap called a *songkok*. It was a strange and unobserved phenomenon that 'modern' Muslim men did not cover their heads. Perhaps they had put all the emphasis on women to cover their hair and had forgotten about doing the same themselves, I thought to myself.

When it came to the subject of men and *hijab*, there was one thing that made me angry on their behalf. Some Muslims described wearing *hijab* as a way of protecting themselves against men's rampant and uncontrollable lust. If women didn't wear *hijab*, they would be ravaged by these poor men who would be driven wild. I felt quite offended on behalf of men by the idea that they were sex-crazed monsters. It wasn't up to women to control men. They weren't wild animals. Men were ethical and moral, and were perfectly capable of treating women with respect. Modest behaviour and dress were for both men and women, to create an environment that was respectful and relaxed, and where both would be judged not on how they looked, but for who they were.

'DO YOU SLEEP IN YOUR HEADSCARF?'

Being beautiful is an inherent part of being a woman. Looking glamorous, smelling fragrant, making the most of one's feminine attributes are all significant components of womanhood. One of the reasons I was looking forward to getting married was to have a man with whom to share these beauties and who would appreciate me. Intimacy of the, *ahem, ahem*, sexual kind, was highly encouraged by Islam, and making the most of your beauty, for both men and women was all but mandatory in the privacy of the home. Stepping out of the modest paradigm was not just with a spouse but for the whole of the private domain. So I would step in the door at home and unpin my headscarf. When it came to bedtime, there was nothing between me and my pillow.

Wearing the headscarf in public was a matter of practising my faith, involving modesty in behaviour as well as clothing. I couldn't separate that out and leave it at home, because that would be leaving my social values in the private sphere, and what was the point of a social value if it wasn't practised out in society? It was like believing that kindness was important, but then not being kind out in public.

'ARE YOU A TERRORIST?'

I wanted to respond 'yes!' and then rummage round in my handbag to pull out an unidentified object, but I had to hold myself back. I limited myself to a response in a deep-baritone voice, 'Are *you*?' and then waggled my eyebrows like the villain from a superhero cartoon.

As a student at school, we had reviewed our career prospects with the local school adviser. I filled out a digital questionnaire about my strengths, weaknesses and interests. It offered me four suggested careers. First, prison warden, as it said I had good nurturing skills and could see the good in people. Second, library administrator, as I liked books. Third, technology design, as I liked new ideas and relating them to people. And finally, a new addition to their list of potential careers, terrorist, as I wanted to 'make an impact'. I wasn't sure what the qualifications or job prospects would be for this last option. I was doubtful that it would be well paid, and was certain there would be no pension or healthcare. Instead I decided to obtain a degree from Oxford and then go on and work in the fledgling technology industry. It was definitely the right choice.

Of course I'm not a terrorist, what a daft question.

I wondered what drove someone to the point where they were willing to end their own life and create destruction around them. What kind of macabre aspiration was that? Was it pure hatred? Was it an evil mind that had got hold of the means to carry out a bloodthirsty act? I couldn't help but think those who had committed the acts of 11 September fell into this category, although none of us would ever know the truth.

I aspired to live a happy life, a good life, a life that might be remembered by just a few, or perhaps by many, for making a positive contribution. I wanted a career, a home, a husband, children, a comfortable retirement, as most human beings do. And I also wanted to make a contribution to reducing the misery and oppression in the world and bring about a lasting change, no matter how small. Every Muslim woman has aspirations, just like every other human being. The clothing we wear or the acts of faith that we carry out do not change any of that. We want to live happy, fulfilled and successful lives.

My aspirations were real and huge to me. They dominated how I lived my life. But there were others around the world who lived in poverty, war, famine, destruction, dictatorship, oppression and occupation. Some of them saw acts like setting themselves on fire or killing themselves as well as others as better than living. I didn't want to imagine the void in their lives where hope ought to have been. What terrorised me was the knowledge that these people had taken a decision that their life could be improved only through death. If their aspiration was simply to end their suffering then we had let them down. I had let them down.

'WHY DO YOU WEAR SO MUCH BLACK?'

I wondered sometimes if people really did look at what was in front of their eyes. With pictures of Muslim women dressed in black used as shorthand for 'Muslim' or, worse still, 'Muslim terrorist', it was assumed that all Muslim women wore black all the time. This was the fashion from the Gulf countries, including Saudi Arabia, which exported its opinions on Muslim behaviour and etiquette around the world. Just as women across the globe had adopted 'Western' clothing, it seemed that a certain segment of the Muslim population was adopting 'Saudi' style to represent the rekindling of their Muslim renaissance. When the black-clad women of the Gulf travelled to other Muslim countries, they stood out like a sore thumb. Muslim women elsewhere, and that consisted of the majority of Muslim women around the world, in countries like Indonesia, China, Malaysia, Nigeria, Turkey and so many, many others, wore brightly coloured clothes, from greens to pinks to blues to whites and every colour in between.

'I wear a pink headscarf,' I pointed out, 'usually in a shade of lilac or soft rose pink. It is my signature colour.'

E-veil-uation

I had a good feeling the day that I met Hasan for coffee. It didn't last long.

'I wasn't very keen to meet you,' he confessed. 'Nothing personal, but I've told my mum and my aunt who are both on the lookout for a wife for me, that I don't want someone who wears *hijab*.'

Oh dear, here we go again: telling me I'm completely unsuitable in his first breath! 'But they just went on and on,' he rolled his eyes in jest, 'about how lovely you are. How smart, how pretty, how nice, until I could take no more!' Who were these women who thought so differently from all the other Aunties? I couldn't place his mother or aunt at that moment, so I was unaware what I had done to impress them.

'They finally persuaded me to meet you. I had no option to say no!' He threw his hands up in mock-protest, ridiculing the process of persuasion. He was affable and laughed at himself and his ludicrous situation.

I smiled sweetly. It was the best I could muster for a man who was honest enough to admit I didn't meet his requirements. I gave him some leeway. He had come with an open mind at least – well, half an open mind.

'They've been pestering me for quite some time actually.'

He seemed nice, well-mannered and intelligent. He was very polite, willing to try new things and open to considering new possibilities. After all the introductions that I had been through, I learnt very quickly to identify someone I would get along with and with whom there was potential. Other than his resistance to my headscarf, everything else was very positive. I had also learnt that it was important to be brave enough to raise the make-or-break issues sooner rather than later. The answer to the question would always be the same in the end: time rarely changed someone's response to a critical issue.

I plunged in: 'So why do you want someone who doesn't wear *hijab*?'

'I think girls who wear *hijab* are probably very religious and stay at home all day praying. They must be a bit dull. I like to go out a lot, so I wouldn't have anyone to go with.'

I repeated his sentence back to him. 'So a woman who wears *hijab* is someone who stays at home all day, prays all the time and doesn't go out. And she is very dull.' I looked at him smiling.

He squirmed, boyish and innocent, smiling too.

'Now, you may have noticed that I am a woman in *hijab*. So what are we doing here? And by the way, you called me dull!'

'I know! I know!'

More wriggling on his part.

'What else?' I asked.

'Well, there are places I want to go that I wouldn't want to take a woman in *hijab*,' he offered, with a note of defiance, concern and naughtiness.

'What kind of places?' I asked. He wasn't getting off so easily.

'Places. You know.'

'No, I don't know.' I raised my eyebrows and took a sip of coffee. 'Anywhere you can go, I can go too.' I paused to see if he would buckle. 'Or are there places that you go where you feel in your heart that you shouldn't go, and seeing me with my headscarf with you would remind you of that and make you feel guilty?'

He changed the subject. 'I just don't feel comfortable with a woman in *hijab*.'

'Really, I make you feel uncomfortable?' I laughed at him.

'No! No!' More squirming.

I couldn't contain my laughter any longer in response to his elusive answers.

'I've just never met anyone like you. I don't know any women who wear *hijab*. I just thought that's why they would all be dull.'

Preconceptions: I had freed myself from one set to find myself up against another. I wondered how Hasan would respond to a tougher line of questioning. I decided to be blunt.

'Is it that you want to show your wife off to your friends to point out how pretty she is? If I wear *hijab* then you can't exhibit me.'

Some boys had brazenly admitted to me that they wanted a pretty wife to show off to their friends so they could compete to see who had the most luscious partner. A woman in *hijab* would never meet that expectation. A woman in *hijab* would never want to.

He looked at me, unsure of this turn in the conversation.

'Or maybe you are worried that they will know that you are a Muslim? Or they will stop being your friends because your camouflage will be blown?'

As Muslim women who wore a headscarf, our faith was obvious to those around us. We were clearly marked out and we had to learn to establish our identities as Muslims who were confident in our faith. We took the brunt of recognition as Muslims. The way we appeared in public was used to epitomise Islam. Stories in newspapers to do with Muslims – even if Muslim women were not involved – invariably carried pictures of Muslim women wearing headscarves or veils. We had to align the way we looked on the outside with what we believed on the inside; we had no choice.

For some Muslim men, who did not want to wear their faith so openly or who did not want people to know that they were Muslim, it was easy for them to hide their faith. They did not have to carry any outward signs. There were some Muslim men who acted like this because they were embarrassed by their religion and did not want to be associated with it. For them, I knew that my headscarf was extremely conspicuous, as though a big sign was appearing over our heads flashing 'Muslim! Muslim!'

I looked him straight in the eye. I was trying hard not to label him unfairly based on my experiences so far of men who did not want to marry a woman who wore *hijab*. I had to fight my own preconceptions.

'You're really nice, and I never knew that Muslim women went out or travelled or worked or could dress fashionably and still look attractive . . .' He blushed, and then I did. 'I didn't realise. It's just, just . . . I'm sorry, I just don't feel comfortable.'

We talked further, and slowly Hasan's real feelings were revealed. My *hijab* fully publicised my faith to the wider world, and Hasan's conclusion was that I must therefore be totally consumed with instituting a highly visual public statement of religion, which would destroy his efforts to keep his own religion private. I explained that even though a woman may have taken the huge step to dress modestly and wear the headscarf, it didn't mean that she was perfect or pious in every, or even in any, way. She was just as human as everyone else. However, his reflexive reaction was that I was forcing him to expose what he had consciously and subconsciously spent so much time hiding.

The different responses I received to my headscarf had revealed how these men felt inside themselves. I remembered my Funny Valentine card and thought about how different men react to women who wear *hijab*, and how a woman's dress can change someone's perception of who she is so dramatically. Hasan had an idea of himself that he kept very private. He was honest in describing that he had a seed of faith that lay in his heart but that he wasn't ready to bring it out into the open and expose it yet.

He and I were at different stages in our journey through life. We were in such different places that we did not even have the language to *talk* to each other about what was important to us.

I liked the fact that he had his own ideas about the world but that he also understood there was space to learn and to grow. Most of all, I was impressed with his honesty and willingness to challenge his own preconceptions. He made me challenge my own ones and ensure that I saw each person with individuality and humanity.

I had started my search looking for a man who would abide by the choice I had made to wear the headscarf; after all, it was my own decision as a woman as to how I should dress. But the more I had to fight the preconceptions of what a Muslim woman who wore *hijab* should be like, the more I wanted a man who understood why I wore it and supported me. I wanted him to *want* me to wear *hijab*. I wanted him to have a vision of a better future for our society, and to understand that the reason that I had chosen to wear *hijab* was a small contribution to that future.

If someone was tied to literal or cultural ideas about Islam and being Muslim then we would never be able to improve the status quo. Instead, we had to create new possibilities, and to do that I needed someone who was magical enough to free himself of the preconceptions that held all of us back.

Wearing *hijab* was not a decision I had taken lightly. *Hijab* is an Arabic word that means 'to cover', which includes covering the whole body in loose clothing, but it was used commonly to refer to the headscarf itself.

When I first made the decision to 'wear *hijab*', I did it simply because it was 'the thing to do'. I went often to the mosque, I read a lot of Islamic books, I read the *Qur'an*, I travelled to Muslim countries, I went on the *umra*, the lesser pilgrimage, to Mecca. I was immersed in wanting to live a fully Islamic lifestyle as part of who I was, and I decided that wearing *hijab* was a fundamental part of that desire.

Wearing modest clothing was described in the *Qur'an* as something that the believing men and women engaged in. I believed in God and I believed in the *Qur'an*, and I wanted to be considered one of the believing men and women. It was therefore quite simple: I believed in the concept of *hijab* and I wanted to wear it.

This decision meant a slow change in wardrobe, my dress sense growing with my *hijab*-sense. It meant taking care over long sleeves, long skirts, scarves that wrapped around the head covering hair, ears and neck, and pinned underneath the chin. I was conservative with my experimentation, as were many British Muslims. *Hijab* was still very new to Britain and to the Muslims who started to wear it here. It was not at this time about being fashionable, but about observing the parameters of modesty.

Many of the Aunties would titter half-embarrassed, half-proud at the 'modern' clothing they had worn before they had 'understood' Islam.

'We had to move away from our homes, and away from Muslim countries in order for us to really understand our faith of Islam,' said the Aunties. This sentiment became more and more prevalent amongst the generations that had arrived as immigrants. 'Back home' it was assumed that culture was 'Islamic'. It was taken for granted. No questions were asked about whether what people really did was Islamic or not. In their new home each action had to be reassessed: there was no longer any assumption that any activity was de facto Islamic. When the new generation like me grew up in Britain, every action that was a remnant from other cultures had to be challenged and justified; it was no longer good enough for an action to be based on 'how it is'. That is what parents found hardest – that they were being challenged. Many saw it as a sign of rebellion against them, when it was far from that. It wasn't them as people who were being analysed, but whether the customs that were being practised were really as 'Islamic' as they claimed them to be.

When the Aunties explained this, it brought them to life as real human beings who had been through their own challenges. I started to understand the tribulations that they had faced in moving geographies and cultures, and in the context of a slow but perceptible change in social values, immigration and the role of faith.

Some of my friends wanted to wear *hijab* but their families did not permit them to do so. They were actually prevented from making this choice for themselves. The families didn't want their daughters turning into 'fanatics'. They didn't want to be seen in society with a 'crazy' or 'fundamentalist' child.

Both post-modernists and many traditional Muslims agreed on one thing: feminism was a dirty word. But I was fascinated by the struggles that European women had gone through to create a society where I was able to choose to wear *hijab* and establish it as a principle of my choice and empowerment. I read writings about throwing off corsets, burning bras and the revolution of the mini-skirt. The questions that women asked then were the same questions that Muslim women were asking now: who were men to tell women how to dress? Why were women being fobbed off with ideas that they had already been given their due, when in fact they hadn't? Why did women not get their voices heard? I agreed wholeheartedly: women had to throw off their shackles, liberate themselves, enter the workplace and establish equality. I punched the air fervently and then asked myself meekly, was I a feminist?

I thought its aspiration was very attractive. I knew that as a child of the 1980s I had not suffered the inequality and oppression or the struggles and sacrifices of the women who came before. But I was indeed suffering at the hands of an Asian Muslim culture that interpreted Western feminism as misguided, and misguidedly interpreted Islam in order to subjugate women.

Feminism had explored one area that greatly intrigued me – how should women behave in the workplace? How should they interact in order to be taken seriously and gain maximum impact? In this area, surprisingly, it coincided with the general thrust of Islamic thinking – that women should dress modestly so that they would be taken seriously for who they were rather than what they looked like.

I wanted to contribute to the social discourse about gender and equality, but Muslim women who wore the veil by choice, and by extension who embraced Islam as a positive force, were not allowed to have a say. Only Muslim women who had openly rejected Islam were allowed to be part of the discussion. I was an inadmissible feminist.

The global discussion about equality for women referred to the veil as oppressing women, a sign of their second-class status. Where women were forced to wear it, I believed it was wrong. But the fact that they were forced to wear it was not the problem itself: it was the symptom of more serious underlying inequality. That inequality wasn't part of the blueprint of Islam. Islam talks about equal value and worth for both genders, both equal as creations.

Each man and each woman will be judged on their own individual merits for each atom of good and each atom of evil that they have done. I was most moved by a verse in the *Qur'an* which says that God 'created you from a single soul'. No left ribs, no second status. Men and women were from a single soul, equal in creation and worth. Everything else had to be interpreted in this context. That meant if there was inequality in interpretation or in practice, we had to go back to this very essence and rethink where we were. Everything in our understanding as Muslims had to be in the spirit of 'created from a single soul'.

I felt that if the ideas of Islam about men, women and equality were scrutinised by Muslims and others, a whole plethora of ideas could be developed to improve the situation of women around the world. Having grown up and embraced my faith, my Asian culture and my British culture, I felt that this gave me and others like me a unique perspective. I wanted to make a difference.

In the gender blueprint that Islam offered, there was one thing I loved above all else – and that was the value that it placed on 'womanly' things. I felt that these needed more status and more recognition: being a wife, being a mum, being a carer, a nurturer. Even though feminism had gone a long way to rebalancing gender equality, it seemed that in many cases it was by opening doors for women to do traditionally masculine things. It needed now to put back value into the inherently feminine things. I watched game shows where women tagged along with their husbands to declare themselves to be 'only a housewife' or 'just a mum'. I knew just how hard my mum had to work to look after me.

When I thought about my mother, and the status of all mothers, I reflected on the saying of the Prophet Muhammad: 'Paradise lies beneath the feet of the mother.' Everything that a believing Muslim dreamed of was there, waiting. The *Qur'an* talked about how a child should never even utter the sound 'uf' to her parents, in recognition of the pain, efforts and anguish that they have suffered to bring up that child. Most striking of all, when the Prophet Muhammad was asked which parent a child should obey, he responded, 'The mother, the mother, the mother, then the father.'

My mother is the closest human being to me on earth, and I know that she loves me more than anyone else. She knows if I am sad, lonely or in pain without even asking. She always puts me before herself, and is constantly praying for my well-being and for my dreams to come true.

As I grew up, and as I embarked on the journey of looking for the One and learning about life and faith, she travelled with me and we grew together. I shared my experiences with her and she shared hers with me. She would sit on the sofa and I would lie with my head in her lap while she stroked my hair. No matter how old I am, that will always be the most comforting, safe and loving place for me. Even if I am married, the love between a mother and a daughter will always be different from and irreplaceable by the love of a partner. As mother and daughter, we have shared a journey through the joys and pains of living in this world as women and sharing in the most intimate moments of our lives.

My mother lives and breathes dedication and commitment to her husband and her family. I have not experienced anyone with as many smiles and as much patience and contentment in the face of adversity as my mother. She is a quiet hero, as most women are.

My mother calls me her *'hiro'*, a Gujarati word meaning 'diamond'. She is *my* hero, my inspiration for all that I do. If I grow into half the woman that she is, my life as a woman will be a success.

Anti-repressant

I had *issues* just like everyone else. I still had to get my head straight about life, faith, men, spirituality, work-life balance, culture, love. All of that just made me a normal human being trying to make my way in the world. When it came to issues of boxes and labels, and people's ideas of 'this is how it's always been' and 'this is how it should be, because this is how it should be', one simple fact became clearer and clearer: the problem was not me.

'Shelina should be more flexible,' the Aunties and matchmakers told my mother.

'What does "more flexible" mean?' I asked my mother, perplexed. Hadn't I already met a man who played a practical joke on me, one who turned up two hours late because he was watching the cricket, and one who claimed that a bolt of lightning had destroyed my contact details?

'You've had an enquiry,' she told me, 'from a very suitable young man. He's also been to Oxford and now has a very good job in the city. He is from a very good family and I remember his father used to be very handsome when he was young. His mother is beautiful too, so I'm expecting that he is probably very good looking. I'm told that he used not to be very religious but he's becoming more and more interested in Islam and he says he would like to marry someone who is also religious.'

'That all sounds very promising,' I responded. 'So we should meet him, no? Sounds like the best interest we've had in quite some time.'

My mother produced an encouraging frown face.

'What is it this time?' I asked, hesitant. After engaging with optimism and hope through numerous matches and introductions, I'd finally learnt to confront 'the catch' at the start. When I first noticed myself doing this, I had tried to put a stop to my increasing pessimism and stay positive. But with more and more introductions under my belt, and less and less fantasy to cling onto, I concluded that it was better to face reality up front – that there was always something that wasn't quite right. After all, wasn't that the point of arrangements and introductions: to think with the head and make a reasoned decision about whether reality could support the feelings and emotions someone evoked inside you?

'He doesn't want someone who wears *hijab*,' she continued. I'd heard this one before. Surely the simple answer was for him to be introduced only to women who did not wear the *hijab*? That seemed the obvious next step in this scenario. I said as much to my mum.

'Perhaps you need to consider him, he is everything you need. He is intelligent and intellectual, he has a forward-looking outlook on life, he's active and sociable, and his family are very open and easy-going, all of which you are having trouble finding elsewhere,' she advised.

Her analysis was right. I *was* having difficulty finding these qualities. I sighed, 'So what are you suggesting?' We'd been through this before, this process of being introduced to men who had specifically stated that they wanted a non-*hijab*-wearing woman in the hope, or taking the calculated risk, that having seen me they would be overwhelmed with my good looks, charm and endearing personality and would immediately say 'yes' in a mesmerised trance of my brilliance and un-miss-ability. They always said 'no'.

'It's not *me* suggesting this,' said my mum with audible italics. 'It's just that Auntie has asked me to put this to you to consider. I have to give you the option to make your own decision.'

'I don't really want to be put up in front of another man for him to measure my looks on a ten-point scale and decide if I am pretty enough to be a trophy wife for him or to judge if my clothes are trendy and stylish enough to "compensate" for my *hijab*.'

There was a bittersweet irony in the suggestion that I should be *told* that I should *not* wear a headscarf. The request to *not* wear it was repressive.

'Auntie is saying that he doesn't mind you wearing *hijab* in the long-term, in fact he says that he would probably want you to wear it. He says he likes the idea that you are interested in religion and he thinks he could learn a lot from you.'

'So then I don't understand what the problem is.'

'Before he gets to that point, he is asking if you would stop wearing *hijab* . . .'

My eyeballs pinged straight out, then off the wall and bounced on the floor. I picked them up, put them back in and let her conclude.

'. . . for a year,' finished my mother.

'Wow.' I was gobsmacked. Was this a gracious compromise on the Prince's part?

'So let me get this straight, he wants me to stop doing something for a year, which he thinks is probably the right thing to do anyway? And which he agrees is part of our faith.'

'Yes.'

This was puzzling indeed. And what was most puzzling was that his parents would have discussed this with him, and then with the Auntie, all of whom would have agreed that they thought there was sense in this proposition. In the interest of getting the boy married, they were willing to ask someone to *not* do something which they all agreed was the right thing to do and to make it seem that I, the poor passive, accepting woman, was inflexible and lacking in kindness and understanding, and unwilling to show a commitment to the ideal of getting married if I didn't do it. If I sounded cross, it was because I felt cross.

I had made a choice about my faith and the way that I wanted to live my life. I had based these decisions on careful thought and what I believed was right. I realised that I didn't have to shape my faith in order to subsume it to this false god of social and cultural acceptability. I didn't have to accede to the trump card of the boy's superior cultural position and the marriage-at-all-costs attitude.

Marriage was important, but it was supposed to complete my faith, not destroy it.

I had changed my own world, and that meant I was ready to push back and change the world itself. I grinned at my mother. And at that, my mother's worried frown turned into a small, conspiratorial smirk and then into a wide, proud grin at the daughter she had raised who had finally learnt to call things as they were. She didn't want her daughter – and by extension herself – to be bullied by an age-old custom where the boy's family held all the cards and where they would insist on incomprehensible requests, even when they knew that they contravened all faith standards.

I blamed the gatekeepers – the mothers-in-law, the Aunties, the matchmakers. They were supposed to be upholding the sanctity of marriage. They had told the girls that it was important to look beyond the superficial, that love would grow with time, that marriage was about more give than take. They told us to be religious and uphold our faith, and yet here they were promoting and encouraging young men to ask Muslim women to stop practising their faith so that they could get married.

'If they really want me to stop wearing *hijab*, which they agree is something that a Muslim woman should do, then I think you should tell them that I will be happy to do so if they will take the responsibility of me giving up my prayers and my fasting in Ramadan for a year as well.'

SEVEN

Love

From a Single Soul, Created in Pairs

☆

Late in the summer I travelled with friends on a tour of Jordan and Egypt. I was excited. Egypt straddled Arabia and North Africa, at the centre of Muslim dynasties that had spanned hundreds of years. I couldn't wait to see the architecture or to wander through its bustling and famous bazaars. Its history stretched back to the great civilisation of Ancient Egypt, which included the Bible and *Qur'an* stories of Joseph and Moses. Ever since I was a child I had wanted to see the Pyramids, walk on the sands that had witnessed the Pharaohs, El-Alamein and the building of the Suez Canal. It was not just its history that I wanted to experience, but also its natural beauty: to travel through its wildly beautiful desert, to take a sunset boat ride along the Nile, the artery of this great nation. I felt a connection to Egypt through the river Nile, as it originates on the borders of Tanzania, my parents' place of birth. I had seen with my own eyes out of the window of the aeroplane on my travels to East Africa the way that the water transformed the desert, winding through it like a thick verdant snake.

We spent several days in Cairo, the capital of Egypt. Despite the incredible whirlwind of activity in the city and the utter majesty of the Nile that dominates its centre, there was one thing that constantly surprised us: the number of marriage proposals we received. We compared notes at the end of each day to tally up our offers. We notched up several proposals from taxi drivers – they had car journeys in which to make and explain the value of their offers; two from shopkeepers and a handful from the owners of the horses that took us for rides around the monuments.

Sulaiman owned a tour company that provided horses and guides for tourists to ride around the Pyramids. All four of us took a horse each, and Sulaiman elected to accompany my horse on foot. I had never ridden a horse before and wondered what the risks were if the horse broke into a gallop. Sulaiman laughed at my feeble urban nerves, chuckling at these soft female tourists who couldn't do a basic thing like ride a horse. The hooves padded rhythmically in the sand and the small dots in the distance turned into high-rise Pyramids. We continued past them and the swarming tourists, and circled round to the other side as the sun slowly dropped towards the horizon. The hot red streaks in the sky reflected on the sand.

We stopped directly in line with the Pyramids and waited for sunset, admiring the ancient vista before us. Sulaiman was diligent in exercising his guide duties by allowing us to fully enjoy the sights.

We chatted about tourists, life in Cairo, his work, London. And then abruptly, and uninvited, he looked directly into my eyes and declared: 'You are beautiful.'

'Thank you,' I muttered, and fell silent. I wobbled on the saddle as the horse swished round to drink from a shallow puddle.

'I have a good business,' he continued. 'Many horses.'

'How lovely,' I answered insipidly, worried now at the direction this conversation was taking.

'And many camels, too.'

'That is very good,' I said unenthusiastically, keeping my gaze fixed on the Pyramids.

Sulaiman strode off and came back a moment later with another horse, and swung himself up onto it. He had been disadvantaged on foot but now he sat eye to eye with me, separated emphatically by two well-behaved horses.

'Isn't this wonderful?' He paused and looked over at me. 'Wouldn't a human being want to survey this kingdom every day?'

I thought about his suggestion, far away from rainy London, the daily commute by dirty, crowded train to sit at a stagnant desk job, which led to more commuting and different desks as life progressed. Just because that was how it had always been, it didn't mean that was how it had to be. Why wait until I was creased and battered by life to have a holiday home in a warm relaxed climate? I could throw out those parameters that I held myself back with and have that joy now. I was already asking myself challenging and unorthodox questions every day about what I was really looking for in a person who would be my companion. I ought to ask the same type of challenging questions about the way I lived my life.

'I have 20,000 camels.'

I pointed to my ring, even though it was on the wrong hand, leaving him to draw the conclusion that I was married or at the very least engaged.

If only I had known that each camel was worth a thousand pounds, I might have agreed, or would I? Could I have spent so many years searching for someone who would complete me and hold my hand on a spiritual path, only to give it all up for a stranger with a large pot of cash?

I was quick to decline: there were too many other things to consider in this case. I would be facing a new country and a new culture with a man who I had known for barely an hour. I saw the risk of being stranded in an unknown place with so many new people. Most of all, and thinking clearly, I had to question whether he really did have this enormous reserve of wealth, and if his intentions really were genuine. I'd heard too many horror stories.

At the papyrus shop, I admired the varieties of tourist memorabilia made from one of Ancient Egypt's most well-known symbols: reed papyrus. The intriguing painted paper made for ideal presents – light, small and cheap. I found myself browsing through the different paintings on my own, but not for long. One of the shop staff came to assist me, and without hesitation spoke to me with frank emotion.

'You are very beautiful.'

Here we go yet again, I thought. I continued to look at the papyrus.

'The men where you come from must be blind not to see how

exquisite you are.'

I paused and gazed at a traditional painting of the Tree of Life.

'I would defend you, and look after you. I would show you how a woman like you should be appreciated. You should be accompanied by a man who treats you as the most important thing to him. I would not let you be on your own like this. I would carry your bags and take care of you wherever you go.'

It was an eloquent and touching speech. I smiled, opened my mouth several times, but could find no suitable words. What could one say to such an outpouring of emotion?

What motivated these men to approach us so directly? Perhaps they saw us as a game of statistics and believed that if they asked enough women, one might succumb. Or were we an easy target to drum up business through flattery? It was possible that we were entertainment for them, as they laughed amongst themselves at the gullible female tourists.

I wondered, what if one of us had actually said yes? Would he have married her, and then would she remain behind in Egypt? Or would the newly married couple have moved to London? We were sceptical: we assumed that they found our passports more beautiful than us. In this context, we thought love was being played as a game.

Was this all part of the tourist service? Despite our complaints about the unwanted attention, did female visitors enjoy the compliments and flattery? I had never been told so often how beautiful I was. I had never been proposed to so often. All that these men were doing was exposing and then feeding the beliefs that we had about ourselves that we were desirable women with status. We had let their compliments go to our heads and it revealed an unpalatable truth: we thought we were somehow superior because we were from the 'West'.

Every so often their words made me pause and wonder if I had been too cynical about their motivations. Were we seeing them as caricatures? I wanted to find out what really lay behind the cheerful banter. I decided to put a stop to their flattery and ask them directly about their lives, and speak to them as one human being who was on a quest to another. They were surprised that I was interested in their lives. As they spoke, the men evoked strong emotions about the way they lived, how they struggled to earn a living, about their families and their aspirations. They described with great passion how much they loved their country and how they longed to make it a better place.

The shop assistant carried on speaking to me. 'I am a Muslim too, and I am looking for a wife who is a good practising Muslim. If you are from London and you wear the *hijab* there, you must be very strong. It must be difficult for you.'

I turned to look at him. The tone of our interaction had changed and we were now two people on the same journey, learning from each other. I was no longer his prey. Instead, he was inviting me to connect with him at my very core – my faith. That was the power of the sense of *ummah* that Islam instilled in all Muslims. *Ummah* was one of the fundamental concepts that Muslims believed in. It meant being part of a single nation of people who shared a sense of community and togetherness, wherever you were in the world. Even though every individual and society within the *ummah* would have different opinions and cultures, it brought everyone together through unity and belonging. What we shared was a journey towards the Divine, and a desire to make the world a better place. Rooted in the very beginnings of Islam, 1400 years earlier, it was the first global identity that existed, before the ideas of 'globalisation' or 'global village'. Like a large family, every member of the *ummah* was of value, and you felt their happiness and their pain. That is why Muslims always seemed to express themselves so strongly about the experiences and troubles of other Muslims in different parts of the world. Each one was immediate and real, like a family member, no matter their physical location.

I smiled at him as I spoke: 'Do you know that there are almost two million Muslims in Britain? We are very blessed, I can wear my *hijab* to university and to work. We can pray and fast. We have our own mosques.'

'Really?' He was surprised and moved. 'Sometimes we wish for that kind of freedom here. We have to be careful of what we say. It is easy to get into trouble, especially if you are too religious.'

I had heard similar stories in other Muslim countries too. In Syria people rarely spoke to strangers about politics. In Tunisia the government tried to ban Ramadan. The Tunisians we met also told us how unusual it was for them to see educated women wearing the headscarf, because it was not permitted to be worn at university. The men even whispered that if they went to Friday prayers at the mosque, they would risk being taken to jail. In Saudi Arabia I met a woman who wept about how difficult things were for her and how she longed for the freedom I had to practise my religion freely. I felt a sense of responsibility in using my freedom to change the situation that these people faced.

One hundred years earlier, most Muslims had lived within relatively defined areas of the world. With the end of all the empires that had dominated the globe, along with changes in travel, migration patterns and a global economy, Muslims were now part of societies all over the world. My own family was one example. The breadth of that existence and the huge contribution Muslims made to all the various countries they lived in was not known by those who remained in Muslim majority regions. No wonder Muslims who still lived in the traditional heartlands were surprised to find out how widely spread out we all were.

'*Inshallah*, I will go for *hajj* this year,' he told me. He was beaming broadly. *Hajj* was the opportunity every Muslim yearned for at least once in their lives, a journey to Mecca. I also wanted to go and experience the phenomenon that changed the lives of so many people.

'I will pray for you to go there and to return safely,' I told him. Prayers were the best gift that I could offer him. We were always advised that if we wanted something, we should pray for others to be granted what they wished and in return our own wishes would be granted. 'And I will pray that you find a beautiful and wonderful wife.'

'Thank you, sister, I will pray for you to go to *hajj* also. And I will pray that you find a very good husband,' he responded. I was very moved by his unsolicited prayers for me to go on the *hajj*. His use of the word sister indicated a change in tone and respect. It made me feel safe and welcome.

Here in Cairo I was forced to ask myself whether all the time, effort and dedication in securing the impossibly perfect man was misdirected. Perhaps the reality of love was much more mundane in its origin than the idealised, airbrushed expectations I had. All that romantic chasing around after a perfect-but-unattainable love: who had time for all of that? As the Imam said, 'Love comes after marriage. You only know the meaning of love after you've made the commitment.'

If love blossoms after the relationship has been formally agreed, then instead of putting all our focus on the 'finding' part, more of our emphasis should be on the 'relationship' part. Less searching and asking; more energy on keeping the relationship alive afterwards, integrating our families together and making the marriage unit a foundation for the community. In which case, proposing should be as easy, quick and straightforward as I had experienced in Egypt. There ought to be no shame in being rebuffed to reach the goal of getting married. Making a formal commitment was the entry point into the real story of love.

I should have learnt from all my encounters that love lies in the most extraordinary people and places. Even if I didn't find love for myself here, it lived here too, in a different shape, fitting its people and community. Was love hiding in those narrow *souk* alleyways? Whatever the heritage and cultures amidst which it found itself, love existed at the very core of the human condition. Love was the spark that ignited the soul and love was also what sustained it.

*

Once we arrived across the border in Jordan, we made our way towards Petra, the mystical setting of the film *Indiana Jones and the Raiders of the Lost Ark*.

If only Indiana Jones was with us, I sighed. I had an enduring crush on him, with his masculine chiselled looks and his fearless chivalry. Who could resist the vast intellect of a professor of history and archaeology who lived a double life as a roguish adventurer from the 1930s?

Petra had been at the crossroads of trade for thousands of years, being inhabited since prehistoric times. I imagined this junction of commerce bustling with travellers transporting silks and spices between China, India, Arabia, Egypt, Greece and Rome.

To reach the 'Rose City' of Petra we had to make our way slowly down the *siq*, a one-and-a-half-kilometre long gorge that was dark and narrow, sometimes only three to four metres wide. The terracotta-coloured cliffs swept frighteningly up to the skyline, leaving only a sliver of light coming down to us as we sweated our way along the enclosed path. Even though we had begun the walk at 6.30 that morning, the heat had already reached intolerable levels. The path we were following grew even more constricted and the deep orange cliffs on either side stretched even higher. Eventually the corridor widened and we were spat out at the entrance.

Standing at the gates to the historical site at 7 a.m., we looked around at what appeared to be a bustling village. There were small cafés and plenty of locals milling around the already buzzing throng of tourists. Long shades extended across low tables and chairs set out in traditional Arabic style to delight the visitors. At this time they were empty as travellers focused on exploring the historical ruins of Petra. Later, as the afternoon grew long and dusk approached, they would fill up with ravenous customers. We too walked past them. The locals who worked there nodded to us, noting our presence.

As the cliffs separated to form a wide arena, our jaws dropped. In front of us was an enormous building almost 40 metres high, half constructed, half hewn from the solid rock. Beyond that we could see entire homes and edifices carved out of a mountain, retained in exquisite detail after thousands of years. The cliffs had been cut into elegantly and in keeping with their spirit and size, so that it looked like the rooms had been there ever since the cliffs themselves were formed. What stunned me most was that a human being had stood in front of these impenetrable mountains that were thousands of times taller than any person, and had the imagination and creativity to envisage a home, a temple, a crypt, a whole human community living in this space.

The *Qur'an* mentions a place which is believed to be Petra, the place of abode of the people of 'Thamud'. It records that 'They carved out houses from the mountains, feeling safe . . .' Who wouldn't feel safe ensconced in this valley under the overwhelming protection of these epic mountains? The people were known for their immense skill in carving rock but the *Qur'an* describes them as uninterested in looking for deeper meaning or the Divine. They built their success through sly monetary means, often cheating others. They were proud of what they had achieved, both financially and architecturally, believing that their success would be infinite and indestructible.

The *Qur'an* recounts their story to impart the wisdom that greatness will come to an end if you are arrogant and engage in acts which are wrong. In the case of the people of Thamud it was cheating people of their money. The *Qur'an* advises people to travel and see the remains of civilisations like Petra, and while it may have described what happened, nothing could match the visual impact of seeing the place first-hand. Wandering around the site and observing the size of the architecture as I stood next to it made the point obvious: even great empires come to an end through corruption. No wonder the *Qur'an* encouraged people to visit historical monuments. The vision was unforgettable.

Petra was one of many stories of the rise and fall of empires, people who built large buildings and thought themselves immortal, impene-trable. Pharaoh was another, a man who killed thousands of innocent babies. In his self-proclaimed divinity he wanted to build a spiral staircase into the heavens so he could reach up and kill God. But when it came to the story of Pharaoh, I was more interested in his wife Aasiya than him. Now there was a real woman.

Since our visit to Egypt, I had been thinking of her a great deal. She was Pharaoh's most beautiful and most intelligent wife, and as a result she was also his favourite wife. Egypt was a great civilisation of its time, and as its queen she was one of the most powerful women in existence. She would have enjoyed all the luxuries, pleasures and status imaginable; the world would have been at her feet. Aasiya could not have wanted for anything: she was Queen of Egypt.

I admired Aasiya because she saw more than just the wealth and power around her. Despite the favour she held with Pharaoh, she knew that he was a tyrant and a murderer. She knew that he did not uphold justice or equality, and killed innocent people. Pharaoh said that he was God but she did not accept that. He was furious: how dare she disobey him! Instead, she followed her own heart towards the truth and did not blindly accept what her husband told her. She chose to believe in a Creator and Cherisher, One God. Her belief was that this Divine Being was the Truth, and all the principles that flowed from that truth – justice, equality, respect – were to be upheld to the best of her ability. So she confronted Pharaoh, and would not accept him and his despicable ways.

She prayed, asking for spiritual closeness to God who has no physical location: *I would like to be near you in heaven.*

Even though he loved her so much, Pharaoh's pride forced him to call for her execution because she was defying him with her belief that there was One God and that Pharaoh himself was not a deity. She should just enjoy being the Queen and not worry about the way he ruled the country. Pharaoh begged her to change her mind but she refused. What kind of wife would she be if she did not point out her husband's heinous errors? What kind of woman would she be if she did not offer her life in the path of truth and justice?

As I looked at the huge buildings around me, my respect for Aasiya grew. She was Queen of all Egypt, Queen of the Pyramids. She could have had anything. But she chose to challenge the most powerful man of her time and gave away her love, her life and her status to make a stand for humanity.

We walked from one cavernous awe-inspiring room to the next, marvelling at the temples, crypts, baths and living quarters, dutifully ticking each one off our guidebook list. We gasped at the individual artistry of each site until the sun began to fall, the heat softened and the shadows grew.

The lights in the little cafés started to illuminate and sparkled romantically in the dusk. We were so wrapped up in laughing, admiring and revelling in the experience that we failed to notice how quickly night was setting in, and by the time we reached the gates it was dark. The local men had gathered in the cafés to relax after their hard day. Once all the visitors had left, their true personalities unfolded and the atmosphere changed. It was a glimpse of local life rather than the Disneyesque charade that they put on to meet tourist expectations. We loitered, chatting to them as we sipped our drinks.

'You won't find any way out of Petra at this time,' they told us. 'You can stay here if you like, and then leave in the morning.'

Tourists were not permitted to stay in Petra. The locals knew this. At their invitation, though, we could enjoy something that no other visitors could experience. A moonlit night in Petra sounded adventurous and romantic!

'Try these pastries,' they said. 'Do you want some tea?'

We shook our heads, deep in discussion about whether to take up this exciting one-time-only offer. Not only would it be an extraordinary experience, it would also save us the trouble of finding transport to our next destination at this time of night. Petra was too far from any town to be able to find a taxi or bus.

There was much rapid whispering between the four of us. We kept our voices low for privacy, but those serving the tourist industry are remarkably adept and seemed to be able to follow conversations in all languages, even when whispered or mumbled. Their faces changed expressions each time we raised a new idea about the merits of staying. We all turned abruptly back to face them and said, *OK!*

There was a look of astonishment on the men's faces. Since all four of us wore headscarves, we were a group of women who were obviously Muslim. And we had agreed to spend the night in Petra. Big smiles spread over their faces and they licked their lips.

'Well then,' they grinned, 'we will certainly enjoy ourselves tonight.' They burst out laughing.

At that moment we knew what we had to do. It was one thing to be adventurous, independent and daring, another to be reckless of our safety. The four of us turned to look at each other and then swivelled back to face the men. 'No thanks!' We reversed our decision in chorus, and then turned on our heels, running out of the gates and up the hill.

The next morning, we piled into the back of a pick-up truck for a tour of the Jordanian desert. We sat out in the open under the increasingly fiery sun. Sara and I sat opposite two English boys and a French girl. The two pasty-faced boys were at the start of a pan-Arabian tour. They wore baseball caps, loose T-shirts and baggy shorts to protect their as yet untanned skin. The French girl was also about our age, wearing shorts and a low-cut vest. Sara and I wore our usual linen trousers, long sleeved shirts and white scarves. There wasn't much conversation as the truck bumped through the desert, stopping every so often so we could look at the bizarre rock formations. We took numerous photos and then oohed and ahhed at these incredible alien creations of the endless dunes and seas of sand.

The French girl, Anne, eventually spoke. 'Aren't you hot wearing those scarves on your heads?'

'It's better to wear them in this heat than not, you'll get sunstroke without one,' said Sara, pointing to the two boys whose baseball caps were covering their heads and casting shade over their faces.

'But there is no-one here to make you wear it,' continued Anne.

'No-one is making us do it,' I responded. 'It's our choice.'

Anne got cross. Choice was not something that Muslim women were supposed to exercise. 'You Muslims are always proselytising.'

I'd never heard the word before but luckily Sara stepped in. 'We're not asking anyone else to cover up.' Then she repeated, 'it's our choice to cover ourselves.'

Both Sara and I had to bite our tongues. It seemed futile to point out that in a country where modest clothing was prevalent as part of the culture, and also a requirement to protect yourself from the heat, that revealing attire was bound to attract attention.

'You people are backward, living in the Middle Ages, with a religion of ignorant Arabs. You should get educated and learn some proper values like we have developed in Europe.'

I smiled at her bare-faced emotion, impressed that she had cut to the chase so speedily. At least she wasn't hiding her true, pernicious feelings.

'Sara,' I turned to face her, 'did you not study "enlightened" European teachings whilst you were at Oxford? I thought you won a first for your essay on the rationalist thinkers?'

Sara switched into perfect French to carry on the conversation and I followed her lead. 'I'm not an Arab, are you, Shelina?' she teased me.

I switched back into a posh English accent. 'I'm a European, aren't you, Sara? I was born in London and have lived there all my life.' I paused. 'Apart from when I studied at Oxford.' Whilst I had deliberately hidden this information from suitors who I did not want to judge me, I used it for precisely that purpose in this case.

Anne was not to be outmanoeuvred. 'You Muslim women are oppressed, forced to cover up and not express yourselves. You have to stay at home and men run everything.'

I pulled out my mobile phone. 'Sara, could you call your husband . . . oh no, that's right, you don't have a husband. Let's call mine. Oh! I don't have one either.'

'Let's call your dad,' she countered. She held the phone to her ear. 'Is that Shelina's father? Yes, yes. I was just calling to check. She is oppressed, isn't she? Yes, yes, understand. You forced her to suggest that she goes travelling on her own to show her how repressed and subjugated she is. Yes, yes, it makes complete sense. And yes, of course you insisted that she should be unaccompanied.'

My intertangled insecurities still reared their head at times like this. I fumed defiantly beneath the scorching sun. How dare she suggest we were oppressed: we were educated at one of the most prestigious universities in the world, we spoke probably ten languages between us, had read a wide variety of literature from numerous cultures and languages, and had also travelled through many countries. Here we were, right in front of Anne, travelling unaccompanied in the Middle East, of our own choice. Surely no-one could count us as oppressed? She looked at us as though we were duck droppings. 'You only think you are free but they are still controlling you women. Stop kidding yourselves. Muslims are evil and Islam is a religion of barbaric people who threaten to kill people who don't become Muslims.'

Muslims would typically respond to someone like Anne with the statement: 'Muslims were discovering the laws of alchemy and algebra and laying the foundations of modern science and philosophy and the European renaissance whilst your ancestors were still in the dark ages, wearing loincloths.' But we could no longer be bothered to point this out to her, nor highlight the absurdity of her passion to travel through the Middle East if she thought it had nothing to offer and was only full of barbarians. She was obviously not in the mood for listening.

Sara and I drifted into thought about whether people like Anne would ever really hear what Muslims said, even when faced with real Muslims who could converse directly with them and wanted to engage, discuss, create connections and perhaps agree to disagree. We discovered that Anne had never met a European Muslim before and her views were based entirely on what she read in the papers and saw on television.

It had never occurred to her that we had *chosen* to be Muslim. Yes, we had been born into Muslim families. Yes, we might never know the answer to the question, 'Would you have become a Muslim if you weren't born one?', because that was an existential question that was impossible to answer. What we were sure of was that we had made a conscious decision to be practising Muslims. Many others who were born Muslims had not done so, and saw being Muslim only as part of their culture and heritage.

We felt our free will choice was a response to the needs of our subconscious and gave us a clearer understanding of our conscience. We believed Islam held simple answers to the big questions of being a human being. It started from a very basic premise: that there was no god. Nothing. Except one unified divine entity. Some called it Nirvana. Some called it Enlightenment. Some named it Truth, or Justice, Yahweh, God or Love. As a Muslim, the Divine Being had all these names but was most commonly called *Allah*.

Finding the divine inside ourselves was the journey we all had to go on. That meant connecting to the Creator. It also meant making the world a better place for the people who lived in it by working towards what all human beings cherished: equality, justice, love, harmony. We believed that Islam outlined a strong way to reach those universal goals. We had chosen Islam because we felt it made us free as human beings. We had chosen to be Muslims, not blindly, but because to us it made sense.

*

The desert in Jordan was a haunt of Lawrence of Arabia. The strange rock formations that we had seen scattered through the harsh golden sands created an eerie, indomitable vastness that seemed to stretch to infinity. The land was mirrored by the most expansive sky I had ever seen. We spent the hot nights there camping in the open air beneath the sparkling stars. I would like to claim to have chosen to sleep *al fresco*, but as a beautifully turned-out city girl this was not something I did by choice. All the beds were booked up. Camping it was.

I reconciled myself to this hardship by imagining I was an Arabian princess. I sketched out my character: dark windswept hair, kohl-rimmed eyes, hidden in my little curtain-covered camel-top seat. I smiled at how nineteenth-century European depictions of Arabian beauties had endured so strongly over time and had even seeped into my own imagination. I could be Princess Jasmine for a few days, I told myself. I wondered where my Aladdin was. My princess fantasy was short-lived.

'Make sure you are properly covered,' cautioned the receptionist, 'there are a lot of mosquitoes out there.' She was pointing out into the dark horizon but there wasn't anything there to see. I squinted in confusion in the indicated direction. After a moment's silence on my part, she cackled.

'*Habibti*, my dear, you have to just sleep in the middle, wherever you want,' she scoffed.

'Just check there are no nasty insects. Better to pick a place with less rocks in the ground, saves on the back pain in the morning.' She arched her body out and then stretched her arms to emphasise her words. 'Don't worry, take it easy. At least it's free to sleep here.'

Sara and I grabbed our rucksacks and walked back towards the open expanse. In the distance I could hear a bass beat. *Dum, dum, doof, doof.* We were drawn to the sound, and walked over, mesmerised by the pounding rhythm radiating invisibly out of the blackness.

Sara fell about laughing, pointing at an enormous luminous rectangle that had just come into view. Here, in the quiet Arab desert where our urban lives with their constant saturation of light, sound and people were a distant memory, was a colossal screen playing a blockbuster Bollywood movie. Despite our Arabian setting, all the songs and conversation were in Hindi with Arabic subtitles. When the dancing sequences appeared, the shoulders and hands of the engrossed audience twitched up and down, synchronised with the movements of the actors.

We walked on and eventually found some open space at a good distance from others who had already set up camp for the night. We pulled out our mosquito nets and the multi-purpose sheets we always carried with us. These were useful as picnic cloths, to sleep on, in or under; we used them as prayer mats or for wrapping ourselves up in when it got cold; in desperate times they even served as towels. We created individual cocoons, protecting ourselves from the infectious flying beasts that were out to suck our blood. And then, exhausted from the day, we lay back in silence.

Instead of closing my eyes, I opened them. There, in the beautiful midnight sapphire sky, sparkled a kaleidoscope of stars. I had never in my life seen so very many twinkling lights, shining in their glory, undimmed by competition. There was no urban light for an unimaginable distance around, and even the nearest city was the relatively tiny city of Amman, the capital of Jordan. The moon sat at a different angle from that which I was used to. The British crescent rested at an angle facing diagonally upwards. Here the moon hung like a smug silver smile, with its complimentary star like a kitten's nose. The horizontal moon and star were the symbol of Islam. They had adorned countless books, political movements, flags, websites, Eid cards and posters. Seeing them with my own eyes was a reality I had never experienced before.

For an hour, all I did was stare. Stare and stare. The stars were not scattered erratically as they seemed to be in London, but they were thick, dense, palpable. Not something out of fairytales and distant dreams, but present, here, part of our lives. The way the stars dominated the desert night, it did not surprise me that Muslims had invented world-leading instruments for navigation and astronomy. The history of mediaeval life, travel and destiny being governed by the stars suddenly felt meaningful and real.

I want to come here on my honeymoon, and sit with my sweetheart beneath these stars.

The spell of the sublime was broken. Why had romantic love intruded into this realm of experience? These minutes should have been mine and mine alone, where only my breath and the heartbeat of the milky starlight should have existed. Where had this misfit thought about finding and loving a man appeared from and spoilt this moment between myself and the universe? This moment was not part of the rush to find the special someone; it was not part of the world of introductions, matchmakers, Aunties, shy smiles and fluttering eyelashes. This moment was an escape from the superficialities of work, clothes, social whirl, shopping, giggling, worrying, planning, stress, tears. Only hope and love remained from that old life in London, which now seemed a distant memory.

The innate sense of love and hope were inseparable. I don't know what I hoped for. Was love, romantic love, mythical epic love, my objective? Would that fill me up as a human being? I don't think I even knew to ask that question as I lay on the sand, staring up at the stars. I hoped. I hoped to find meaning, to find out who I was and what I was supposed to do. And in the thought about my honeymoon I had crystallised the idea that love was what I hoped for deepest in my heart. The one that I was searching for would find some connection here. The stars on their own were not enough. The man alone would not suffice. There was something in the combination of the two that would create sparks. This was the search for love. It was not the one-dimensional search for a tall, dark, romantic heart-throb. Nor was it the mono-focus devotion of the ascetic, of the monk or the nun.

The two searches – for the love of a partner and for the love of the Sublime – these two loves ran intertwined. I didn't have the words to explain this, but only later would I understand that these were the same search, the same love, which could not exist or be nurtured or thrive on their own. That is why romantic love seems so fulfilling to start with, because it reaches for another, deeper love. And that is why romantic love feels so empty as it runs its course unless it is replaced by a more profound long-lasting love.

Romantic love was a stepping stone in that paradigm, the love of a Prince Charming. I wholeheartedly believed he was out there. Of course he was. For without him, what was life? What did love mean, if there was no-one to love? To find a man, fall in love and live happily ever after was a simple formula. Wasn't this what people dreamt of? Perhaps as young women we could describe it better and feel confident to articulate it, and we would not be laughed at for our sentimentality; but I knew that men wanted this too.

I wanted a soul-mate who tapped into my spirit and through whom my soul would grow, would learn about Love, with a capital L, and be part of that Love. It was only much later that I discovered the idea of yin and yang, which explained how a man and woman were only halves on their own and could only be whole together. I had sat through innumerable lectures and seminars at the mosque, as well as countless weddings where the theme was always about romantic human love being part of the love for the Creator, but it hadn't sunk in until now. The desert landscape reflected the sky. The desert needed the sky and the sky needed the desert, but they both had to be what they were themselves and not try to be the other. The two extraordinary horizons merging together made it clear: each was beautiful in its own existence, but when connected together, they created a new holistic meaning.

Lying under the stars was the first time the seeds of sublime love were laid in my heart and that the very principles of my faith as a Muslim seemed to take root. I'd heard the words 'love comes after marriage' so many times and in so many ways, but it was this spectacular moment that illuminated the meaning of how the search for love of the Divine could help me find the love I was looking for in a man. My faith was trying to tell me that if I found love for Him, that would create the love I searched for in a person.

'And one of His signs is that He created pairs for you from amongst yourselves, so that you find peace in each other, and He puts love and mercy between you.' I could hear these words from the *Qur'an* being sung deep in my heart. These words always made me shiver. I yearned for this pair of mine, and to experience this new and unknown kind of love and kindness. I didn't yet understand the idea of balance and partnership, of harmony. I thirsted for these things. But what was mirage and what was real? I had been given a cookie-cutter description of love in order to find it. I was the same as all the women I knew, Muslim and otherwise. But we weren't satisfied with the relationships we found, instead suffering malaise and discontent, finding that romantic love was not enough.

I thought about how the *Qur'an* describes the sun, the moon and the stars. Each one follows its own course, not outstripping the other. And the *Qur'an* described how everything comes in a pair: day and night, earth and sky, light and dark. Human beings were no different. The stars twinkled in contentment, at peace, knowing their place. I smiled. It was rare to see that in the world I lived in. One of the stars was particularly piercing. I couldn't yet decode the sign that it held for me but I would one day understand its gift.

I mused again on the words, 'He created a pair for you.'

I was ready.

The 3 Ms of Love:
Method, Manner, Meaning

He was tall, but not too tall. And handsome, too, with features that were chiselled but not harsh. His hair was cropped and dark brown, ruffled haphazardly with the hands of a quiet genius. His small goatee beard framed his face along with metal-rimmed glasses that he took off every so often to expose his chocolate-brown eyes. They revealed his thoughtfulness and offered the perfect setting for his rare but infectious smile.

His dress sense was stylish but understated, hard to describe in detail, as each garment blended into the other, underlining his good looks but not outstripping them. He had studied engineering at Cambridge; he 'put his head down and got on with it' as he had described it, in order to get a first. He was good friends with a family friend, existing discreetly and anonymously all this time in our extended social circle. He was hugely passionate about Islam, devouring books on philosophy, meditation, prayer, wisdom, dialectic. He reflected, pondered, smiled. His name was *Mohamed*, the chosen one, *Habib*, the beloved.

We met at the fifth birthday party of a family friend's daughter. She was wearing a pink sequinned dress with three frills, her face painted like a butterfly. I saw him early on. He oozed charm and gentility. He was engaged in discussion with another man with similar dark hair and glasses. They sat facing each other on the corner of a dining table, tête-à-tête, eye to eye, their hands clutching heavyweight Denby mugs filled with philosophical black coffee, a plate of raspberry frosted cake untouched in front of them. They were discussing *sayr wa suluk* and pondering on the spiritual trajectory of the wayfarer on the path of the Divine. *Whoosh!* Past the end of my nose and skimming over the top of my headscarf. I had never heard the word 'wayfarer' before.

'I have been studying the inner meaning of the *qiyam* at the beginning of prayer for the last three months. The more I study, the more is revealed, the more questions I have,' said the other to Mohamed. Each ritual prayer begins with the standing position of *qiyam*, straight and still, facing the direction of *qiblah* towards Mecca. I stood this way every day many times, sombre and completely still, before bowing and prostrating. What was there about this action that could take three months to ponder?

'I'm still studying the first lines of the *adhaan*,' responded Mohamed Habib. *Adhaan* is the call to prayer, which could be sung out to call a group of people to prayer or for an individual alone to engage in their daily ritual of prayer, the *salat*. What was there to study in a single line?

I wondered what layers of meaning hid beneath the simple and straightforward opening words of the *adhaan*, 'God is Greater, Allah is Greater'. I wanted to interject in their conversation and ask what was concealed underneath the apparent meaning of this phrase.

I had always been given a simple and compelling explanation for this most central of Islamic statements, 'God is Greater'. I could still hear the voice of the Imam explaining it: 'God is Greater than anything you can imagine. The Divine is All-Present, All-Eternal, All-Existing, All-Merciful, All-Just. Imagine anything and Allah is Greater, because anything you can imagine is imaginable only within the limits of your mind. God created mind. The Divine created your imagination.'

Up to this point, there was an echo with St Anselm's proof of God. Anselm had suggested that God must exist because God was perfect, and a quality of perfection is existence so, *piff paff pooff*! God must exist. I liked this proof of God because of its logical neatness. Its elegance always made me laugh. I wasn't sure I should laugh about a proof of God's existence.

Despite the graceful rhetoric of this proof, it was too limited, because even imagining the Sublime in this way was limited. The word

'God' also felt too narrow, because the word itself was so loaded with meaning already.

'You cannot understand the "how" of God, because God created "howness". You cannot comprehend "what" about God, because God created "whatness". You cannot understand "why" of God, because God created "whyness".' These were the words of the son-in-law of the Prophet Muhammad, whose spiritual insights left an enormous heritage in Islam for mystical experience and wisdom. God was not limited and could not be comprehended within the constraints of the mind. But at the same time Islamic wisdom stated the following: 'God cannot be contained anywhere in the universe, except in the heart of the believer.'

Simply overhearing this conversation about unwrapping layers of hidden meaning started to challenge my assumptions that I was a knowledgeable, practising Muslim.

At that moment, the parents of the birthday girl appeared and introduced me to the two men whom I had been pretending not to listen to. I smiled nervously as I was told that their names were Mohamed and Yasir. Yasir wore a wedding band. Mohamed did not. We exchanged platitudes about jobs, universities, birthday parties, and compared our acquaintances and families along the way. Mohamed was an accountant, having concluded that despite its reputation for tedium, accountancy had better long-term prospects for career and pay than if he had continued with the engineering he had studied at university.

'It allows me to concentrate on more *stimulating* and *important* things,' he said, more to Yasir than to me. He looked over at Yasir, encouraging him to rekindle their conversation. Mohamed was pleasant and polite but he looked thirstily again and again at Yasir as all of us continued to chat. I was called to cut the birthday cake, and the two of them resumed their conversation, intent and lost.

I forgot about Mohamed and I forgot about the conversation. Forgetting what is important can be easy.

*

I met Mohamed again a few months later, at an adult's birthday party. He was sitting alone as the group conversed, laughed and sipped tea. He looked absent, his shoulders hunched, a darkness in his eyes. He began by telling me that he had always been very focused on his studies, his job and most of all on his spiritual journey. Mohamed was the first man I had met whose career was a means to an end for him – to make sure he was well provided for so he could pursue his spiritual quest. Others spoke of balancing *deen*, religion, with *dunya*, the world we live in. Most people we knew saw *deen* and *dunya* as something that needed to be given equal value, and celebrated those who appeared to have reached an equilibrium.

Mohamed's words and actions seemed to reject striking a trade-off between the material and the spiritual life. They were not two separate things to him, rather material living *was* part of spiritual living, and he was bent on integrating the two so very tightly that they became the same thing.

Mohamed had been brought up on a teaching of Islam that was formal, traditional and well studied. Living the life of a good Muslim as explained at the mosques and by the Imams was his entire universe. It had held him in good stead and fashioned him into a good human being of whom his family and community could be proud. 'Upstanding citizen' would have been an apt description of him. Up to this point, I was very similar to him.

Then he had discovered that there was something more, something deeper hidden underneath what he had been taught. A new door had opened for him. Beneath the rules and founding principles of Islam that he knew, and the solid scholarship that had formed the basis of his knowledge and understanding, he had discovered a new layer of meaning. He explained that what he had found was built on the foundations he already had, but created a new paradigm: 'Like moving from Newtonian physics to Einstein's quantum theory.'

He changed topic abruptly. His expression became weary as he told me that in the last few months he had met a woman and had been swept away by her. 'I didn't expect it to happen, didn't think it could happen. I've been brought up very sensibly and I have lived a very sensible and moderate life. I had never felt the emotions that she made me feel. I wasn't supposed to have all those strong feelings. So quickly, so very quickly we knew that we were meant for each other. I proposed within weeks and she said "yes".' He didn't even lift his head, just stirred his tea mournfully. I wondered what could have gone wrong.

'I had already met her parents and she had met mine. We had done everything by the book. She was the perfect match, right family, right background, and I felt so much for her.' His stirring paused.

'And then one day she simply said that she wasn't interested anymore.' He looked at me haggard, like Majnoun roving the desert to find his beloved.

Majnoun was the man in the classic Eastern love story of Layla and Majnoun, an equivalent to Romeo and Juliet or Orpheus and Eurydice. His name was Qays, and as a child he fell in love with a girl at his school, Layla. They were from different tribes and were prevented from marrying by their families. He spent his whole life absorbed in his longing for her, and roamed the arid desert in despair at being separated from the one he loved. A wise man advised him to declare war on Layla's tribe in order to secure her, but her father arranged her marriage to another man. This pushed Qays further into madness, so he was given the name Majnoun, mad man, because to everyone else his commitment to Love was utterly crazy. When Layla's husband died, Majnoun was advised this time to pretend he was sane in order to secure her hand in marriage.

He replied, 'How can one who is in love, pretend not to be in love?'

Layla and Majnoun were only united in death when they were buried together.

Majnoun's story is the perilous tale of a lover who is utterly consumed by his search for love. He is devoted to Love itself. Is Layla the beloved of the story or is there a deeper meaning about Divine Love? Majnoun's love is the unattainable love for the Divine, which can only be reached when no longer held back by the body. Eric Clapton was just as moved as I was when he read the myth of Layla and Majnoun. He wrote his song 'Layla' about her. I wish he hadn't; it ruined the story for me.

Mohamed carried on talking about his heartbreak. 'She just said she didn't care anymore. How could that be? How could she have turned my life upside down by taking me out of my safe, solid existence, and then suddenly just walk away? She ripped out my whole being and for what? Why?'

He looked so vulnerable. Here he was heartbroken, like a child. He had experienced emotions that he had not known he could feel, and this had opened his eyes to dimensions of the universe that he had been unaware of. He was a Muslim who had been trying to walk the difficult path of being a moral spiritual person, which he called 'Islam'; and on this journey he had seen the possibility of someone completing him and allowing him to fly.

He was a good man, on a spiritual quest. Why had I not seen this so obviously before? His emotions touched me deeply. Despite all the chatter around us, a shrill voice inside my head demanded to know why I had been blind to the possibility of considering him as a suitor when I had first met him. I had noted his intelligence, his faith, his spirituality and, of course, his good looks, and yet I had walked away unmotivated to find out more about him. I could easily have asked my family to find out if there was a possibility of securing a meeting, a match. Safura and Moses popped into my head again, and how Safura had grabbed her opportunity and was confident enough to create a meeting herself. Instead, I'd only noticed Mohamed when he was already heartbroken and when all he wanted was a listener to hear his painful story.

Every so often, Mohamed and I would speak a few words to each other at the weddings and get-togethers of friends and family. I listened to his agonising but gradually diminishing pain. In return he explained slowly and in detail the spiritual quest of the seeker. I had already realised as I lay beneath the starry skies in Jordan that my pursuit of love was one significant part of my ultimate goal to find Love itself. I was the seeker, and I was determined to pursue this quest.

I stood firmly on that path as he described the journey towards Love. I had never felt as energised and moved as I did in those conversations. I felt free to be the very kernel of a human being that I always wanted to be. It was not him that I was mesmerised by, but the fact that all the information and book knowledge I had about Islam suddenly felt like it truly meant something in my real journey as a human being living in this world of ours.

He told me that some called this journey he was describing 'the path of *tasawwuf*'.

I asked him, 'Is that like being a Sufi?'

He smiled. 'It's very fashionable these days to be a Sufi. No-one is quite sure about the origin of this word. Some think it refers to the woollen clothes Sufis used to wear, some say it is about their dedication to purity.'

He paused to chuckle to himself. 'People think being a Sufi is all cool, hip mysticism, chilled out, easy-going, no rules.' He leaned forward. 'Sufis are the people who change the world. They understand how the journey of the spirit makes you live a life that is dedicated to making the world a better place.'

I was wide-eyed. 'Are you a Sufi?' I asked with surprise. Sufis did not always have a very good reputation amongst those within mainstream Islam, who saw them as giving the mystical experience more importance than the day-to-day rules of behaviour and actions like *salat*, prayers.

He laughed wisely, his eyes crinkling with affection. 'The name is not important in the search. We are all too obsessed with words, names, labels. In order to avoid all these complications, I prefer to call it *irfan*, which means spiritual knowledge. The ultimate goal of *irfan* is to gain *ma'arifah*, knowledge of the Divine. *Irfan* and *ma'arifah* come from the same meaning of "knowing".' As soon as he said the words, I knew that it was what I had been searching for all this time.

According to Mohamed, everything in relation to the Divine seemed to come in threes. The first thing to know about the universe was that every dimension was made up of three points – two extremes and one middle point of balance.

'Think about courage,' explained Mohamed. 'This is an excellent quality. Most people think of it as "good" and then say that it has an opposite, cowardice, and say that it is "bad". But courage is not part of a pair, it is part of a "three". At one end is indeed cowardice – the absence of courage, but at the other extreme is foolhardiness, an excess of courage to the point of madness. Courage is the middle path – the right balance of knowing yourself and your situation. When you set out on your path as a Muslim, you must know that your goal is to avoid extremes, and to be a human being of the *middle* path. This is called the *siratul mustaqeem*.'

Knowledge was also of three kinds. The first type was knowledge that you gained by what people told you, second-hand knowledge. That was the starting point for all of us: teachings from parents, school, lectures, books, conversation. Mohamed explained that this was comparatively weak, all just hearsay. It only gained weight based on the authority of the person delivering the message.

Then there was the knowledge of seeing with your own eyes. This was always much stronger knowledge – after all, seeing is believing. This was how most of us constructed our world. I thought about the authority given to those who were at the scene of an event. Those who saw something knew it for sure, while someone who only heard about it could never be completely certain.

'The ultimate level of certainty,' he went on, 'is the knowledge that you have tasted for yourself. No-one can ever persuade you away from something you have experienced yourself. And if you have experienced it, your knowledge carries the greatest weight of all. People respect knowledge that comes through experience: that is why they stop and listen to such individuals. Someone who speaks from experience creates a resonance that someone who speaks only from book knowledge will never achieve.'

I interjected, 'That's why we say "practise what you preach", because that is the only way to have an impact.' I wondered what my behaviour revealed about me. Did it reflect good manners and did it inspire others to the same?

'Exactly!' He threw his fist up passionately into a small air-punch. 'And that is why the Prophet Muhammad caused such a stir with his words. When he explained the importance of good manners, kindness and etiquette, people listened because he practised it himself. His behaviour was so exquisite, we're still listening today. More importantly, if you want to achieve *ma'arifah*, real knowledge of Love, then the Prophet's words have the greatest impact because he had seen the Divine for himself.' Seeing was not with the eyes, but the heart. That is why love underpinned all our experiences.

'In fact he had tasted it. He had experienced Love in its purest form himself, and that is the final stage of knowledge.'

I looked perplexed. This was all so complicated. And what was all this about 'tasting Divine love'?

My confusion was apparent, so he tried to explain. 'Imagine someone tells you that there is a fire in the next room.' I found out later that he was quoting this from a well-known philosophical example. 'You may believe them, you may not. What they have told you is the first level of knowledge.'

I nodded, understanding the idea of second-hand knowledge.

'Imagine if you walked into the room and saw the fire yourself, then you would know for sure that a fire is there. But imagine you actually sat in the fire, then you would have certainty of what fire is. You would have tasted and experienced it yourself.'

I gazed intently at him, slowly realising that simply knowing was not enough. That was far away from understanding the secrets of the universe – the secrets of Love that I had been searching for. I wanted to 'taste' it myself.

'These are like the three kinds of knowledge of the Divine. If you reach the truest heights of experience, you can be utterly lost in it. That is when you will reach the place that the "I" that you are, or the "I" that I am, is completely annihilated. You have reached a stage called *fanaa*. Once you go through that stage of getting rid of the separation between you and what is around you, you reach *baqaa*, the eternal remaining. That is the immortality that we all yearn for.' The elixir that so many myths had been written about to meet that human longing to live forever was right at our fingertips. But to get there, the journey that Mohamed was describing was at once passionate and perilous.

The verses echoed the statement that a person speaks when they declare that they want to become a Muslim. First, 'There is no god.' This is the nothing. 'Except the Divine.' This is the everything that remains after the material world we see around us.

I recalled some verses from a chapter called 'The Loving Compassionate One' from the *Qur'an*: 'Everything will end in nothing.' It was a stark and sobering truth that all human beings agreed upon. The verse continued: 'And the face of the One that cherishes will remain forever, full of majesty and honour.' Our souls would also remain forever as part of the One.

Mohamed continued to speak passionately. 'The arrogance of the "I" separates you from the Divine and puts veils between you. The bigger your ego – the more we all talk about our superiority as human beings – the further we recede from the secrets of the Divine and the universe. You have to remove the barriers between your heart and the Divine. Be Nothing in order to be reborn into everything.'

This was starting to veer into unnerving terrain. Be nothing? But the words made perfect sense. After all, wasn't getting close to the Creator a natural progression from believing in the Divine?

So I asked the question that critics of the mystical path raise: 'What about the rules?' I enquired. 'What of limits, guidance, laws and rituals? This is all embedded into our learning of Islam. You can't just abandon those for this goal of annihilation.'

He smiled. 'That is the misunderstanding that people have about belief and inner meaning. The idea of losing our pride and reaching this point of annihilating your inner demons is not about fluffy love and chanting.'

I raised my eyebrows in mock offence on behalf of those he appeared to dismiss so easily: 'Those people who follow the inner path are also trying to the best of their abilities to reach God.'

'But the inner is meaningless on its own,' he responded. 'In order to reach the point of "knowing", you have to be able to live in the physical world around you. You have to be in harmony with the environment and with other human beings. That is what is meant by being a balanced human being. To do that you need to follow rules of behaviour and laws, otherwise how can you live peacefully with other people?'

I nodded in agreement. It was true that by interacting with others, you learnt how to be a better person.

'You need law, compassion and love.' We were back to the threes, I smiled to myself.

'There are three paths,' he explained. This time I laughed out loud at his numbering.

He looked up at me, surprised that I found humour here but pleased that I was paying such close attention.

'The first is *shari'ah*, a word thrown around in all discussions about

Islam but without people really understanding what it means. *Shari'ah* is not something vulgar that means chopping off hands and locking up women.'

He was right. I was always deeply hurt when *shari'ah* law was described in a category along with mediaeval horror stories. It was used lazily as verbal shorthand for 'backward' Islam. In day-to-day parlance *shari'ah* was used to refer to the legal code that was used in local law and which jurists spent many years studying, just as they might study British law in universities and at the Bar. Such local law varied across the Muslim world due to the different interpretations that scholars placed on the sources of law, as well as the different perspectives and needs that their cultures required.

'None of this is the *shari'ah* that we are concerned with at the moment,' Mohamed pointed out. 'On the big picture scale, *shar'iah* means the principles on which the universe is organised, the Divine code. It's how the whole amazing world around us works, and the physical as well as spiritual laws that make it all hang together.'

'So would a commonsense law like "what goes around comes around" be part of *shari'ah*?' I asked him.

'Yes, of course. It is also a commonsense rule that "one good deed leads to another". It's one of the rules of the world we live in. How the universe operates and stays balanced: that is *shari'ah*. And when Muslims say they want to live by *shari'ah*, it just means following the "outer" code so that you are in harmony with everything around you.'

This made it quite clear – *shari'ah* offered guidelines for yourself as well as for managing your interactions with others. It prescribed how to look after your own body in the best possible way. The idea of eating only meat that was *halal* meant eating good wholesome food. Fasting helped you to keep in shape and detox. Not drinking alcohol kept your body healthy. Not being intoxicated allowed you to see clearly and be in control of your actions at all times, all the while being able to have a direct clear-headed conversation with the Divine. *Shari'ah* also explained some things relevant to personal life as a Muslim: how to pray, how to marry, how to fast. Finally, *shari'ah* regulated how you lived with other people: not stealing or killing, trying to fight for equality and justice, treating people well, observing your duties and responsibilities to the people and environment around you.

Mohamed then put into words one of the great challenges for people of faith: 'The hardest thing about *shar'iah* is the basic idea of working towards justice and equality. That is the whole point of the rules. People just think it's about the rituals, but that is one element that builds up into the greater outer code. Muslims seem so obsessed with the details that they forget the point of observing the details: to reach the final goal of a just society and happy human beings.'

I was tiring of this obsession with rules. I had followed a lot of rules, but how would they offer me freedom? As though reading my thoughts, Mohamed said, '*Shari'ah* is only the stepping stone to *tariqah*, the *way* you do things. It's not enough to stick to the letter of the law: you have to apply its spirit too. That is why kindness and compassion are so critical.'

This reminded me of Karim and his lightning story. He could have just told me that he wasn't interested rather than spinning me along and then suggesting his preposterous story that lightning had intervened. Or Khalil, who had rejected me before we'd even met because I was too short but wanted to meet me anyway; and then took my money from me.

It was easy to forget that along with what you do, it is *how* you do it that is important. It is the difference between following the rules begrudgingly and softening life with a smile, a small kindness, generosity, compassion. If you fulfilled your duties by the book, you had only observed the method, the *shari'ah*. *Tariqah* was the manner in which you carried out your responsibilities. *Tariqah* was doing things in the best way possible.

Mohamed became most alive and passionate when we spoke about the third way: *haqiqah*.

His eyes lit up. 'This is when you truly know the Truth. You can taste the Divine and witness it. This is the inner path, where the soul has already been freed by following the *shari'ah* and the *tariqah*, and now it can soar into the arms of the Beloved.'

Beloved? Who spoke about God as the Beloved? It sounded very romantic, but maybe that was the idea. There were many names to describe God. God was Just, Compassionate, Merciful. God was Beauty, Majesty and Life. I agreed that he was also Love. But really, who used an affectionate name like Beloved?

Mohamed then told me something that I had heard thousands of times before, but this time it changed my life. 'Allah says that He created the human being in order to be *known*. To be known requires someone or something to do the knowing.' He paused to let this sink in. 'Allah also says that He created the human being in order to be *loved*. To be loved requires someone or something to do the loving.' I waited, wanting to hear how it all came together. 'For God to be known, to be loved, someone or something has to *do the loving* and *do the knowing* of the Creator. Human beings are the best of all creatures, and they exist to know and love the Divine. We've been created for the very simple and single purpose: to love.'

I had found my place, my meaning. I now understood how my search for the one, my Prince Charming, made sense as part of my search for the One, the Beloved. I was a human being who was made to Love, we all were.

Through all the searching we did in our modern lives, through films, music, books, arts, life and dreams, we were all looking for the same thing, whether it had a human, Hollywood or Divine face. It was a sense of completion that came from being in balance with our surroundings. It came from giving love and being loved.

Every human being has a yearning for a partner, a companion, a lover. For what is a heart without someone to love it? What is life without someone to share it with? And that is why I knew, with certainty, that I would find the one. I knew that my heart was fashioned from the intricacies of love, and I had plenty of love to give. All I had to do was find him. What I hadn't known until now was that this cry inside for love, for him, was also a search for Love and for Him.

Love is the Divine principle, and to Love is to Know. That is why the human heart can contain the secrets of the universe.

Quantum Theory

Searching for a husband had distracted me from exploring my own inner world. As a human being my focus should have been on making my spirit blossom. Finding a companion and getting married was part of that journey towards flourishing as a person: that was the Islamic thinking behind marriage. But I had focused too much on the outer search for Mr Right, convinced that this was the best way to fulfil my responsibilities. As a result I had put my inner life and spiritual development on hold. The conversations with Mohamed had ended all of that, and I had made a quantum jump in the journey of discovery.

Slowly, I began to truly live my life once I realised that my companion and my faith were intertwined. I still had value as a human being without him, and I could keep learning and growing as an individual. He would appear when I was ready, and we would begin a journey together, hand in hand. Unshackled from the ideas held erroneously in my mind, I gradually started to open my heart to the potential of life around me.

Talking to Mohamed helped me to open these doors that had stood in front of me for many years. He unlocked a different kind of freedom for me, inner freedom. I did not want to marry him because of the gratitude of a student for a teacher or because of a crush on someone sharing knowledge. Instead, I felt that this was a man I could go on a spiritual journey with. He would be able to take care of me materially and spiritually. The more I spoke to him, the more certain I became that this was a man with whom I could spend the rest of my life.

Little by little, he was recovering from his heartbreak, yet I felt too nervous to broach the subject of my idea with him. My parents had known about him all along, and in any other circumstance I would have asked them to take the formal route of approaching his family through a matchmaker. Given his delicate situation, we all felt that he might feel cornered if his family was involved.

I confided in Jack at work, and asked his advice. 'You can help me, you're a man, just like Mohamed,' I pointed out to him. 'What should I do?'

I explained to him that Mohamed had asked his friends to start on the process of introducing him to women with a view to getting married. After his meetings with them, Mohamed would lament to me how the women were wrong for him, picking out their flaws one by one. But he never asked me if I would like to consider him. I waited, hoping.

I consoled myself with the fact that he was still emotionally vulnerable and that he would have rejected me for the same reason he rejected all the other women: because he wasn't ready. He felt that the more women he was introduced to, the more quickly he would recover from his loss. This made me angry. These women were meeting him with hope and open hearts, and he was using them to provide solace for his pain. I should have taken note.

Jack listened carefully and then paused dramatically before he delivered his opinion: 'If you really like him and you think that he is the right husband for you, then you should tell him.'

'But it's obvious that he doesn't like me, otherwise he would have said!' I wailed.

'Would he? Maybe he feels just like you and is scared to say anything.'

I pouted. Jack continued. 'Think about it like this. If you want a job or a house, you'll go after it, won't you? Think about how much effort people put into their careers. On the other hand, when it comes to their personal lives – and, after all, a partner is the most important part of your life – they are passive and just hope it "happens". You have to *make* it happen.'

I was surprised that his wisdom was so similar to that of the Aunties. I could hear their voices. 'Good men are hard to find, my dear, you need to grab him.' It was clear that their advice would also be to prioritise finding a partner above all else. Tradition and common sense were of the same opinion in this case.

I felt chastened. Even though I had followed the process for so many years, I hadn't yet understood the key universal principle behind it: to think clearly and rationally about how to pursue the right partner. I had let the ideas of all the traditions that I was part of dictate my behaviour. Notions from Hollywood to Bollywood that 'the man has to do it' and that 'it should just happen' had taken root inside me much deeper than I had imagined.

Despite my criticisms of those who upheld all these different traditions over what Islam was trying to teach, I found myself doing the same. I loved the story of Khadijah, the first and most beloved wife of the Prophet Muhammad sending someone to approach him directly to see if he would be interested in marrying her. Safura, too, had taken things into her own hands, asking her father to invite Moses into their home and into their business. I held up these empowered, independent and determined women as inspiration for Muslims, and yet I was falling short.

Jack explained that if I shared my feelings with Mohamed, it would not be an ultimatum, and I should not fear it as such. I realised that I could have the same conversation with Mohamed that I had in introductions with other men. It would be the beginning of a discussion about whether we could see ourselves as a married couple. I had been through so many of them already, I should not be scared. If I really believed that Mohamed was the one, I had to grab this chance to talk to him about the possibility of spending our lives together.

I had been through so much, met so many different suitors, worked with the process, rejected culture and then found my own place in it again. I had learnt about what love was and what love could be. If I did not take this opportunity, I would let myself down. I decided that I would not abandon the journey that had brought me to this point. I had learnt too much about myself to do that.

Over coffee, Mohamed and I chatted aimlessly about work, mosques, literature, art, holidays, food. And then, in a quiet moment as we sipped our drinks, I told him.

'I like you.'

He squinted curiously at me.

'I just thought I should tell you, you know . . .' I stuttered, not sure what to say next.

Be brave, I told myself, *you've come this far*.

'And I was wondering . . .' I lost the nerve to ask him directly if he liked me too. My voice deserted me at that moment, absent without leave. I managed to croak, 'I was wondering what you thought about that.'

There, I had said it. I picked up my cup and hid my face in the dark, opaque liquid. It felt very quiet in the room.

His silence continued. At first, I thought it was because I had made such an unexpected statement. Perhaps he was reflecting on what I had said, perhaps my words had stirred emotions that he had hidden deep inside. He still said nothing. Now that he had reflected, he might be crafting his words to express the depth of his feelings. I started to feel uncomfortable. Surely his feelings couldn't be that majestic and ponderous that he needed this much time to work out how to convey them to me?

I fidgeted, wanting to break the silence. But that would mean I would have to reiterate what I had just said – which would exacerbate the silence further – or I would have to change the subject. I had expended so much energy and bravery to make him this offering of my feelings that I would just wait to see what he said. I would not change the subject now.

I should have known that the silence was foreboding. But I wanted to hear it, to know for sure. A rejection would hurt but at least I would go away in the knowledge I had tried. I would have to find a way to recover from having been so close to the husband I had been searching for and then being turned away.

Being brave enough to ask him about his feelings openly was about to pay off, because his response revealed more to me about his emotional state than years of marriage could have uncovered. As I had learnt, people reveal their true character at times of intense emotional duress.

His answer was even better, even more informative, than I could have expected. It showed me his obliviousness to my bravery and vulnerability, and that made it starkly obvious that he wasn't as suitable for me as the life-companion I had hoped him to be.

The answer was worse than I had anticipated. Not only did he crush my feelings, but he did it without respect or grace.

'Shelina,' he said, looking at his coffee, 'I am a scientist. I have just discovered that Einstein's theory of relativity might not be true. This has turned my world upside down and I can think of nothing else at all. Nothing. I'm consumed.' And with that he continued sipping his coffee.

EIGHT

Multiversal

View from the Shelf

PITY

The Aunties started to feel sorry for me. '*Such* a nice girl,' they would exclaim. '*So* well-mannered.'

'I *can't* understand *why* she isn't married,' said one to the other, emphasising the words.

I expected them to lay the blame at my door for not marrying earlier or for not choosing one of the inappropriate men that had been *recommended*. I italicised the words in my own head for irony. Instead, the Aunties surprised me.

'So *pretty*, so intelligent, so lovely and *religious*, I just can't *imagine* who could be *right* for her,' sighed the other in return.

I was unnerved by their compassion. Had they forgotten their complicity in the tortuousness of my search? Or had they too been on a journey of their own?

They turned their heads to face me whenever I appeared and then stroked my hair lovingly.

'When you find the right person, then you'll know it has been worth waiting for,' they consoled me. 'You're still young and so pretty, plenty of time! A man would be *crazy* not to want to marry you.'

I felt tearful. I felt that I had achieved so much: education, independence, career, travel. Through all of it I had retained a close relationship with my family, my community and my faith. Like many other single Muslim women, I had negotiated the complexities of growing up in a new environment, of wanting to excel in education and career, and of keeping my respect for the importance of ethnicity, faith and identity. I was at once 'independent' and 'community-minded', 'modern' and 'traditional'. In short, I had earned the Aunties' respect.

Whether their words were hurtful or compassionate, the Aunties still pointed to that one thing I wanted most – companionship. For them, a husband had secured them social status and perpetuated tradition. The structure of marriage had worked for them and they had found their place through it.

There was something about marriage that they had only begun at this late stage to explain clearly and which I wished that they had spelt out from the start: the satisfaction of having Someone To Be With. My parents echoed their sentiments: 'We just want you to have someone of your own so you can have some company, someone to go out, someone to do things with.'

They were right. I had already done all the things I wanted to do on my own. I hadn't let expectations, gossip or stereotyping hold me back. I had discovered that I could do all the things that I wanted to do on my own. I just didn't *want* to do them on my own anymore. The experiences would be richer and more meaningful if I had someone to share them with. Once I wanted Prince Charming. I still did, but now Cosy Companion would have sufficed, someone to spend time with, to move on in life with, someone, anyone, *anyone at all?*

Auntie Jee: We must find someone for Shelina.

Auntie Aitch: What about that nice doctor? What is he called? Something beginning with 'Muh'. Is it Mehdi? Masood? Malik?

Auntie Jee: Maazin?

Auntie Aitch: No, no, let me think . . .

Auntie Jee: Muna?

Auntie Aitch: No, not Musa, not Munir.

Auntie Jee: Malcolm?

Auntie Aitch: Malcolm? Who is Malcolm?

Auntie Jee: Sabin's son. You know they were very modern when the kids were born, called them all sorts of things. Now she is more religious than the Maulana himself! Do you mean Mahbub?

Auntie Aitch: Yes, yes, that's it! Mahbub!

Auntie Jee: But he is almost 50 years old! Much too old! And previously divorced with three children who live with him. *No, no, no!*

Not suitable. And you know there were terrible rumours about why his wife left him. Girlfriends, affairs, *drinking*.

Auntie Aitch: She can't be too picky you know, at her age, and having turned down so many very good boys. Fussy is as fussy gets. You know what they say about the fussy crow?

Auntie Jee emits a weary sigh of knowledge.

Auntie Aitch: The fussy crow turns his nose up at the rich pickings and ends up sitting on the pile of dung.

ANGER

Wherever I went I was looked at with sadness. The community couldn't understand why I had not been snapped up. In my head I played back the conversations I would like to have had with them.

'You said I was too educated to make a good wife . . .'

'You said that the boys wanted a younger girl . . .'

'You said I was too religious . . .'

'You said I wasn't religious enough . . .'

I felt angry and let down. To make matters worse, I was not the only woman on the shelf. It was a veritable riot up at this height.

The community had finally started to recognise that there were problems and that it was harder for people to find a suitable match. Although there were plenty of young unmarried women, there was still a mysterious lack of young men. Some really had disappeared. Others were continuing to go 'back home' to marry. This was their prerogative of course; the choice of a partner is an entirely personal matter. The consequence of their decision, though, was that the gaps they would have filled in making wonderful matches for women like me, based on compatibility, life experience, identity and our new British Muslim values and culture, remained vacant. Why did the men not feel the same way about what a good match we would make for them?

It seemed to me that the answer was that women had been forced to redefine themselves through the opportunities and experiences they had lived through. Femininity had changed and been updated by the challenges we had faced, and the outcome was stronger and more centred women. What appeared to be missing was the challenge to men to trigger them to update their own notions of masculinity. Instead of rising to the challenge, some of them now felt at worst threatened by the lively, energetic women who wanted a proactive spiritual and material life, or at best uninterested in them.

What we needed was a collective reassessment of what it meant to be a man and what it meant to be a woman, a new gender reconstruction going back to the very roots of Islam, where men and women were partners and companions rather than disjointed and dysfunctional. After all, as the *Qur'an* said, men and women were created in pairs. The gender constructs that we needed to operate as a fully functioning society – and that was within my own small community, as well as in wider society – had become blurred, or even lost, and that meant we had lost the ability to love each other for who we were.

Was the social pressure and pain that I and my friends had endured the price of being a pioneer and creating change? We had had no-one to point to as role models or leaders, but had to break the mould ourselves. Even some of the mosques and Imams needed changes: not only did young women need to be taught about relationships and marriage, but men, too, in order to redress the asymmetry of marriage and the search for a partner. What good was berating women for being single or for the growing divorce rate if men were not ready or did not have the skills to deal with being married?

The Community Leaders got together to discuss the issue. They agreed that there were huge problems around arranging suitable marriages and keeping them together. They agreed that they must get together again and discuss the problems. They reconvened and discussed that the problems were growing and that solving them was a community priority. After all, a community is made up from the building blocks of solid families. They planned out a series of seminars to brainstorm ideas and engage the community. The community duly held the meetings and agreed that the problem was now of significant magnitude and that Something Must Be Done. They concluded that it was important that young people should get married. They would discuss further with experts. The experts agreed that the situation was dire and that doing nothing was Not An Option. If nothing was done then things would go from bad to worse. Action was demanded. They would reconvene to discuss the matter.

SADNESS

My parents visited a number of local mosques to recruit help from the Imams, Shaikhs and Maulanas. In one of them, the gentle Shaikh pulled out a large tome from under the desk. It was an enormous binder, which he turned to face towards my parents, who were sitting on the opposite side of the desk. Each page contained a piece of A4 paper inside a clear plastic holder and listed the details of someone who was looking fervently enough for a partner to place an advert in the Big Book. It showed a photograph and then listed their biodata.

There were pages and pages of young men and women who were looking for a partner to complete themselves and their faith. It was a post-modern journal of community woe that captured both collective failure to secure happy marriages and individual angst in finding the One. The Shaikh suggested to my parents that I should create my own one-pager with a photo and then come into the mosque to review the binder with him, as he was Custodian of the Best of the Singles Book. I couldn't face the thought of putting an advert with a photo in the marriage catalogue for all to see. Should I have de-prioritised my pride in favour of finding a man? I realised from my reaction to the book that I still hadn't acknowledged in my heart that admitting that you were looking for a partner was perfectly acceptable.

Singledom was growing around me as well – women across wider society seemed to be suffering. We moped collectively at work. Emma was single. So were Elaine and Nicola. The men, peculiarly, were all married or in long-term relationships. Why suddenly this universal explosion of singleness?

To revel in our womanhood we would buy glossy women's magazines at lunch time and share the headlines, laughing at their larger than life claims and mourning at how they subtly pitied our status as single women.

Emma picked one up. 'We have to love ourselves before anyone else can love us,' she read out.

Elaine responded, 'So that means if we're single then we are *unloved*, and that means we are not even *ready* to be loved.' She paused. 'That's *awful*. I should just give up now.'

Nicola read out a whole series of commands from another magazine: 'Who needs a man?' 'Independent is best!' 'Live your own life!' 'If he isn't the one then move onto the next!'

'This is crazy, you ridiculous magazines,' I ranted at the glossy publications, 'we tried being single and we've decided we *do* want a man! We *can* be independent *and* in a relationship. What if there is no such thing as the One? Maybe we have to turn him *into* the One?'

I had always noticed that married men seemed more attractive to single women because they were more balanced, well-rounded and able to relate to women. Maybe this was precisely because they were married and had spent time with a woman in their lives? Maybe we should pick a man who had potential and hope that simply being married to him would turn him into Mr Right? As the Aunties said, it was like a river and the river bed moulding into each other over time to become a perfect fit.

Maybe my father, too, had been right all along. He had said to pick out a man with four out of the six qualities and then work on perfecting the rest later. It meant accepting that no-one is perfect, not even me.

'Maybe I'm being cynical,' began Emma, 'but perhaps the advertisers in the magazines *want* us to be single so that we spend our money on keeping ourselves all primped up because that is what the elusive Mr Right is looking for. But I have spent all my money and I still don't have a man!' Emma was letting her depression run amok.

Emma had had a good solid Germanic upbringing. 'Maybe they want to distract us away from being homely wives and we've fallen for it! Maybe they should be teaching us the old-fashioned habits of wifely budgeting and spending our pennies wisely on Tupperware and jam?'

We all giggled at the idea of attending Tupperware parties. 'I suppose they are not *quite* as glamorous and attractive as designer clothes,' Emma added.

Perhaps there was a happy medium the magazines hadn't recognised or didn't want to admit – that on the one hand we could be happily married to Mr-Nearly-Perfect, knowing that we were not perfect either, but at the same time we could also be stylish and glamorous. Most importantly, the magazines didn't offer us the possibility or aspiration to be contented. No wonder we felt constantly under pressure.

Emma turned the conversation to her failures at the weekend: 'I was a bridesmaid at a wedding and everyone was all loved up in couples. Apart from me. Even the Best Man was taken! What is *wrong* with me?'

Jackie responded, 'The only single men are the sleazy ones who have been dumped more times than a rubbish bin.' It was an awful analogy but we let it go – she looked too distraught. 'They all look like George from *Seinfeld*.'

We shuddered collectively in disgust and sympathy.

Elaine turned to me jealously: 'At least you have people trying to find someone for you.'

'It's true,' I agreed, 'It's hard enough trying to find a man when you have the world and their matchmaker-wife looking out for you and arranging meetings, I can't imagine how difficult it must be on your own.'

I turned my head away and blinked back tears. Whilst it was the case that my family had asked many people to help find a match for me, the introductions these days were rare. There was much nodding when we asked for help but little action, and the few suggestions were wildly unsuitable. I was forced to consider them because it seemed imperative to be grateful.

I met Arif, who had been living in Hungary on his own for the last ten years. He was now back to recruit a wife. He was in his early forties and had been ordered by his long-suffering mother that he was not permitted to remain single any longer and must marry and multiply *tout de suite*. He had struggled to get a job in the UK and instead had found a post as the financial director in a small investment firm based outside Budapest, in one of its outlying suburbs. Despite his decade of residence there he recounted proudly that he kept himself to himself and had no friends, had no idea where the local mosque or community was and didn't feel the need to spend time participating in Hungarian life or getting to know the locals. He saw himself living there long term and thought his wife would be happy to slot into his one-bedroom flat. Learning Hungarian, working or having a social life were not important factors in Arif's consideration of his wife's comforts.

At least Arif had all his own papers and citizenship. Nabeel was visiting from a small community in Kuwait in order to trade in his current passport for a British one. I was advised that this was advantageous for me – he wanted to meet someone and arrange a wedding quickly in order to secure his papers, which meant that I would not have to wait too much longer to secure my own visa into Marriedsville.

Asgar, Sadik and Jabir followed soon after, all *un*-visaed, *un*-jobbed and *un*suitable. Their expectations of a woman and wife – and of marriage – were completely different from mine. They had been brought up with a 'traditional' model of marriage from 'back home', and hadn't shared the strains of the new culture and challenges I had faced, leading to different expectations of social and family life. A wife was a wife and marriage was marriage as far as they were concerned, and the nature of the relationship and the expectations would be the same whatever the geography and culture. It's just that this one would have the advantage of a British passport.

I had never thought my best feature would be British citizenship. I wondered if my biodata had been reduced to *single female passport holder*.

SHAME

One of the kindly uncles slipped a piece of torn-off paper into my father's jacket after Friday prayers. He was discreet, checking that no-one was watching. It was important that no-one should see him passing on this information, nor see my father receiving it. 'Tell Shelina to have a look at it,' he whispered elusively to my father. 'We all want the best for her,' he added, and then swept out of the prayer hall and never turned to look back.

I unfurled the rough-edged scrap with my father in the privacy of our home. It had a website address on it. But this was no ordinary website, it was the address of a *marriage* website. At that time the internet was relatively new, untested and untrusted. There was general hysteria about the internet itself, and so a marriage website unreasonably carried a double shame. The uncle was a reliable source and had great stature in the community. This new cyber-option therefore came with authority and credibility, and my parents backed the idea of searching for a partner through the internet.

I visited the website, which listed over a thousand profiles. There were no names, only numbers. There was a huge amount of detail, an online Biodata Bank. You could search by age, country, city, even height, although the latter was still a very sore point. Then there was a freeform section to describe yourself and a further section to describe the person you were looking for.

I decided to conduct a search. I selected 'Female looking for male'.

I then picked a wide age-bracket, as I wanted to see what was out there. It was possible if I limited my parameters too strictly I might miss out on someone who was just one tiny step outside the boundaries of perfect. I chose 'United Kingdom' under country, leaving the city blank, and deliberately avoided choosing a height option.

The search returned a few hundred results. I should have felt elated at the pool of potential husbands who were just waiting for a cyber-bride. Instead I wilted beneath the weight of the profiles that I would have to trawl through one by one to see if they were a good match. I steeled myself for a long, arduous marathon facing the computer screen.

Reading through the profiles was surprisingly addictive. I read one, and then another, one more, just one more, and then just one more. I experienced a 'light-bulb moment': here was a captive pool of single Muslim men! But what kind of men were they? Was there something wrong with them if they were searching online? If I was about to put my own details onto the matrimonial site there were only two possibilities: I was normal, therefore they were normal too; or they were very strange and something was wrong with them, and so was I. I gave myself the benefit of the doubt and assumed we were all normal. It was also the most logical analysis in response to my doubt.

Some of the men had left the space for their descriptions completely blank. It seemed that they were not bothered enough to spend the time describing themselves or what they were looking for. I dismissed them immediately, as they weren't taking this process seriously. Others had written long essays. I studied these carefully. Some were prescriptive, some arrogant, some downright ludicrous. They reminded me of the wildly unrealistic and unbalanced matrimonial adverts we used to listen to on Sunrise Radio when I was a child. Sometimes the adverts were posted by the parents of the boy.

Every so often there would be a profile that looked appealing, both sensitive and sensible, and that reached out from the screen and touched me with its intelligence, humour and spirituality. I would clip the advert and add it to my list, but I was still hesitant to take things further and fully commit to cyber-searching.

Even at this point I felt that the internet search was a shameful secret. If I proceeded, I would need to expose myself and share some details. I would be anonymous but I would still be committed. I would need to share information about myself, and I fully expected people to deduce who I was and then propagate the knowledge that I was searching through the InterShame to find a man. Perhaps I felt that my urgent desire to be married had reduced my dignity and I wanted to hold onto as much of it as I could.

For a few weeks I watched proceedings from the sidelines. One day, one of the profiles caught my eye and I decided to take the plunge. He was about my age, lived in London and wrote an engaging description of himself that showed he was committed to finding someone but was not self-centred or arrogant. In order to send him a message I had to post my own profile, which I finally decided to do.

It was biodata hell all over again. This time I had the opportunity to capture my aspirations and myself in as many paragraphs as I wanted, and send it directly to the people out there who might be interested. I was also able to describe in more detail the kind of person I was looking for. It would help him to decide if he resonated with my ideas. I spent a few anguished hours carefully crafting my words, and then hit the 'submit' button. There I was, officially looking for marriage in public on the internet.

The search became more and more addictive. Apart from the obvious fact that there were so many potential suitors online, I saw profiles of men across the country and even the world, and I started to learn about what else was happening in places I'd never previously had insight or access to. It was a new universe, populated entirely with people in the same situation as me. Reading profiles, sending the odd e-mail, scrutinising each word for meaning and nuance to see if the owner of the profile could hold the key to something special – the process became all absorbing. There were no introductions at all through the 'old' channels, and yet here I was swamped for choice, ranging from ghastly to full of potential.

I spent many hours each week reviewing several different marriage sites, reading through new profiles, re-reading old ones, and then submitting my requests or responding to requests from other people. Every so often there would be a two-way match and then an initial e-mail, and if that went well, a period of frenetic e-mail exchange. The usual shyness of meeting in person, of not knowing if the person is looking to marry, and whether they could be interested in you, were all gone.

Occasionally I exchanged an introduction with a prospect who had either been rejected or not suggested in the traditional channels by a third party who was busy interfering. We cyber-laughed, sharing an understanding of the flawed matchmaking process. It was remarkably heartening to be able finally to share the trials and emotions of the search so openly. The detachment and anonymity created by the internet were remarkably cathartic. I felt I was not alone.

There were profiles from the Middle East, Canada, America, Australia, in fact any country you could imagine. I exchanged e-mails across time zones and learnt what was happening around the world, and came to one simple, obvious conclusion: that we were all looking for the same thing. We all had a strong desire for a partner and the desire finally to find someone to love, and we pursued this with enormous gusto. The global connections opened up a whole new world for me and for the Muslims that I was in touch with. I learnt about new places and new experiences, and found far-flung cyber-pen pals. The globalisation and easy access to people all around the world changed all the parameters. I had met men from abroad before who had travelled to the UK to meet prospective wives, but this was the first time that I could proactively choose to introduce myself to a man from almost anywhere on earth. It marked a general change in the world, and in the Muslim community, that we were so easily and quickly connected to anyone, anywhere.

As my confidence and sense of self kept growing stronger, I found this global connectivity very liberating and exciting. I could go anywhere and talk to anyone in any location. It melded with my sensibilities as a global citizen. And it enhanced my sense of faith because the language and values that I used as my currency were cross-border and cross-cultural. The worldwide connectivity reflected a change in the wider Muslim community, too. Cheaper phone calls, widespread internet and the sharing of news tightened connections between the already existing multitudes of Muslim Diasporas. It also reflected the general trend of globalisation and creation of cross-territory communities. No longer were national borders a defining factor; instead it was about interests, faith, extra-curricular activities. News, events, trends, humour were all shared across the global village. One of those villages was SingleMuslimsville, which I was inhabiting, temporarily I hoped.

The internet also opened up opportunities for Muslims like me who had grown up in Britain or other Western countries to explore the new multifaceted identities which we had been developing in private without knowing who to share them with. Newsgroups, bulletin boards and blogs exploded onto the cyberscene with an exponential growth of activity, writing and opinion. If I had once felt lonely with my British Asian Muslim Woman multiversal identity, I knew now that there were other people out there who felt the same.

It was extremely exciting to find messages from different places in the world, respectful and direct approaches from men who were searching and who found your profile interesting. They were usually polite and conscious of the context of the marriage search. No longer was there the need to go through a third party; instead you could get to know someone directly. Messages would tell you unexpected things, from people who were interested in getting to know you. The sweetness and charm of receiving a message sometime in the middle of the working day are exquisite, and at some point, after the volume of e-mails exceeded a certain threshold, there came the moment of seeing a picture of that person or picking up the phone to hear their voice.

I tried not to decide too rapidly upon seeing a picture – photos were deceptive. Speaking on the phone was more revelatory. I never gave my number to anyone but asked them for theirs and then had a brief conversation. I learnt that e-mails were misleading. It was too easy to read into them what you wanted to read. Even on the phone you lacked their physical presence and non-verbal cues to really know if the person had genuine potential.

Talking to someone unknown on the phone or meeting an unknown in person were skills I had already honed through the introduction process. But I felt a greater need to be cautious. These were people who had not been vetted and who I had no background information about. On the rare occasion that I finally arranged a meeting in person, I was careful to ensure that my safety was paramount. I would always have someone with me or be in a public space, and, of course, have the fail-safe of all blind dates, a get-out excuse.

GUILT

After several months, I came across Tayyab's profile. He was American, about my age, working in the technology industry. He showed healthy humour about the online marriage process and his description made me laugh out loud. He didn't take himself too seriously but sounded sensitive and interesting. I submitted a request to be put in contact with him and he accepted, so we began exchanging e-mails. He lived in Houston, by all accounts a cosmopolitan city with a large Muslim population. At first we just shared facts and opinions, and then slowly we talked about our hopes and dreams about getting married.

Tayyab was of Indian origin, born and brought up in the USA and very much an active member of one of the more progressive mosques in Houston. He played sports, loved writing and wanted to make the world a better place. And he wanted someone to share it with. He had reached his late twenties and he wanted a companion, a wife. He had discovered that he was lonely. He had some interesting political and social opinions. He loved watching the news and was clued up about what was happening around the world. We exchanged ideas about the US presidency, modern science, Islamic jurisprudence, emotional intelligence. I was stimulated and challenged. And I was totally hooked. I really believed that he might be the one.

We spoke on the phone, and he was everything I imagined him to be during our e-mail exchange. He was funny, sensitive, emotional, warm and intelligent. He sent me a photo where he was a small speck in a dark night sky. He looked like a normal twenty-something. The only thing that worried him was that he was only five foot five tall. He was small, only a couple of inches taller than me apparently, but I reassured him that was fine. I had already faced height discrimination and was not about to do the same.

'I'm going to come and visit you in London,' he told me in an e-mail one day. This was big, this was huge, this was momentous. Tayyab had never been outside America. Despite the fact that I had received several suitors who had visited London from abroad on their bride-finding tours, no-one from the internet had yet done so.

It took Tayyab some time to organise his travel arrangements. He had to get himself a passport and arrange with work to take some time off. He grew more and more excited, and I grew more and more nervous. Deep inside me was a mounting trepidation. Even though my parents had conducted some preliminary research about Tayyab and his family, we didn't know a great deal about his background. My parents were therefore just as concerned as I was but encouraged me to give it a try. This was uncharted territory for them as well.

When he arrived he was introduced to my parents, and each day he would meet them, just as he met me, so that we could all get to know him together. His persona was sharper and more angular than when we had spoken on the phone. The mystery of absence had vanished, and instead I saw his own expressions face to face. The biggest challenge was to get to know him almost as a totally new person, because he was different from the character I had created for him when we spoke on the phone. I had experienced this with other people I had met, but with the epic travel across the Atlantic, and his certainty that our meeting in person was just a formality before getting engaged, the contrast between Internet-Tayyab and In-Person-Tayyab was heightened. He was also much more short-tempered than on the phone; the distance and our intermittent interactions had hidden this from me, but in person it was constantly evident, and this is what eventually signalled the end of any potential.

He started to annoy me: he seemed more excited about being in the UK as a tourist than meeting me. He jumped up and down about how our number plates were different, how we drove on a different side of the road, how everyone spoke with cute accents, how our houses were smaller, our cars were tinier, our streets were narrower. Most of all, though, he started by trying to make a show of being well paid. I was more than happy to contribute or even cover our shared expenses, especially in light of the fact he had paid to travel across the world to London. He insisted on paying but then very quickly began complaining about how expensive our coffee was, how expensive our food was, how expensive everything was! And soon his offers to pay, or even share, were deliberately and pointedly withdrawn, despite his initial showmanship about his financial liquidity and his own chivalrous qualities. It was the dentist all over again. This did not bode well for married life.

It was Tayyab's unpredictable temper that finally sealed the decision for me. I felt enormously guilty that he had travelled so far to see me, but I told myself that I had no reason to feel guilty. I had not forced him to come. Every individual did what they had to do to find a partner. And Tayyab had taken a calculated decision to make this journey, knowing that things might not work out.

Was it my fault that it didn't work? Should I have tried harder? After all, everything else seemed to fit so well and my parents were already tracing further references. I ought not to feel guilt – after all I had been the catalyst for Tayyab to do something he had never done before and might not have done if the prospect of marriage had not enticed him. I ought to have felt satisfied with my contribution.

Instead, everything I did made me feel guilty. And it wasn't just about Tayyab, it was with my family too. They wanted so much for me to be married and live happily that I felt guilty I was unable to fulfil their wishes. It would have made them overjoyed if I had got married, and it was almost worth getting married to anyone who seemed broadly suitable just to see the happiness they would have felt. Not to give them that made me feel guilty. But if I had married any old Mr Mediocre, they would have known that I had compromised my hopes and ideals, and in that process compromised the hopes of my family, too. They had supported me in my search through the difficulties, the heartbreak and the loneliness, and if I gave up now, I would also feel guilt.

After so many years of my parents supporting me to make my own choices, it was only fair that I kept up the search. So many Muslim women were denied the free choice and support that I had been offered by my family, which they gave me based on their Islamic principles that every person has the free choice to marry whom they wish and not be forced to marry against their will. I tried to uphold those values, and yet a bitter voice inside sent droplets of guilt running through my veins. Was it all my fault? Had I deluded myself with dreams of Prince Charming and Happily Ever After? Had I put myself and my whole family through this misery for nothing? Had I missed out on any opportunities? The answer was clear: no. Regret was definitely not on my shelf menu.

Marvellous Mary

I decided that if I couldn't find a man, then I would have a wedding anyway. I hadn't lost hope – just started to prepare myself for the idea that it might not happen. Pretty dress, romantic venue, lots of good food, wonderful company. It was time for me to be the centre of attention. Without Prince Charming I may not be able to reap the benefits of marriage, but at least I could have a lovely wedding. Did I need a groom? I was tempted to buy my dream wedding dress because what if I never got to wear one otherwise? I pictured a long, white flowing robe, encrusted with sparkling crystals all over it, and a translucent ephemeral veil to reveal my smile of pure happiness. I imagined ivory silk and hand-embroidered beads.

Mary, the mother of Jesus, was a wonderful inspiration to me during this time. She was mentioned with great reverence in Islamic traditions and was considered to be one of the 'women of paradise'. Even a chapter in the *Qur'an* was named after her. Mary's father had desperately wanted a child and prayed to God that if he was blessed with one, he would dedicate his offspring to serving God in the temple. Mary's father was delighted when his wife gave birth to a child, but he was surprised that it was a girl. He pointed out to God that being given a girl rather than a boy was an unexpected turn of events. He had made a vow to dedicate the child to God, but only boys used to serve in the temple.

God was fully aware of this fact, obviously, as God knows everything. In His wisdom He had created a girl, to be dedicated in His way, and this challenged people's ideas at that time, establishing that a woman was equally worthy in the eyes of God. Her presence destroyed the cultural traditions that a female was a subservient creature and not worthy to worship the Divine. Those who excluded women from the act of worship did so because they believed only 'real' human beings could worship God, and women were not considered to be fully human. Mary's birth itself was a stand for equality for women, and established by Divine Decree that women were of equal value and spiritual worth.

Despite the traditions of that era, Mary was given to the temple and grew up to be a woman known for her exemplary character and immense spirituality. Her being was entirely focused on creating a strong relationship with the Divine. Her uncle would come to visit her in the temple, and was surprised to find her eating delicious fresh food. When he enquired as to its provenance, she told him that whilst she was engaged in prayer, the food was brought to her by an angel, as a gift from God.

Since Mary was considered amongst the purest of all women, God chose her for the most amazing of miracles – a virgin birth. But in Islamic tradition, there is no Joseph involved in the story of the birth, no man to diminish the central role of the woman in this story. Instead, she is in her own right a shining independent icon, a woman leading her own life.

When Mary is about to give birth, she finds a quiet place under the shade of a tree. Her response to being in labour is described in the *Qur'an* through words that all women can relate to. She is not a distant unattainable figure, but shares the same experiences of womanhood as the rest of us. During the pain of giving birth, she cries out, 'I wish I was dead.' Many women seem to say the same thing in the agony of labour. My mum says she wished it as well, right up until the second she saw me in her arms, and then forgot about the pain. Mary holds on to the tree and squeezes it with all her might to be able to get through the pain.

Despite her unblemished reputation, the gossiping Aunties of her time accused her of immoral behaviour and they are supported by the power-wielding patriarchs. In order to protect her character, the little baby speaks by a miracle to explain that Mary is pure and untouched, and that he is the baby Jesus, sent as a prophet from God to deliver the truth and the scripture, and the message that people should pray, give charity and worship God.

I don't believe Mary ever married but in fact brought up Jesus on her own. I admired her because she was the very embodiment of the equality of women in worship and in social life. God had deliberately sent her as a sign of the worth of women. Her challenges were also very real, living with the people around her as a single mother, as a woman being talked about, as a human being living the best life she could. And if she brought up an amazing child like Jesus, then she must have been quite some mother.

I particularly liked the story of Mary and her role as a mother because my own mother's name, Maryam, was the Arabic version of Mary. She, too, had been unperturbed by the gossiping of those around her, and had supported me through my search and given me inspiration. Both of them gave me hope that as a woman, whether a man was present or not, I could still pursue magical dreams and be a marvellous human being.

The groom-less wedding was never to happen. Instead, I kept hoping that the new methods of meeting someone that were blossoming would eventually deliver Prince Charming to me. And that is how I found myself one evening, with Noreen, at a speed dating event. We decided that if on arrival it was too awful, we would leave together. The speed dating event organisers promised us something that we couldn't get elsewhere: men in the flesh, and plenty of them. The event was due to have twenty men and twenty women, and every participant would spend three minutes with each person of the opposite gender to decide if that person might be the one.

We eventually located the obscure address for the venue, only to discover it was a nightclub-cum-bar. This immediately made us feel uncomfortable. Were we in the right place to find a suitable husband?

As teetotal Muslims we did not spend time in bars. And since we were both looking for practising Muslim men, we were dubious as to whether the men who attended would meet our expectations. The room was large and low lit, with red and orange lanterns and luscious exotic fabrics giving the whole place a sensual feel. It immediately made the whole speed dating concept even more challenging than we had anticipated.

The organisers handed each of us a card. Down the left-hand side were the numbers one to twenty. Then there were three columns: definitely, maybe and no. Finally there was a column for notes. We wrote our own profile numbers in the top right-hand corner. All participants had a sticky label that they attached to their lapel with their profile number in big writing. No-one was permitted to share their own name.

Each woman was given her own table, and every three minutes the men would stand up and move onto the next table. Eventually each of the twenty men would have spoken to each of the twenty women. We were advised to take any notes on the card to remind ourselves about a particular person, and then to decide if that person was a 'definite', a 'maybe' or a 'no'. The cards would be collected at the end, and if a two-way match of 'definite' was detected by the organisers, they would swap e-mail addresses and leave the participants to continue their conversation directly. If one was a definite and one a maybe, they would investigate with the 'maybe' to see if he or she wanted to pursue an e-mail address exchange.

Eventually a critical mass of participants had arrived: twenty women and sixteen men. As always, there were fewer men. The women sat by the tables which formed a perimeter round the room while the men hovered nervously around the closed bar in the centre. I noticed that I was the only woman in the room wearing a headscarf. Some of the women looked as though they had come after work in their suits, others looked dressed up to attend a Bollywood awards ceremony. After an introduction from the host, the men were dispersed randomly to take their places, one at each table. We were advised not to ask the usual 'what is your name and where do you come from?' questions but rather to open with conversation pieces so we could get a feel of personality rather than vital statistics.

The first few men who came to my table looked superficially enthusiastic. The next girl on from me was a glamorous, curvaceous entity who had caused a mass sweep of eyes as she had entered the room. The boys who sat at my table had to scoop their tongues into their mouths in order to maintain even a courteous conversation with me. At first they tried, but it was obvious that my headscarf had turned them off completely. And besides, with the Aishwari Rai lookalike next to me, they didn't have much blood flowing through their heads. As the evening wore on, it became plain – because I eventually decided just to ask them directly – that they had come to find a wife who was Muslim for cultural or family reasons, not for reasons of faith. Therefore I was not an option they would consider. As an experiment, I ticked every single 'definite' box to see if anyone had shown any interest in me. I got no responses.

Although disheartened, I told myself that I would not have chosen any of the men who attended. However, the pit of my stomach was sore from disappointment, no matter how irrational that feeling was.

Inspired by Mary's determination, I picked myself up and decided to try again. I assumed that this was the wrong speed dating event for me, as it was aimed at a different audience. Perhaps others might have more appropriate suitors for me.

I came across another company that claimed to conduct a more sophisticated method of speed dating. The organiser insisted that all prospective attendees should be first cleared through a vetting process. Only if an individual met the criteria for right attitude, realistic expectations and good quality of intellect, personality and personal success would they be permitted to attend. He said that this avoided timewasters and those who were not looking for 'the kind of marital relationship' that we had in mind. It sounded very promising, like an all-encompassing Auntie process where every suitor – male or female – would be of an appropriate calibre.

I was given a time to call the assessor, and rang at the appointed slot for my interview. I was grilled for about 30 minutes on all aspects of my views on marriage, what I was looking for and what I had to offer. At the end of the session I was congratulated on being admitted to the event. I felt smug and validated in my womanhood. I had been anointed as a catch. It was great marketing by the speed dating company. The organiser offered me a selection of dates and quoted a price to attend. It was high, very high, but not much above the cost of a good night out. And who knew? Perhaps I would walk away with a well-vetted, high-calibre, potential husband. It wasn't an exorbitant amount of money, but it made the event much more serious than 'it's not too expensive, I'll give it a go, and if it's horrid I'll leave'. He sensed my nervousness and said that if I booked to attend three or more sessions to start with, I would get a discount. I was tempted, but something niggled about the assumption on the part of the organisers that I would want to – that I would need to – attend several sessions. After my previous disheartening speed dating event, I decided I would try one out on its own to start with.

Again I decided to attend with Noreen, to ensure I had moral support. This event was much smarter than the previous one, with formal round tables for six set out. Once the proceedings had begun, each table would be composed of three men and three women. After twenty minutes the men would rotate tables. The group setting was designed to make it easier for conversation to flow and the longer session should allow for deeper discussion. Based on my previous experience it made good sense and I felt hopeful.

There was a delay to the start of the proceedings. Again there were about twenty women, yet at the appointed start time only a handful of men. We were advised that since it was a weekday, some of the men were running late from work and would be joining us imminently. We waited patiently for them to arrive but about 45 minutes later, as the women were starting to get agitated, we were informed that some of the men had pulled out at the last minute. Apparently they were scared and too nervous to attend.

The organisers disappeared and tempers began to fray. Many of the women had experienced several other events with poor male turnout and demanded a refund. The organiser ran hurriedly hither and thither, scraping his hair back from his worried brow. Another 45 minutes later and a trail of men trickled into the hall. Despite the rising anger, the women started to look more hopeful. Men! Finally!

The evening slowly changed gears from apprehension to activity. There was something strange about the attitude of the men, they seemed too relaxed and not engaged enough in the process. They didn't ask many details about the women, instead they talked between themselves. As we met twelve or so men – not the twenty we had been promised – I realised that again I was the only woman in a headscarf and that none of the men present were interested in a *hijab*-wearing wife. I felt conned by the whole evening: a promise of high-calibre candidates but a delivery of a few mediocre specimens. At least I wished it had been even that – one of the men let slip that in fact they had been paid to attend.

Round and round the speed dating tables, getting giddy, raising hopes, falling harder each time. It felt like ever decreasing circles, with ever-diminishing hope, spinning round, hoping that one day a man would appear and the maniacal haunting music would stop.

The circles of speed dating and the marriage circuit were utterly forgotten as I stood in front of the Kaba in Mecca, ready to perform the *hajj*, the pilgrimage that each Muslim should undertake at least once in their lifetime. The circulating movement of the ocean of humanity evoked emotions from the very depth of my being. This was the place the Prophet Muhammad had grown up in. It was the place which cradled the footsteps of Abraham, who had built the Kaba; it was the location for the birth of Islam as we knew it today; and it was the place which I faced every day when I carried out my *salat*, the ritual prayers. Round and round went the enormous swirling crowd.

The Kaba towers above all its surroundings, at fifteen metres high, twelve metres in depth and ten metres wide. This large, cube-shaped construction is usually covered in black cloth, which is what gives it its iconic look. It is known as the House of God, but since God has no physical location, it is more a concept for Muslims to focus on than an actual abode for the Divine. In one corner is the Black Stone, a meteor believed to be a piece of rock from heaven itself. Around the Kaba is a vast courtyard with white marble flooring, which is the setting for the hundreds of thousands of people that walk around the Kaba in anti-clockwise direction. When they have walked around it seven times, they have completed the *tawaf*, which is the first component of the *hajj*.

Around the edge of the courtyard is a vast mosque built in a circle around the Kaba. It ushers in the pilgrims and offers shade and rest from the extreme heat of the Arabian desert during the daytime. As I stood on the steps of the great mosque looking at the point that is the focus of all Muslims around the world, I saw wave upon wave of thousands and thousands of men and women dressed in white, walking slowly around the black cube. They had come here – just like me – to perform the pilgrimage of the *hajj*. Were it not for the requirement to perform *hajj*, they might never have travelled outside their villages or countries. For many Muslims from less affluent backgrounds it would be a dream to be here. For those of us who had grown up in comfort in the West but outside the traditional old Muslim heartland, it created a new view of Islam, one that was holistic, ever present and in the majority.

The *hajj* was a physical as well as a spiritual journey. Almost three million people were all trying to focus their spiritual energies towards the Divine. They found themselves also having to be physically part of the world's most global and diverse community. Everyone was instructed to wear white, in as simple a fashion as possible. Men wore two white unstitched cloths to cover themselves, women wore simple, long white dresses. Whether it was a queen or a commoner next to you, you would never know. And that was the idea: the inequalities of the material and physical world were erased and replaced by spiritual status. What you knew of the person next to you was not their wealth or job title, but whether they smiled in greeting, whether they pushed or shoved, how nicely they treated you. With everybody wearing white clothes, with no decoration, styling or accessories, they were no longer judged by fashion, style or wealth. Everyone was just a soul.

Across the Muslim world, although Muslims were loath to admit it, racial prejudice was rife, and yet here, at the height of religious devotion, people of all ethnicities imaginable mixed on a par. The interconnections were immediate and proximate. You might find yourself next to someone from the game parks of Africa one moment, the next from the Uyghurs in China, a second later circulating with someone who had grown up in the foothills of the Incas, or being given a helping hand by a Bedouin Arab, blonde-haired Bosnian or a bright-smiled Nigerian. The moment I realised, it seemed obvious: we were all human beings. All the confusions I had faced growing up living a life divided into tangled and disconnected identities all suddenly became clear. I saw the reality of how it could work in front of my eyes: so many different identities occupying the same place, flowing into each other. You could pick each of them out separately, bold and proud of what they were.

'That's how we need to live in Britain,' I thought to myself as I watched all these different people from around the world walk on the same journey, 'side by side, working, studying, living, communicating, respecting, whatever our ethnicity, religion or belief. Seeing the people around us as "other" is not an option.' At the heart of it, we were all like the white-clothed souls that walked in front of my eyes – we were the same underneath, human beings.

On my search for a husband, and for my faith, I had learnt to be comfortable in myself and to see the connections to other people as human beings, no matter what their faith or belief. We were all on the same search to find meaning and truth. Looking in front of me at the crowd swirling past, I knew that I was different because I was me, but I was also the same as everyone, because I was a human being. Each of us occupied so many spaces and identities, and that made us multiversal, not identical.

I had been searching to find a partner to love and had been trying to learn about Divine love. In front of me now I realised that there was one more kind of love that was essential: the love for other human beings. Each of the men I had encountered was just as much part of that human diversity as the crowds I saw before me. I had to love, accept and learn from each of them, whether I liked them or not. The saying that I had heard before that 'Islam is to serve the Creator and to serve Creation' rang true, because love for other human beings was a fundamental part of Love for the Divine.

Right next to the Kaba is the grave of Hagar, the wife of Abraham and the mother of Ishmael. As the pilgrims circle the Kaba to complete their pilgrimage, they must walk round the area designated as the place where Hagar is buried. Hagar was a slave before she married Abraham, which in the eyes of chauvinists the world over would relegate her to the lowest of low positions. And yet those same chauvinists would have to include her as part of their worship, as a symbol of high status in the eyes of God. I smiled at the deliciousness of the irony. In fact I laughed. There was no man included in this way in the rites of *hajj*.

After circling the Kaba, the pilgrims proceeded to a nearby plain about half a kilometre long between two small hills, called Safa and Marwa. On the command of God, Abraham left Hagar in this place with their young child Ishmael, asking them to wait until he returned. Hagar, needing to find water for the boy, ran backwards and forwards between the two hills to see if she could see a spring or river. As part of the *hajj*, the pilgrims walk between the same two hills to emphasise that looking after your worldly needs is just as much a part of getting close to the Creator as acts such as prayer. The whole event of the *hajj*, including this part of emulating Hagar's run between the two hills, is one of the pinnacles of spiritual devotion for a Muslim.

How had the fact that it was in a woman's footsteps that Muslims had to follow been overlooked in giving Muslim women their rightful elevated status? The cultures of many Muslims chose to ignore the obvious facts and pretend that Muslim women should be weak, subservient and oppressed. Here, right in front of our eyes, around the Kaba and walking between Safa and Marwa, it was most obvious that women were of the highest ranking. What had gone wrong?

As well as the clear message that women had an extraordinarily high spiritual status, Hagar inspired something specific in me that I had found hard to balance: an understanding that looking for food and shelter were just as much a part of worship as prayer. Circulating round the Kaba established that the Divine was the focus of being a Muslim, round and round each day as the sun rose and the sun set. The universe was a repetition of cycles, each one following its set orbit and finding its place in the Divine order. But Hagar's run, backwards and forwards, was the day-to-day rat race, to work, from work, to work, from work, literally mapping out my life. The two parts balanced each other perfectly and I realised that both the sublime and the mundane fitted together.

Despite the fact that the pilgrims came from far and near for a spiritual journey, it was, of course, a wonderful opportunity to meet other potential suitors. Wasn't that the case in every situation where new people might be present? The wise Aunties pointed out that marriage was a spiritual act, and that finding a suitable partner was even more apt if he was presented to you at the footsteps of the House of God. It was a compelling argument. And with everyone dressed down, make-up stripped to the minimum and the swagger of daily life removed, it was an opportunity to meet and get to know someone for who they really were. Some couples came after getting engaged, trying to maintain a respectful distance so that no-one could accuse them of too much smiling! Others came with the hope that they would go home having completed their *hajj* with the additional gift of a fiancé.

Fatima and Abdu were one such couple who found each other during the *hajj*. The Aunties on the trip were always prepared for any opportunity. I did not know when this meeting between them, or the proposal, had happened. I had been too busy spiritualising to plug myself into the hurly burly of marriage matches at this special time. I simply wanted to enjoy finding my place and experiencing this amazing whirlwind of global togetherness.

I also wanted to fall to my knees and into prostration and weep. For the joy of being at the focus of Muslim life, and at a place where the Creator had said we are as pure and innocent as young children, I wanted to demand that the pain of loneliness and desperation be put to an end. I refused to relinquish hope, but I had run out of places to look for Mr Right. John Travolta had not come to my door. The Milk Tray Man had most likely eaten all his own chocolates by now. Even the most mediocre of men I had met seemed to have got married. Humbled at how small a speck I was in this huge sea of human beings, I hoped that my pride had been crushed, leaving only a lonely soul waiting to connect to another. I added another emotion to the list of experiences on the shelf: patience.

In my Yin

There is one thing that a state of extreme endurance gives you the freedom to do: to consider possibilities that you may otherwise have dismissed. It forces you to re-evaluate the potential of a situation that at first glance you thought had no merit. To be blunt, I was open to consider anyone. But my experiences in *hajj* had softened me as well, pushing me to look beyond my initial assessment to the deeper soul of the person. Each individual I met, whether in an introduction or in day-to-day life, I looked at differently, exploring the human spark that might lie underneath.

For men I might have normally dismissed through irritation or personal dislike, I wondered what hidden universes lay underneath. Was he a Mohamed Habib, hiding mysteries of the universe for me to discover? Did a quiet, ordinary-looking man hold secrets of the Divine, with contentment and love lurking beneath his calm unprovocative exterior? Or if he was at a different place in his journey from me, was he heading in the same direction at least? If I wasn't attracted to him physically to start with, would the connection of ethics, personality and time together reveal an attraction that would run deeper and more passionately? As the Prophet had alluded, physical beauty may be present now, but it only heads in one direction with age – away. Inner beauty was the key search criterion (if only the online marriage sites offered a grading on this point), for that only grew with time.

I started to take an interest in people simply for who they were. I was more reflective, gentler, more inquisitive and open in my demeanour. What made this person tick? Each person was a delicious moment to be savoured with respect for their humanity. There was no need to assess them as a potential suitor; instead I was more interested in seeing them as a window to a new world. I enjoyed getting to know people as human beings.

I realised that my bumpy ride across hills and potholes to look for love had allowed me to understand the universe around me in the most effective and enlightening way – through getting an insight into the microcosms that lay inside each unique and amazing human being. If the Divine could not be contained by the universe but was to be found in the heart of the human being, wasn't that the place to look for the Divine spark? Each person represented a path to God that I could not have seen on my own individual journey.

The ecstasy of the spiritual discoveries I had made created a glow on my face that somehow should have been eradicated by my arrival at Desperation Stations. Instead I felt more contented than ever and shone with an inner happiness that I had not felt before. I enjoyed my life, and a husband would be a partner in an ongoing exciting chapter towards further self-discovery and fulfilment.

And so you would expect me to say that love struck at the moment I least expected it. The glossy magazines would diagnose that I had learned to love myself and I was now ready for someone to love me. However, I had *always* loved, *always* been ready, but now I had a different insight. I had enjoyed living my life and was happy being myself, but I could not help but think that had I got married younger, shown more interest in Ali at the very start – and I realised that he did have all the qualities to make a wonderful husband – then I would have had a very happy life on that path too. I didn't agree that I 'wouldn't have changed a thing' in the journey I had taken. It was a meaningless statement. If I had lived a different life, I might have discovered different things that I hadn't found on this path, and I might have been just as happy, perhaps happier. I would never know the answer to that question.

Waiting for love to strike 'when you least expect it' is a wonderfully fatalistic cliché, which allows you to relinquish control over the most important part of your life: who you spend it with.

Hollywood and Bollywood rom-coms would write into my script an unexpected fairytale ending with Prince Charming arriving to sweep me off my feet. Or, in a more cerebral genre of film, the story would wind down and I would accept that I was not to find love. I would submit to my destiny and move on towards productive spinsterhood. I would reflect wisely on the wonderful path I had trodden and all the people I had met. I would end my story with the cathartic analysis that it was the taking part and not the winning that was important. I would realise that 'finding the one' had been the wrong prize, for living life was the prize.

I had learnt so much. I had sat at the sharp point of British culture, Islamic faith and Asian culture. Through my journey, the sharp point had turned into a vantage point, where I could observe, enjoy and share the multiverses that I was part of. And this experience had revealed one very simple truth – that love comes in multiple layers, from the carnal, through a partner, and parents, through community and society and all the way to the underpinning universal Love of the Divine.

My journey for my own Mr Right had revealed that in an era of abundance, extravagance and hedonism, the very intangible search for love was the thing that bound us all together. When science and the need to prove everything through fact alone dictated our social mores, it was most incredible that the least tangible, manageable or definable quality – Love – was the thing that created most tension, most excitement and most human togetherness.

We were exposed to so many heritages and traditions driving towards love. The god of Romance was all-dominating on one side, the weight of tradition dragged heavily on the other, and the principles of faith hidden beneath cultures and geographies on a third side, if such a discussion can have three sides. The awkward point where they collided had always poked me uncomfortably, causing a confusing pain. But this prodding and these tensions revealed what could not be discovered elsewhere. It threw up a new confidence in the multi-layering of love. It could allow both men and women to ask previously taboo questions, and there were so many vital questions that needed to be asked. Should tradition dictate how a partner is chosen? Should an individual be solely responsible for finding a mate or should the community step in? What were the priorities and criteria for selecting a partner, and had modernity got it wrong? If not, why were more and more people single, and why were divorce rates rising, while we were all still desperate for love and companionship? How were romance, companionship and relationships interrelated and which should be prioritised? Were we being short-changed by the fashion to eschew long-term companionship in return for high adrenaline, short-term romantic excitement?

Why did we need to be constantly at the height of the adrenaline rush? What was wrong with simply hanging out and being contented and happy with a partner who could fulfil you? Adrenaline meant instability – breaking relationships off before the beginning of the End, picking bad boys, having affairs because they were exciting. Why not make stability and contentment fashionable again? Traditions and faith cropped up uncomfortably to remind people that these values could actually make us happier. But that wasn't a sexy message, and being sexy was very important. There was a cultural insistence that everything, especially women, had to be constantly and utterly sexy.

You had to be sexy in the public domain to be accepted. If you were interested in love, then it had to be a beautiful, glamorous, sexy kind of love. That was difficult to reconcile as a practising Muslim woman wearing *hijab*. That is also why a Muslim woman talking about love is such an incongruous idea. It jars with our notion that love is only romance or love only means sexuality. 'Sexiness' in public is fundamentally opposed to *hijab* and the headscarf, because the headscarf is about being sexy only in private. 'Being sexy' was definitely an essential part of being a woman, but it is part of her mystique, to be retained in her control to reveal as part of the companionship and journey of love with a partner. For me, love for a companion was not a shared public experience and neither was sexuality. Like other Muslim women, I was interested in love, but not the kind that forced me to define love only and exclusively as being sexy. My mission was to understand love in all its facets and to define it on my own terms.

People ask me, how did you find him? Did you do anything special? Or was it fate just stepping in, in which case, they say, we can do nothing and we must just hope for the best. It didn't happen for me when I least expected it. I was waiting, ready.

There are some that say that once you are confident and complete in yourself, when you stop being needy, then your partner will find you. I *was* in need. I *did* want a partner. I *hadn't* resigned myself to 'least expect it'. It was still my priority to find a companion and to learn what love really is through the reality of living with someone.

Living life to the full allows you to discover uncharted territories at the tops of mountains or in the valleys of long-forgotten civilisations. It allows you to find the Divine, whether it is in the great gatherings of people like *hajj* or in the hearts of the human beings we meet in our lives like the Karims, Khalils and Mohamed Habibs, or our friends, fathers and mothers. Above all, life allows you to gather experience to find and know love – that thing that eludes our modern gods of science and yet still dominates human existence entirely and completely.

Love brings compassion, justice and an understanding of the self and of others. You can only ever be complete when you've seen yourself through someone else's eyes. Then only can you truly know yourself. Love brings contentment because it means understanding and accepting yourself, and understanding and accepting others, because love can blind you to their imperfections. In our rush to find perfect fairytale love, we seem to have forgotten that kind of gentle, unhurried love that grows over time and requires careful nurturing. Love reduced to romance is flighty and unfulfilling, and it has left us insecure, un-nourished and un-whole. It only feeds our surface needs, not the inner hunger for a long-term, stable, fulfilling love. Romance is high calorie, quick fix, low nutritional value.

The more that people told me he would turn up when I least expected it, the more I became annoyed. There was no moment when I did *not* expect to meet him. I expected it all the time.

That's why I chose a Coco Chanel-style dress to wear that day. I wanted to be prepared, just in case. It was a good thing I did wear a dress that he liked. He commented later that he was drawn to the fact that it was different, quirky. It was a simple, stylish number, carefully tailored in black with a cream border at the bottom, which finished just above the knee. It was a cute dress, feminine and confident. I complemented it with some elegant cream silk trousers and a matching black and cream headscarf. I added some height with black platform shoes and finished the look with a quick dash of almost imperceptible lipstick.

I had planned to attend a Muslim charity conference being organised by a group of friends. I hadn't seen them for some time and it was the perfect way to say hello. And of course there was the possibility of meeting a suitor there. I arrived in the large auditorium when the speeches were already in full swing and the hall was packed almost to capacity. The lights were dimmed and I scanned my eyes across row upon row of bearded uncles, thoughtfully stroking their facial hair whilst listening to the speaker who sat on stage with his co-panelists. I looked again and realised happily that he was accompanied by several female peers. The men had occupied the first fifty rows, and at the back on the right-hand side were ten rows laid out for the handful of women who had chosen to attend. I was disappointed that there were so few of them.

There were several empty chairs, and after a few minutes evaluating if there was anyone I knew who I could speak to, I decided to sit down and try to locate them during the interval. I sat at the end of the row, next to some Aunties I did not recognise, and started looking around. I tucked a few wisps of wayward hair back underneath my headscarf. After a few minutes I saw a colleague of mine, Abdullah, with whom I had worked on a charity project recently. We had some follow-up work to engage in, so I stepped carefully over to where he was sitting. He, too, was at the end of a row, close to mine.

SATURDAY, 21 MAY, 2.31 P.M.

And there he was, sitting next to Abdullah, a young man with thick dark hair and a small, neatly kept beard. He was dressed in a dark suit, and even at a distance I could see that he had an endearing dimple in his right cheek. I felt like I knew him yet I was certain that we had never met. I stared at him, watching him whispering earnestly to Abdullah. As he spoke he ran his fingers through his hair in a thoughtful way. His face looked intelligent and warm, full of character. I was mesmerised. As I walked over to talk to Abdullah, I was hoping to have a chance to speak with this mysterious stranger, not realising the huge impact these steps would make. Fortunately, when I arrived he was still there. I greeted them both with a shy smile. The tall dark handsome stranger pulled out a chair for me.

Almost imperceptibly Abdullah slipped away. Whether that was coincidental or deliberate I will never know. He claims that he already had the match in mind and that we were meant to cross paths that day, and he had arranged our meeting deliberately. Abdullah would go on to offer a glowing reference for him.

I asked him how he knew Abdullah. 'He's a family friend,' he responded. 'What about you?'

'We worked on a project together. I was coming over to talk to him about a few outstanding matters but . . .' I looked around me, to emphasise that Abdullah had abandoned us, '. . . he seems to have disappeared.'

We paused awkwardly, unsure of what to say next. He was

extremely handsome but unaware of his charm. I was urgently evaluating new topics for discussion, to keep his attention and stop him from walking away. Fortunately he continued speaking.

'Have you been to this conference in previous years?' he asked neutrally.

'No, this is my first one,' I told him. 'It's a very impressive affair,' I added, realising that he was one of the organisers.

An unknown man walked past, and seeing him, stopped and shook his hand, giving him a warm friendly hug. He sat down to restart the conversation, and a second man arrived, introduced by the first man, who also gave him a hug. He was clearly well respected and much loved.

He turned back to face me. 'I'm sorry, that sort of thing happens a lot. I don't want to be rude to them.'

'It's OK,' I smiled at him, 'I understand that I'm interrupting a big occasion for you. I can leave you to it.'

I thumped myself on the inside of my head for making that last comment. I did *not* want to leave him to it, and I should not have offered to do so. I was an idiot.

Fortunately, he did not take me up on my offer. 'No, no, it's fine. They can manage without me.'

As we sat at the back of the hall chatting, I hoped again and again that he wouldn't be called away to run an errand or speak to someone. With each breath I willed him to stay so I could speak to him more. What if he left? What if he politely, courteously took his leave and the conversation ended abruptly, cold turkey. He says now that he was worried that it was I who would stand up and walk away and he cannot believe I remained and spoke to him all afternoon.

Although the hall was filled with a thousand other people, we later both confessed that during that first conversation we forgot that anyone else was there. As we spoke, there was an innocent pleasure in learning about another human being. He had picked a career outside of the typical Asian portfolio, which immediately made him more interesting to me. He also devoted much of his time to charitable work. The fact he was not typical, that he was complex and multifaceted, wrapped up in a courteous warm package, gave me a feeling of hope: that the world held hidden people for me to discover whom I could admire and who filled me with optimism for humanity. I dared not think he might be the One.

We had exchanged nothing but names during the conversation, and so a few days later I Googled him. I nervously typed in his name, not knowing what to expect. The internet delivered his profile to me, which gave me his e-mail address. I decided to send him a note. Despite the free-flowing and friendly conversation we had when we met, I wasn't sure what he had made of it, so I kept my e-mail short and playful.

> After we spoke, I was curious to find out if you were really who you said you were, and not really a spy. I found this, is it you?

A few minutes later, a response pinged onto my desktop.

> Yes, it's me. Sadly I'm not James Bond. Just an ordinary man, in an ordinary job. I'm sure my work isn't nearly as exciting as yours.
> P.S. It is in fact possible that I'm a spy, but I can't reveal that information to you.

I smiled. This was going to be fun. As we continued to exchange short e-mails that day, he remained bright and warm in his tone but just as nonchalant. Now he admits he had spent the previous days in a heightened sense of anxiety, worried that he might never see me again.

Over e-mails and phone calls I started to realise that we shared values and ideals and were trying to tread the same path. What if we walked the middle path hand in hand, supporting each other? Besides all of which, his smile made my heart race and I couldn't wait to spend more and more time with him. One day he sent a huge bouquet of flowers to my workplace. They were stunning, and I felt breathless as I collected them from reception. Despite my joy at receiving them, I felt nervous. Did he feel as strongly as I did? I suddenly knew deep inside that this one would last. There was definitely something special about him, but the reason that this would turn into something more permanent was that we had both shown our commitment to making a partnership work. He was the one because I was going to make him be my one. He said that he felt the same.

My parents were delighted at the smile that spread across my lips every time his name was mentioned. They were sure it heralded a new chapter in my life. He revealed that he, too, could not stop smiling every time he heard my name or saw a message pop up on an e-mail.

The same checks and references were carried out on him as with any other suitor that I was introduced to. My parents invited him for a formal meeting at our home. Then they spoke to their contacts until they had traced reliable sources to offer critical information and references about him. No matter how the relationship began, it was subject to the same assessment of security and stability. He was given a full and extensive vetting, and passed through the entire process.

I realised that we could become companions and partners, 'garments for each other' as the *Qur'an* described a married couple. The possibility of having a partner in life suddenly looked real. I felt that he might shape himself round me and I round him until we created a complete circle, like the male and female of the yin-yang symbol. In that circle the masculine and feminine are equally balanced, black and white, active and passive, earth and sky. The circle was the whole, and its value and impact blossomed when the male and female flowed into each other. The two halves were not created by a line drawn across the diameter. Instead, each half melted into the other, a curvaceous, infinite sweeping. And even more alluring and perplexing was that in each half was a droplet of the other. The feminine held a contrasting circle of masculinity at its very heart: the masculine cherished a sparkling jewel of femininity at its core.

When he asked my permission and the permission of my family to marry him, I drew a simple innocent fairytale heart to represent our feelings as our wedding approached. Each time I doodled a heart between our names it made me smile.

When Love picked up the pen to sketch out our futures, its gentle strokes painted in firm ink a partner, companion and lover who would complete me and whom I would complete in return. And then it painted in that final drop to remind me that we were interlinked. Wherever I would turn, there he would be: romantic, divine, exquisite Love.

Epilogue: The Beginning

I am standing in front of my mirror this morning, ready for the day ahead of me. I have stood in this same place so many times before, on the days that suitors were brought into my home. I have looked myself in the eye, full of nerves and anxiety, wondering whether this time my suitor would be the one. Today I am not feeling nervous or apprehensive. I know that it is time for my beginning.

Love is always the beginning of the story. No matter how intricate our existence before love, it is Love that transforms it from black and white, to breathtaking, beautiful inspiring colour. That is not to say that life without love has no meaning, far from it, life in all its minutiae is Love itself. Each man and woman exists because we are Love, and we already have Love in our lives. When we recognise Love with a heart that is courageous, open and honest, when we invite Love into our lives without conditions, that is when the story truly begins.

I am not dressed in pink or purple, blue or green. There is no frantic search for what to wear. This moment is timeless, because I have hoped for it for so long. I open my eyes and gaze into the mirror. My heartbeat is calm and what I see in my reflection is a woman who has grown from a girl with so many dreams and hopes, and so many ideas and challenges, into a woman who is ready to embrace faith, life and love.

My dress is ivory silk, just as I have always dreamed. It was created with my own personal designer, then cut, sewn, tailored and embroidered by hand. The bodice fits me perfectly. At the waist the luxurious fabric is encrusted with hundreds of sparkling crystals, which open up into an exquisite silk and organza skirt that trails with twinkling beads. I have a matching *dupatta*, a long ivory organza veil with embroidery and crystals that match my dress. It is pinned into my hair and floats magically over my shoulders.

I am upholding thousands of years of bridal tradition by having my hands and feet intricately decorated with henna. An artist spent five hours painting the patterns onto my skin last night, and now they have deepened in colour into a unique piece of art that will last only a day.

It is a beautiful day for a beginning. The sky is clear blue and the sun is shining brightly, as it often does as one season changes to another. The mood at home is relaxed and joyful. I feel light-hearted and contented. I have found myself, and as I look in the mirror, what I see staring back with clear eyes is me. I am here, present, myself. Over breakfast I drank my last cup of coffee with my parents, in their home, as their daughter, basking in their parental love. In a few hours I will still be a daughter, but I will also be a wife.

My aunts have arrived, and with my mother and sister-in-law they start fussing over me, admiring my dress, and complimenting me on how beautiful I look. There is a feast of feminine indulgence as each one of them recounts stories of their own wedding day. I let myself enjoy the moment.

My parents gather around me. This is a moment of love, as my family circle me in their protection. We recite a small prayer together, which is especially for blessing the bride as she leaves her home. I feel tearful, realising that I am at the cusp of a huge life change. I look at my father, who has always believed that I can be anything I want to be; and my mother, my heart, who was all of these things, as well as patience, hope and belief.

My mother and father kiss me and leave ahead of me for the wedding, ready to welcome our guests. My sister-in-law smiles at me as she drapes my long bridal-white headscarf over me and pins it in place.

She holds my hand to help me walk to the wedding car. As we step out of the house, the sun is radiant. I'm smiling, I can't stop.

She steps in front of me and opens the door.

'Your carriage awaits,' she winks mischievously at me.

I turn to look at the house, my home. I feel emotional but not sad, because I'm not leaving it behind. It is still all part of me, and always will be. I'm not moving to a different life: I'm expanding the multiverse I live in.

She teases me, 'Come on then! We've waited long enough for this day!'

I step into the car, about to begin the journey, and say as I always do at the beginning of any action: *Bismillah Ar-Rahman Ar-Raheem*, In the name of Allah, the Lovingly Compassionate, the Kind.

This is a journey that each human being makes, from being one, to being part of a pair. The promised experience of being part of a pair is peace, contentment and love. Will I find these things? The journey itself to seek these things may be rewarding, or perhaps it will be the reward in itself.

I turn to close the door of the car. I look back at my home, and then forward to the road that lies ahead.

Acknowledgements

It would be impossible for me to write my *thank yous* without mentioning the one, with a little *o*. This is mainly because he insisted that he be first in the list, and that I acknowledge him for being a very patient man through this period of creative madness. Anyone who knows him will be aware that he is indeed a patient and caring man of extreme gentleness and gentlemanliness. He is also intelligent, handsome, quietly funny and sensitive, with great vision and enormous heart. Amongst his many talents, which I have been fortunate enough to benefit from, are his abilities to create, inspire and encourage, and simply to be his gorgeous self. Of course, it is thanks to the fact that he took his sweet time in appearing, that this book was written. Thanks for showing up. Eventually. *Mithu*, it was worth the wait.

My parents are just as inspiring, and it is through their unconditional love, belief and encouragement that they have instilled in me the constant aspiration to create new things, try new ideas and to share everything I have with the world around me. It is their optimism, faith and prayers that have guided me through my life. With them standing behind me, nothing has ever been impossible and their confidence continues to drive me forward in the belief that it really is possible to make the world a better place, and to fill it with love. I could not have asked for more incredible and amazing parents. Mum and Dad, I pray that you are blessed abundantly.

He and she, who don't want to be mentioned, but know who you are, thank you for your support, as well as your raised eyebrows at some of my madcap ideas. They are just as helpful and just as needed, in life as much as in writing. Just knowing that you are there when I need you is a huge blessing for which I am deeply grateful. You may not know this, but I've learnt many things from both of you, which have made me, and continue to make me a better person.

To my grandparents, uncles, aunts and cousins, thank you simply for being you, and loving me and supporting my work. Every bit has made a difference.

There are a number of people without whom the book would simply not exist in the form it is today. It is the Aunties and the suitors who come first to mind. They were incredible characters, real and intensely human, and who, one realises with hindsight, were lovable and frustrating in equal measure. The wisdom I gained from them in apparent and hidden ways is irreplaceable, and for that I thank all of them. The Imam that I mentioned, too, has a strong presence in my life, even though he is no longer with us. May mercy be showered on him for his passion, knowledge and vision.

All the girls who shared tears and laughter over their equally perilous journey, thank you for making me realise I was not alone in my quest. Remember that you, and anyone who is on this journey, are not alone either.

Others who walked with me and held my hand cannot be forgotten either, in no particular order: Malika Chandoo, Shaheen Bilgrami, Masoma Khoee, Tim Lloyd, Gary Ellis, Remona Aly, Peter Hobbs, Gillian Cargill, Mukul Devichand, Emily Buchanan, and Irfan Akram.

Ahmed Versi deserves a special mention for asking an untested novice like me to write for his newspaper *The Muslim News*, and crazily agreeing to give me a regular column. I was bitten by the writing bug, set up my own blog, won a couple of awards and have now written a book. Thank you also to all my readers, each one of you makes a difference to my work and I value your support and comments. Luqman Ali cannot be forgotten either, for his serenity, eloquence and creative inspiration and for simply understanding everything.

Abdulaziz, you share some of the blame too. We know what you did, and we thank you wholeheartedly for it.

Finally, when it comes to the book, there are a few people who must take credit for seeing the potential of a sample of raw writing from a first-time author and believing that it could be a beautiful piece of writing. Dan Nunn, you were the first; I'm sorry we couldn't make it happen together. Diane Banks, my ever cheerful and talented agent who is definitely going places, when you told me that you were glued to your screen when you read my story I nearly hugged you. I love the fact that you are persistent and tenacious, and (despite being an agent) completely human. Thank you for believing. To Karen, my ever patient editor, thank you for seeing what the book could be, and my, what a long way we've come, In particular, I congratulate for not strangling me over our 'creative tensions'. Luckily, cyberspace and the trek across London helped.

And, there is no way to forget the wonderful, intelligent and beautiful Nahla El Geyoushi and Elaine Heaver. Without them the book might not have made it out into the world so confidently and with such excitement. They believed, supported, wept and laughed with me through this process, and made me realise that I am a very fortunate person to have such close and dedicated friends.

To all of you, and all those who have made my life and my writing a joy, thank you.